Healing Wisdom

Depth Psychology
and the Pastoral Ministry

Edited by

Kathleen J. Greider,

Deborah van Deusen Hunsinger, &

Felicity Brock Kelcourse

William B. Eerdmans Publishing Company
Grand Rapids, Michigan / Cambridge, U.K.

© 2010 Wm. B. Eerdmans Publishing Co.
All rights reserved

Published 2010 by
Wm. B. Eerdmans Publishing Co.
2140 Oak Industrial Drive N.E., Grand Rapids, Michigan 49505 /
P.O. Box 163, Cambridge CB3 9PU U.K.

Printed in the United States of America

16 15 14 13 12 11 10   7 6 5 4 3 2 1

ISBN 978-0-8028-6254-9

www.eerdmans.com

For Ann

Contents

CONTRIBUTORS   ix

Introduction   xv
    Kathleen J. Greider, Deborah van Deusen Hunsinger,
    and Felicity Brock Kelcourse

Healing Wisdom for Ministry Practices

Ministry in Depth: Three Critical Questions   3
    Rodney J. Hunter

Flowers on the Altar: Initial Pastoral Visits and
Communication in Depth   16
    Russell H. Davis

Much Depends on the Kitchen: Pastoral Practice
in Multicultural Society   34
    K. Samuel Lee

Healing Wisdom for Human Flourishing

The Ministry of Everyday Life: Psychological
and Spiritual Development   57
    Ana-María Rizzuto

Contents

Sacred Space and the Psyche: Reflections on Potential Space
and the Sacred Built Environment   72
    Pamela Cooper-White

A Wisdom Model for Pastoral Counseling   94
    Daniel S. Schipani

Knowing and Unknowing God: A Psychoanalytic
Meditation on Spiritual Transformation   109
    James W. Jones

Healing Wisdom for Suffering and Evil

The Question of Evil: An Answer *from*, Not *to*, Job   125
    David W. Augsburger

Scapegoating in Congregational and Group Life:
Practical Theological Reflections on the Unbearable   141
    K. Brynolf Lyon

Resistance Is Not Futile: Finding Therapeutic Space
between Colonialism and Globalization   157
    Cedric C. Johnson

Ann Belford Ulanov: A Brief Biography   176

Ann Belford Ulanov: Selected Bibliography   178

Contributors

DAVID W. AUGSBURGER, Ph.D., is Professor of Pastoral Care and Counseling at Fuller Theological Seminary in Pasadena, California. His research and teaching interests include cross-cultural counseling, communication and conflict reduction, forgiveness and reconciliation, spirituality and ethics, interfaith dialogue, systems theory of family and community, as well as the broader field of pastoral counseling. He is the author of twenty-five books, among the most recent of which are *Dissident Discipleship, Hatework: Working through the Pain and Pleasures of Hate* (2006) and *Helping People Forgive* (1996). An ordained Mennonite minister, he does continuing supervision of pastoral counseling as a Diplomate of the American Association of Pastoral Counselors. He travels widely doing seminars and training in China, India, Russia, Australia, and the United Kingdom.

THE REV. PAMELA COOPER-WHITE is Ben G. and Nancye Clapp Gaultier Professor of Pastoral Theology, Care and Counseling at Columbia Theological Seminary, Decatur, Georgia. She is the recipient of the American Association of Pastoral Counselors' 2005 national award for "Distinguished Achievement in Research and Writing" and the Samaritan Counseling Center of Philadelphia's 2007 "Spirit Award" for community service. She holds Ph.D. degrees from Harvard University and the Institute for Clinical Social Work, Chicago, and is the author of four books, including *Many Voices: Pastoral Psychotherapy and Theology in Relational Perspective* (2006), *Shared Wisdom: Use of the Self in Pastoral Care and Counseling* (2004), and *The Cry of Tamar: Violence Against Women and the Church's Response* (1995), which won the 1995 Top Ten Books award from the Academy of Parish Clergy. An Episcopal priest and pastoral psychotherapist, Dr. Cooper-White is certified as a clinical Fellow in the American Association of Pastoral Counselors. She serves as Editor of the *Journal of Pastoral Theology.*

RUSSELL H. DAVIS, Ph.D., is currently the founding director of the School of Clinical Pastoral Education at Sentara Hospitals in Norfolk, Virginia. He obtained his Ph.D. in the Program of Psychiatry and Religion at Union Theological Seminary, New York City. Ann Belford Ulanov was his mentor and dissertation adviser and from 1986 to 1991 also his colleague during the time he taught Psychiatry and Religion at Union Theological Seminary. Later he taught at the University of Virginia, having a joint appointment on the General Medical Faculty and in Religious Studies. He is certified as a CPE Supervisor by the Association for Clinical Pastoral Education, Inc., and served as its Executive Director from 1995 to 1998. He is an ordained Baptist minister, endorsed by the Alliance of Baptists. In addition to articles, chapters, and reviews, he is the author of *Freud's Concept of Passivity* (1993), which appeared in the prestigious Psychological Issues series published by International Universities Press.

KATHLEEN J. GREIDER is Professor of Pastoral Care and Counseling and a therapist and clinical supervisor at The Clinebell Institute for Pastoral Counseling and Psychotherapy at Claremont School of Theology in Claremont, California. Her research and teaching interests include spiritual care, pastoral theology, interculturality, the interplay of social and personal change, and depth psychology. She is the author of *Reckoning with Aggression: Theology, Violence, and Vitality* (1997) and *Much Madness Is Divinest Sense: Spiritual Wisdom in Memoirs of Soul-Suffering* (2007). Ordained in the United Methodist Church and a Fellow in the American Association of Pastoral Counselors, she has clinical pastoral experience in general hospital and in-patient psychiatric settings, pastoral counseling and psychotherapy, spiritual direction, and parish ministry. She holds the M.Div. degree from Harvard Divinity School and the Ph.D. from Union Theological Seminary in New York City, where she was a student of Ann Belford Ulanov.

RODNEY J. HUNTER is Professor Emeritus of Pastoral Theology, having taught for thirty-five years at the Candler School of Theology, Emory University. He is most widely known as the general editor of the *Dictionary of*

Pastoral Care and Counseling (1990 and 2005), though he has also authored many essays in pastoral theology and co-edited the volume *Pastoral Care and Social Conflict* (1995). His research interests focus on methodological issues in practical and pastoral theology, the theology of pastoral care and counseling, personality, religious experience, and theology, personal devotion, loyalty and commitment, and the teaching and practice of ministry. A Presbyterian minister, he holds B.D. and Ph.D. degrees from Princeton Theological Seminary and is an active clergy affiliate in Central Presbyterian Church, Atlanta.

DEBORAH VAN DEUSEN HUNSINGER is Charlotte W. Newcombe Chair of Pastoral Theology at Princeton Theological Seminary. As a young college graduate, she matriculated at the C. G. Jung Institute in Zurich for one year. After obtaining her M.Div. from Yale University Divinity School, she studied at Union Theological Seminary with Ann Belford Ulanov, earning her Ph.D. in Psychiatry and Religion. An ordained Presbyterian minister, she is interested in educating clergy and laypeople to offer theologically sound, psychologically informed, and contextually relevant pastoral care in the church. Her current research interest is in bringing the knowledge and skills of nonviolent communication and restorative practices to the church and wider community. As a Fellow in the American Association of Pastoral Counselors, she founded the Bangor Pastoral Counseling Service in Bangor, Maine, and worked as a pastoral counselor for nearly fifteen years before she began teaching. She is the author of *Theology and Pastoral Counseling: A New Interdisciplinary Approach* (1995) and *Pray without Ceasing: Revitalizing Pastoral Care* (2006).

CEDRIC C. JOHNSON is a Ph.D. candidate in pastoral theology at Princeton Theological Seminary. He holds the M.Div. degree from Princeton Theological Seminary and the M.S.W. degree from Hunter College School of Social Work. His research and teaching interests include spirituality and mental health, cultural trauma, postcolonialism, and pastoral theology in African American and other diasporic African contexts. He has over fifteen years of experience in the field of community mental health working as a psychotherapist, Clinical Supervisor, and Clinical Director in various outpatient settings. Ordained as an elder in the Church of God in Christ, he presently works as a consultant for pastors and congregations on issues related to the provision of pastoral care and counseling in urban settings.

James W. Jones, Psy.D., Ph.D., Th.D., holds doctorates in both Clinical Psychology (Rutgers, 1985) and Religious Studies (Brown, 1970), as well as an honorary doctorate from the University of Uppsala in Sweden. He is distinguished professor of religion and adjunct professor of clinical psychology at Rutgers University, a lecturer in Religion and Psychiatry at Union Theological Seminary in New York, and a visiting professor at the University of Uppsala in Sweden. He has also taught at the Drew Theological School and the General Seminary of the Episcopal Church. He is the author of twelve books including: *In the Middle of This Road We Call Our Life* (1995), *Terror and Transformation: The Ambiguity of Religion in a Psychoanalytic Perspective* (2002), *The Mirror of God: Christian Faith as Spiritual Practice* (2003), *Waking from Newton's Sleep: Dialogues on Spirituality in an Age of Science* (2006), and most recently *Blood That Cries Out from the Earth: The Psychology of Religious Terrorism* (2008), as well as numerous professional papers. He is a Fellow of the American Psychological Association, from which he received a special award, in 1993, for his contributions to the field of psychology of religion. For six years he was co-chair of the Religion and Social Sciences Section of the American Academy of Religion. He currently serves on the governing board and as the vice-president of the International Association for the Psychology of Religion. He is a priest in the Episcopal Church, and he maintains a private practice of psychotherapy.

Felicity Brock Kelcourse is Associate Professor of Pastoral Care and Counseling and Director of the Doctor of Ministry Program at Christian Theological Seminary in Indianapolis, Indiana. A recorded Quaker minister, she earned her M.Div. degree at Earlham School of Religion in Richmond, Indiana. She served congregations in Indiana, London (England), Jamaica (West Indies), and Ohio before completing her Ph.D. in Psychiatry and Religion at Union Theological Seminary under the direction of Ann Belford Ulanov (1998) and clinical training at Blanton-Peale Graduate Institute in New York. She is a Fellow in the American Association of Pastoral Counselors, a Supervisor and Clinical Member of the American Association for Marriage and Family Therapy, and a Licensed Mental Health Counselor, and her 20 years of clinical experience include chaplaincy, counseling, and spiritual direction. She edited *Human Development and Faith: Life-cycle Changes in Body, Mind and Soul* (2004), and has published numerous articles and chapters focused on the dialogue between depth psychology and theology. Her research interests include cross-cultural approaches to healing, psychological and religious dimensions of discernment, religious experience, and the spiritual value of dreams.

KYUNGSIG SAMUEL LEE, Ph.D., is Associate Professor of Pastoral Care and Counseling and Executive Director of The Clinebell Institute for Pastoral Counseling and Psychotherapy at Claremont School of Theology in Claremont, California. He previously taught at Yale Divinity School and Wesley Theological Seminary. He holds the M.Div. degree from Yale Divinity School and the Ph.D. in counseling psychology from Arizona State University. His research and teaching interests include pastoral theology, counseling, and ministry in multicultural contexts. He is the author of many articles. His work significantly contributed to the development of the multicultural competencies in the Association for Clinical Pastoral Education, and he currently serves as the chairperson of the Multicultural Competencies Task Force of the American Association of Pastoral Counselors. Ordained in the United Methodist Church, he served numerous local churches in Arizona and in California.

K. BRYNOLF LYON, Ph.D., is Professor of Practical Theology and Pastoral Care at Christian Theological Seminary in Indianapolis, Indiana, and a psychotherapist in private practice. He received his Ph.D. in religion and psychological studies from the University of Chicago Divinity School (1982). He is a Licensed Mental Health Counselor, a National Certified Counselor, and a Certified Group Psychotherapist. His research and writing over the past several years has focused on practical theological perspectives on group dynamics and congregational life, particularly concerning group conflict, identity, and the challenges of learning from experience in group life. His earlier work includes *Toward a Practical Theology of Aging* (1985) and serving as one of the co-authors of *From Culture Wars to Common Ground: Religion and the Family Debate in America* (2000) and as co-editor with Archie Smith Jr. of *Tending the Flock: Congregations and Family Ministry* (1998).

ANA-MARÍA RIZZUTO, M.D., is a Training and Supervising Analyst at The Psychoanalytic Institute of New England, East. She is a native of Argentina, where she obtained her medical degree. She was Professor of Child and Adolescent Psychology at the Universidad Católica de Córdoba, in

Córdoba, Argentina, from 1961 to 1965. In 1964, she was Professor of Pastoral Anthropology at the Seminario Pontificio de Nuestra Señora de Loreto, also in Córdoba, Argentina. After immigrating to the United States, she trained in psychiatry in Boston and in Psychoanalysis at the Boston Psychoanalytic Institute. She is a member of the American Psychoanalytic Association and of the International Psychoanalytic Association. In 1987 she was a Visiting Lecturer in Psychology and Religion at Harvard Divinity School. Her books include *The Birth of the Living God: A Psychoanalytic Study* (1979), *Why Did Freud Reject God: A Psychodynamic Interpretation* (1998), and *The Dynamics of Human Aggression: Theoretical Foundations and Clinical Applications* (2004), which she co-authored with W. W. Meissner and Dan H. Buie. She has published numerous articles on the psychodynamics of religion, language in psychoanalysis, aggression, the clinical situation, and other subjects. She is a practicing Roman Catholic.

DANIEL S. SCHIPANI is Professor of Pastoral Care and Counseling at the Associated Mennonite Biblical Seminary in Elkhart, Indiana. A native of Argentina and an ordained minister in the Mennonite Church, he also serves as a pastoral counselor (volunteer) at a local community health center for economically vulnerable care-receivers. His research and teaching interests include formation and transformation processes and intercultural and interfaith pastoral care and counseling. He is the author or editor of over twenty books on education and practical and pastoral theology, including *The Way of Wisdom in Pastoral Counseling* (2003), *Spiritual Caregiving in the Hospital: Windows to Chaplaincy Ministry* (2006), and *Interfaith Spiritual Care: Understandings and Practice* (2009). He lectures widely in North and Latin America and Europe. He holds a Doctor of Psychology from Universidad Católica Argentina and a Ph.D. in Practical Theology from Princeton Theological Seminary.

Introduction

Kathleen J. Greider,
Deborah van Deusen Hunsinger, and
Felicity Brock Kelcourse

Excellence in ministry is hard won. In addition to a thorough knowledge of biblical texts and exegesis, the history of the faith, and the habit of theological reflection, a well-prepared minister is one who is not afraid to face the depths of human suffering. The latter capacity cannot be acquired through intellectual effort alone. The ability to offer a "non-anxious presence" to those in need, to bracket the pain of one's own woundedness while listening empathically, to face head on the purifying fires of human transformation — these are a few of the qualities in ministry we designate as "healing wisdom."

Healing wisdom is best appropriated through active engagement with what Anton Boisen called "the living human document." As we learn to deepen our own self-understanding, including an acceptance and acknowledgment of those aspects of our being that are usually distant from conscious awareness, we develop receptivity to deeper, more honest encounters with one another. Both head and heart must be fully engaged for this type of learning to succeed. One must hold fast to the saving grace Jesus promised his disciples, that "you will know the truth, and the truth will make you free" (John 8:32). Without this promise of liberation, the knowledge that hard won wisdom does in fact offer freedom and healing, the price of a ministry that mines the depths of human experience might appear too great. To brave the "valley of the shadow of death" (Ps. 23:4a) with another we must first face it in ourselves. And nothing imparts courage for the journey as thoroughly as the example of a mentor who has faced her or his own depths and gained, in so doing, the wisdom to heal.

Those of us who have had the privilege of studying with Professor

Ann Belford Ulanov at Union Theological Seminary in New York know firsthand what *healing wisdom* looks like. It is the kind of wisdom that Ann herself embodies. It pays attention to the specificities of a person's culture, unique history, and family. It responds to suffering with compassion and respect, giving both support and space to the one who suffers, never distant, yet never invasive. It bears witness to the reality that religions sometimes support human flourishing, but sometimes do damage, and so it neither withholds nor forces spirituality — instead, it respectfully discerns with care-seekers what ultimate values most meaningfully ground and order their lives. It waits patiently in the presence of painful symptoms, trusting that hidden meaning dwells in the affliction. It carefully builds a sturdy human relationship to hold and witness all that the suffering one brings: her guilt, shame, and regret, along with her longings, ambitions, and unlived life. It offers hope, not a hope that ignores evil, anguish, or loss, but that fully enters into it. It is ready to rejoice, when joy comes. It is humble, down-to-earth, imaginative, multifaceted, *real.*

As former students of Professor Ulanov, the three editors of this volume seek to honor our teacher by bringing this kind of healing wisdom more directly into ministry. We are teachers in theological schools and so prepare students for many forms of religious leadership — especially for work in congregations, chaplaincies, seminaries, and pastoral counseling centers. The field of pastoral care and counseling has emerged within the Christian tradition, but the students in our classrooms increasingly represent religious diversity and are seeking to learn how to offer in other religious communities or in religiously diverse settings what Christianity has called the "care of souls." With these diverse students and communities in mind, we set about to create a textbook for religious leaders that would capture many of the multiple strands of our work and weave them together, as Ann Ulanov does in her teaching, psychotherapeutic work, and writing.

What does it mean to speak of ministry in depth? To approach ministry conscious of its "depth dimension" indicates a willingness, first of all, to pay attention to those things that usually lie only at the fringes of our awareness. Psychotherapists sometimes speak of "the unconscious" as if it were "a something" residing within us. With a richness and multiplicity of example, Ann Ulanov's teaching and writing make it clear that our "unconscious" thoughts, feelings, motivations, and needs constitute the unlived life that belongs to us, but to which we lack conscious access or refuse to live into and claim.

Our inability or unwillingness to live out our wholeness affects not only our own life path but also that of our family and community. Painful losses, unmetabolized suffering, even talents that go unattended can contribute to an inner deadness. By contrast, those who risk living the fullness of who they are, are generative of aliveness, not only in themselves, but in others as well. Like a good plant, writes Ulanov, "the oxygen each of us makes is breathing space for all the rest of us."[1]

This volume is designed to bring what is normally unconscious into fuller awareness in the tasks of ministry. Often ministers learn pastoral practices without fully appreciating the depth dimension of what they are encountering. This includes not only theological and spiritual depth but also psychological, historical, and cultural depth. Which of us serves our first congregation as fully cognizant of the culturally specific context in which we are working as we need to be? Do we attend to each person's personal and cultural specificity with the insights of power analysis, knowing that social dynamics and personal dynamics are never unrelated? Do we fully appreciate the multiple dimensions of even a single encounter with a parishioner, including an awareness of both the limits and the opportunities implicit in our role as a new pastor? While most of us studied questions of theodicy and evil in seminary, what happens when we encounter it in the actual lives of those in our care? Do we fall back into clichés, hold forth with philosophical speculations, or otherwise break the empathic connection with those we serve? In the chapters that follow, authors experienced in ministry share their own specific understandings of what it means to minister in depth, appropriating wisdom that heals.

The volume begins with three essays that focus directly on questions of *ministerial practice*. Recognizing the creativity involved in all ministry, Rodney Hunter raises fundamental questions that will lead ministers to a depth of understanding if asked with seriousness of purpose and in collaboration with others. Russell Davis examines the deceptively simple practice of offering flowers on the altar in memory of loved ones and finds a mother lode of spiritual and emotional depth in his parishioners. Davis analyzes a verbatim record of two actual pastoral visits and comes to some surprising conclusions. The honesty of this account (and what he calls his "faulty pastoral technique") will be reassuring to students just learning

---

1. Ann Belford Ulanov, *The Unshuttered Heart: Opening to Aliveness and Deadness in the Self* (Nashville: Abingdon, 2007), 8.

how to listen. The third essay deals with the need for a depth understanding of what it means to practice ministry with multicultural competence. Through a personal reflection on his first pastorate, Samuel Lee introduces the importance of knowing the cultural specificity not only of the congregation's history and cultural setting, but also of one's own unique ethnic identity and history. Such depth of knowledge will engender preaching that is more prophetic (and more honest) through pastoral care that attends to burning issues of difference and misunderstanding that often go unspoken or appear taboo.

The next four essays look at models of *human flourishing* through the lenses of both time and space. First, Ana-María Rizzuto considers what she calls "the ministry of everyday life" practiced by parents, teachers, and mentors in providing the "emotional nutrients" needed by young people in order to grow. This hopeful essay lifts up the importance of respectful and honest dialogue between the generations about things that matter. Pamela Cooper-White brings into awareness the depth dimension of the spaces we inhabit, in particular, the sacred spaces where we worship. She explores how these spaces shape us not only as individuals but also as communities. They are deeply personal spaces that mirror the immensity that lies within us, but they are also collective, culturally rich spaces that have meanings that transcend not only the individual, but also the community in any particular historical period. Our buildings embody a storied richness, as generation after generation pass through their doors to offer prayers of lament and songs of praise.

The volume then looks at two cultural forms current in the United States and closely allied with practices of pastoral care, namely, pastoral counseling and spiritual care. Daniel Schipani has developed a model of pastoral counseling that draws on the clinical perspective of psychotherapy but relies conceptually, not on a medical model of pathology, but on developing healing wisdom in the light of God. Emphasizing spiritual and moral discernment, Schipani discusses a case study which illustrates his approach. James Jones takes an alternative approach to spiritual care by examining a fourteenth-century text called *The Cloud of Unknowing*. He asks a set of evocative (and provocative) questions about any pastoral encounter and then raises the question of how we come to know God. The *via negativa* that is described in *The Cloud* is set forth as a viable approach for those whose well of faith has gone dry.

The third section of the volume deals with the human encounter with *suffering and evil.* David Augsburger surveys Jung's *Answer to Job,* but offers an alternative conclusion to Jung's own. Attentive to the cultural location of the reader, he brings contextual sensitivity as well as theological depth and pastoral ingenuity to his reading. K. Brynolf Lyon looks at the painful practice of scapegoating in congregational and group life. This phenomenon arises out of a group's unwillingness to deal with ambiguity, to contain opposites, and to sustain an empathic imaginative connection with the Other. The last essay of the volume, by Cedric Johnson, exemplifies the need for pastoral practice to develop a rich appreciation for history and politics in the service of personal and cultural survival, especially for oppressed or marginalized groups.

While their training and backgrounds differ, all of the contributors have pursued a vocation that involves intensive reflection on matters of theology, psychology, and spirituality. Though these essays reflect their Christian heritage in the field of pastoral care and counseling, all of the contributors aim to engage readers with respect for spiritual and religious diversity: consider these essays in relationship to the healing wisdom needed by persons of all religious traditions (and none) to live lives full of wholeness, vitality, and engagement. Most fundamentally, in this book we seek to show and explore the constant interplay between unconscious dynamics in human relationality, life in society, and spirituality to better understand and embody religious leadership. In recognition of Professor Ulanov's contributions to the field of pastoral theology, it is our hope that these essays will assist students to reclaim the rich legacy of depth psychology in their ministries of pastoral and spiritual care with persons and communities.

We dedicate this work to our beloved teacher, Ann Belford Ulanov, with deep appreciation and gratitude, in hopes that the wisdom we have gained through her example may continue to offer a source of healing for others.

Healing Wisdom for Ministry Practices

Ministry in Depth: Three Critical Questions

Rodney J. Hunter

Spirituality is a popular and widely used concept today, but strangely it is also an especially problematic one even for those who use it deliberately to describe their ministries or professional services. What exactly constitutes a "faith dimension" or "spiritual depth" in, for example, an institutional chaplaincy in a public hospital in which patients, families, and staff persons represent a kaleidoscope of religious and non-religious backgrounds and traditions, or in a pastoral counseling practice that attempts to meet the psychological and interpersonal issues of persons of all faiths and of no faith from a "faith-based" perspective? Nor is the uncertainty of "spirituality" limited to these extra-ecclesiastical settings. Spirituality is also, and perhaps especially, a problem for traditional ministry as well, even if in many instances thought not to be. There is much in the Western church's practice of ministry, especially in the American church, to suggest that it has become strangely and, one must say, sadly difficult for pastors and congregations to find and practice the core spiritual meanings of their faith in the midst of the relentless demands of institutional church life and the pressures of a powerfully materialistic, competitive consumer culture that not only surrounds the church but invades it in myriad ways large and small.

While it is difficult and perhaps impossible to say precisely what spiritual depth even looks like, we generally know it when we experience it, as Jesus' contemporaries learned in their encounter with the rabbi from Galilee who "taught them as one having authority, and not as the scribes" (Mark 1:22). At the very least, we can point to a degree of freedom from the compulsive pressures of society and its prevailing value system, as well as a tendency to be in touch with a dimension of experience that is both deep within oneself, yet transcends the self as a source of insight, moral authority, and formative impact on others. Some have called it an "inner transcendence," though the language of inwardness can be misleading. Spiritual depth is not mere introspection or self-centeredness. It is, rather, a profound sense of living within a mystery that encompasses and reaches beyond the self yet grounds it and inspires it for meaningful, courageous, and creative action in the world. It means having a sense of participating in a process of becoming a more full, complete, and meaningful human being, and equally of participating, in one's unique time and place, in a movement of history that exceeds one's ability fully to understand or control, yet is felt to be aimed at the fulfillment of some as yet undisclosed purpose.[1]

Ministry or "spiritual practice" in depth therefore points to a kind of activity that opens up and inspires a sense of the ineffable wonder, mystery, and purposefulness of life in the midst of its practical challenges, perplexities, suffering, and absurdity. It enables us to experience our lives in larger terms, to put things into a seemingly ultimate perspective, to get free of the narrow, anxious concerns of the ego, and to give ourselves to the intangible yet real and powerful movement of life toward fullness of being.

There is no technique for developing spiritual depth in ministry or in any comparable professional or lay practice. "Life in the Spirit" grows and flourishes, if at all, quietly and mysteriously in each individual life, like Jesus' grain of mustard seed that begins inconspicuously but emerges one day as a full-blown tree (Mark 4:30-32). No doubt each person must discover the path in ways unique to himself or herself. This is as true of spirituality in ministry and all forms of spiritual care and guidance as it is of the spiritual life itself. No seminary curriculum or educational program can

---

1. Jungian psychology, significantly represented in pastoral and religious literature by Ann Belford Ulanov, provides a particularly powerful and much debated psychological interpretation of the meaning of depth (or unconscious) experience and its relation to religion. See (e.g.) her co-authored work (with Barry Ulanov), *Religion and the Unconscious* (Philadelphia: Westminster Press, 1975). See also Romney M. Moseley, "Analytical (Jungian) Psychology and Religion," and James E. Dittes, "Analytical (Jungian) Psychology and Pastoral Care," in *Dictionary of Pastoral Care and Counseling,* Rodney J. Hunter, gen. ed. (Nashville: Abingdon Press, 1990, 2005). For a theological critique of and search for a postmodern alternative to this concept of depth, see Catherine Keller, *Face of the Deep: A Theology of Becoming* (London: Taylor and Francis Group; New York: Routledge, 2003), especially 161-71.

manufacture it. However, we are not without some guidance, some pointers growing out of the church's and our own common experience of the spiritual quest. In what follows, I wish to suggest a few such pointers that I believe can be helpful to theological students, pastors, and all who provide spiritual care, who hunger and thirst for a ministry that is practical and realistic yet spiritually deep in relation to God and the things that pertain to the life of faith. Specifically, I will suggest three simple questions that can be asked in every situation of ministry, the pursuit of which, if undertaken with a true and earnest desire for ministering in depth, can help such a ministry to take shape over time.

These are not magical questions, yet their power in each set of circumstances rests in our ability to resist what may be the most obvious, immediate answers that spring to mind in order to search for more profound and significant ones. Such a search requires not only a willing and courageous heart, but also an informed and inquisitive mind. This approach will not appeal therefore to ministers or other spiritual practitioners who want simple "how to" directives for "handling" this or that pastoral situation, whether in traditional pastoral care and counseling, preaching, worship, or church administration, or in the many forms of faith-based service outside the traditional church. If we can get past the felt need for a "quick fix" in any of these contexts of ministry, these three questions can be genuinely helpful in enabling forms of service that have authentic spiritual depth, and are therefore able to resist the siren calls of our hedonistic, competitive culture and to speak more truly and realistically to today's spiritual hunger.[2]

---

2. These questions are based on the more or less commonsense observation that all mental activity is continuously concerned with making at least three psychological determinations: perceiving and knowing one's environment, evaluating the situation (Is it good or bad for me and for what I care about?), and forming appropriate and effective action. Thus what I am proposing as a simple guide to ministerial practice is a professional and religious refinement of fundamental mental operations that everyone performs continually. By the same token, all ministers can be said to operate in practice with the three-question framework presented in this article, whether or not they are consciously aware of doing so. Depth and sophistication in the practice of ministry can be said to vary according to the degree to which these critical questions are recognized, differentiated, and intentionally addressed. For a roughly comparable theory of general professional practice, see Donald A. Schoen, *The Reflective Practitioner: How Professionals Think in Action* (New York: Basic Books, 1983).

Rodney J. Hunter

Three Critical Questions

The first thing that many pastors and most theological students and other professionals think of when confronted with any situation of need and service, is "How can I handle this situation? What should I do?" It is, perhaps, a natural first question, since clearly something *must* be done, and the pastor feels on the spot to do something helpful, indeed, something pastoral. But in fact *what to do* is usually not the *best* first question. In fact, in my experience, *what to do* is usually the wrong first question, however urgent and unavoidable it may feel. The best first question, I submit, is in a sense more reflective — something like:

1. What is going on here?

Before a course of pastoral action is undertaken or even contemplated, the prior need is to make at least a beginning attempt to *discern* the nature of the situation more fully than what first impressions provide. First impressions are important and must be noted and taken seriously, but over time they can lead to superficiality that misses the truly significant issues at stake. They can also be wrong, and first impressions are seldom in any case sufficient to ground and guide a deeply relevant ministry of faith.

This principle applies to all situations of congregational ministry, including preaching, leadership of worship, pastoral care, organizational leadership and administration, and educational events, but also to non-traditional and non-ecclesiastical forms of spiritual service. Though these various expressions of ministry and service may seem rather different and call for distinct skill sets, which is true to a point, at bottom they have much in common. Each entails particular circumstances, needs, and problems within which ministry attempts to provide spiritual guidance and care. Understanding the distinct nature of each situation is critical to fashioning a ministry that is relevant, effective, and faithful to the theological purposes of the church, whether in its traditional congregational forms or its many other related expressions in contemporary society. Sermon preparation, for instance, must include reflection on the congregation and its larger social context as well as the text and its universal meanings, and seek ways of integrating the two. Acts of pastoral leadership and administration are likewise at risk of failure or irrelevance if they do not take into account "what is going on" in the group and work out creative ways of engaging it in relation to the larger goals one hopes to accomplish. But equally so must the institutional chaplain or spiritually oriented psychotherapist or counselor consider carefully the particulars of "what is going on" in any actual situation, whether that situation be defined in religious terms or not.

It is especially important, however, to understand that *What is going on here?* is not a question that pastoral persons alone can ask, as if they were the sole authorities or sources of insight in the situation. Far better, it seems to me, for them to find ways to help the persons or community involved to begin asking this question for themselves. This is because inviting others into the inquiry *empowers* them as participants in the life of faith that any true spiritual practice seeks to enhance. But if the pastoral person alone asks the question, it tends to put him or her in a privileged position of authority and control and to relegate parishioners or clients to the role of passive recipients, however well intentioned the pastoral figure may be.

Whether or not this is a good thing is, of course, a matter for theology to determine, and no doubt much ministry over the centuries has operated on assumptions of just such a dominant pastoral authority and the subordinate role it assigns to parishioners. Many churches, today, however, like many forms and philosophies of professional practice, seek ministry or spiritual service that is more egalitarian and democratic, emphasizing the values to be had through the empowerment of full participation for all persons involved, lay and clergy, professional and non-professional alike. There still need to be specific roles and duties for clergy and cognate professional persons to be sure, but a truly *servant* ministry or professional practice on the model of Philippians 2:5-11 is one in which those with formal ordination or other specialized authority enact their ministries not as a means of exercising dominance but as a way of strengthening the appropriate power, participation, and authority of all members of the body. "How do *you* see what is going on here?" (or words to that effect) can initiate a shared search for truth and wisdom which might in fact revise, expand, or even negate the pastoral person's first impressions. More important, putting this open-ended question up front signals to everyone that our present understanding is not immutable or definitive, that there may be more going on here than meets the eye, and that we should not presume to know too much — or indeed, to know too assuredly what should be done in the situation. A little humility about ourselves and our knowledge therefore opens the door to deeper spiritual inquiry and the possibility of coming to an understanding of the situation that is informed and guided by our discernment of God's work among us.

The first question in any form of ministry can of course be asked from a variety of perspectives, and it is important to do so. We have already suggested that our first impressions may be limited in scope and depth and shaped by our own needs in the situation. As such, they can be a source of both brilliant insight and grievous error. That is why it is necessary to view the situation from wider angles, including social, historical, and psychological points of view. It is important to recognize, for instance, the age, generation, and historical cohort of the participants, their gender, economic status and pressures, the power dynamics of the situation (its politics), and the cultural meanings and values by which the participants generate their understanding of a situation. One can and should ask all the same questions of oneself as pastor or spiritual guide. Most of these factors operate silently, in the background, outside of explicit awareness, though they are often of considerable importance in shaping the way each person subjectively experiences the situation and influences the flow of events. These wider perspectives often offer valuable clues about the situation's future possibilities.

When we think in terms of "depth" perception, however, we also mean the more profound levels of personal, subjective meaning that events and situations are given that are normally hidden from awareness and not easily made conscious, like a dream that one can "almost" recall but proves too elusive to grasp. If we think along the lines of the "depth psychologies" that emphasize the importance of such unconscious imagery, thought, and feeling, we can assume that in every situation of ministry, however mundane, simple, or difficult, there is a largely unrecognized set of psychological questions pertaining to who its participants understand themselves to be and what they are seeking in life. This level of the human mind is known mainly through dreams and fantasies, and indirectly through the symbolic character that simple, ordinary actions sometimes disclose, as when we "accidentally" leave a personal object in someone's home as an unconscious signal of our fear of losing our relationship to that person or what he or she represents to us. All spiritual practice is greatly enriched to the degree that these more personal and often hidden meanings, fears, questions, and desires are recognized. Much of what we mean by "ministry in depth" entails connecting with people at these elusive, profoundly personal levels. It is particularly important to recognize the ways that *religious* symbols, imagery, feelings, and ritual performances touch upon and influence these issues, and the way the deeper levels of the mind shape how religious meanings themselves are perceived, understood, and valued (or devalued).

As these comments suggest, such specialized angles of vision can be greatly enhanced if one knows certain kinds of *theories* about human behavior, individual psychology (including its unconscious processes), and social experience. In fact, the very word "theory" comes from a Greek root that means *to see,* as in the word *theater* — a place where one *sees.* Psychological and scientific theories of all kinds, including those of depth psychology, are intended to help us see the world more clearly, more deeply, in greater detail, and with a degree of explanatory power. Ministers and priests, like other professionals, are often distinguished by having specialized education in such theories to enable them to understand *what is going on here* more fully and to contribute this expertise to the common search for a way forward. But laypersons often have as much or more expertise of this kind as well, and their gifts and abilities should be elicited.

It is especially important to note that *What is going on here?* is also a theological question. It is not solely up to psychology or other secular theories to define the situation. In fact, it is essential to the nature of ministry or any spiritually oriented professional practice to ask and answer this question as best we can theologically. This can take various forms, such as asking how God may be present (or absent) here, what God may be seeking to bring forth from our situation, or how it is to be understood in theological terms. How might the concept of sin apply, for example, or forgiveness, justification, or sanctification (to give but a few possibilities)?

This question (or some version of it) is not asked once but again and again, almost continuously, as ministry moves forward. It weaves in and out of the other two questions, as they weave in and out with it. One never wants to lose touch with "what is going on"; indeed, an ever deepening sense of what is going on continually shapes and reshapes ministry, including the answers to the other two questions. But it should also be noted — and here the plot thickens — that an ever deepening understanding of the situation often carries us beyond our comfort zone. What we find when we attempt to look honestly at ourselves and each other may threaten our self-esteem or idealized pictures of ourselves or provoke resistance, at least initially. Whether this is *always* the case is a matter for theory and experience to decide, but there is indeed much evidence to indicate that anxiety and fear, as well as attempts to deny or evade or overpower them, are never far from serious efforts to understand ourselves. Finding ways to live with our anxieties and resistances is therefore integral to any serious form of help, whether in ministry or any other field of leadership and care. Thus ministry entails the fine spiritual art of seeking the very truth that we may often wish to deny. At the same time, however, we also find that coming into deeper levels of reality may also disclose beauty, strength, and blessing where none was expected.

2. What is God's will for this situation? What can we rightly hope and pray for?

This may seem a presumptuous if not impossible question, and in a very real sense it is. Who can know the mind of God about any particular situation? "Thy will be done on earth as it is in heaven," of course, but it certainly seems easier to leave our prayers in general terms than to attempt to know God's will for the immediate here and now. However, in ministry as in all forms of truly spiritual practice we do not have that option. One way or another, whether intentionally and by forethought or by unreflective assumption, we engage in such situations with some sense, however inchoate and uncertain, of which direction things *ought* to be going. In life as in ministry, there is no escaping the need for a sense of direction or purpose; human action in every form and expression presupposes some kind of ideal or normative orientation. The only questions are therefore whether to be theologically reflective and deliberate, or to fly blind; and whether, if the former, our reflections and deliberations are theologically informed and grow out of an earnest desire to know and do the divine will.

I have phrased this second question in two forms intentionally, either of which will do. Asking about God's will puts the matter more objectively, in relation to God, while a more subjective form is given by the second version in terms of what we, in our perplexities, desires, and fears, might rightly hope and pray for. "Rightly" of course implies the possibility of "wrongly," which requires a word of explanation. There is (in my view) a spiritually valid sense in which we may indeed pray to God for *anything* that is on our hearts, however impossible, selfish, or ill-considered: "Take it to the Lord in prayer," as the old hymn says. The whole tradition of lament in the Psalms gives voice to a faith that God is not unable or unwilling to hear our anguished cries. It is important to remember, however, that the biblical paradigm for all such prayer, Jesus' own anguished prayer in the garden, concludes with "yet not my will but yours be done" (Luke 22:42). This qualification, rightly understood, does not mean that God is ultimately unconcerned about our needs, fears, and desires, but precisely the opposite. In faith it assumes that God's will is truly *pro nobis* — "for us" — that in some ultimate sense our true happiness and welfare lie infinitely close to the heart of God even though God's larger purposes exceed our finite understanding and our present petitions inevitably fail to conform fully to God's will. A way of stating this theologically is to say that, at the deepest spiritual level, we pray "in the name of Jesus," meaning that our imperfect, often fear-ridden, self-limited prayers are offered through the intercession of Christ who lovingly perfects and completes them for us.

What makes this second question difficult in ministry is not only the ultimate mystery of discerning the divine will itself even in general terms but the more precise task of trying to know it for the immediate ministerial occasion. God's will, what we can rightly hope and pray for, must always be sought in relation to a particular state of affairs. At the same time, the particular will of God for this situation, however humbly and dimly intuited, must be sought, theologically, in the context of a more general engagement with the classical sources of theological knowledge — scripture, tradition, reason, and experience. Individual judgments about God's will are always to be tested against these larger historic norms, even if the norms themselves may require revision and correction in light of ongoing ministerial and ecclesial experience. All of this reflection is integrated with insights and perspectives gained from the immediate circumstances of ministry. It is a complex business requiring multiple forms of knowledge, a growing, searching faith, and a charitable wisdom and sense of humility.

We search for the "deeper," less obvious, more fundamental, and more hidden or mysterious movement of God within or beneath visible events and circumstances — something like "the Spirit of God . . . moving over the face of the waters" (Gen. 1:2). This is no ordinary perception; it requires spiritual sensitivity and "discernment," understood as a spiritual gift. It requires time, patience, humility, and a pure heart to "see God." In fact, the whole enterprise of discerning God's will is fraught with danger as well as difficulty, as we know from a long and often violent religious history. Arrogance, self-righteousness, a compulsion to dominate, and a willingness to do violence in the name of God often lurk in the shadows of pious endeavor. Therefore this second critical question, like the first, should not be quickly or too confidently answered. It must be allowed to emerge from the depths of the discerning community in the context of historical perspective and scriptural witness, and to be continually subjected to the critical and spiritual scrutiny of the community.

3. How then can we most effectively proceed?

This third question is, quite frankly and unapologetically, the "how to" question. As the situation begins to be seen and understood in its richness, complexity, and mystery, and as we seek to discern God's will for it and to shape our ministry in that direction, the practical question inevitably arises of how to get from here to there, however obscure both the "here" and the "there" may still be. This is a question, at one level, about practical knowledge and skill: for example, how most effectively to organize, illustrate, and preach a sermon, provide pastoral leadership in conflicted or multicultural situations, lead congregational worship and prayer, minister to a grieving family, teach a church school class, or make a witness of faith on a public issue. Or how to provide authentic spiritual care and guidance in public settings to non-Christian or to secular persons, particularly in relation to difficult situations of social conflict or psychological complexity or pathology.

Such "how to" knowledge is essential to all dimensions of ministerial practice, yet it is important to see that the work of deepening practical knowledge and improving skills is also an art form that comprises a fundamental spiritual discipline of any spiritual practice or ministry. For instance, the development of pastoral skill in the professional arts of ministry applies to all three questions, not just the practical how-to question. It takes skill, practice, and experience to gain understanding about *what is going on here* from multiple angles, theological and non-theological. Over time, with training, patience, wise counsel, and devoted practice, however, one can become more adept at seeing deeply into situations and grasping their underlying patterns, issues, and dynamics, intuiting what might rightly be hoped and prayed for, and determining how to proceed in the most faithful and effective way.

Moreover, it is important to recognize that pastoral skills, like skills in other professions and the more general skills of life itself, take numerous forms, vary in subtlety, and complexity and often require an element of imagination and creativity. A beginning student of preaching or pastoral care, for example, can generally master the simple elements of these ministerial arts — biblical exegesis, focusing, developing, and illustrating one's ideas or listening attentively and entering empathically into what suffering people are experiencing. As one becomes more experienced and adept, however, these elementary skills broaden and deepen into a kind of wise, intuitive wisdom and nuanced modes of pastoral action. Such mature functioning cannot be easily described and cannot be directly taught. It must develop uniquely for each practitioner through experience and the trial and error that inevitably marks the formation of any complex practical skill. Pastoral or spiritual ability is therefore something of a creative art form that can grow (or wither and die) over time, depending on how authentically artist-practitioners devote themselves to their calling. There is an old saying that with practice and patience, skill development moves from unconscious incompetence to conscious incompetence, then to conscious competence, and finally, if all goes well, to the promised land of unconscious competence!

At what might be called the deepest level of skill — unconscious competence perhaps — something quite remarkable and spiritually significant occasionally happens. In such rare events, one has the sense that the skillful practice is not so much something one manages or controls, deliberately or with effort, but rather is experienced as a kind of participation in an action larger than oneself. A musical or dramatic performance, or an athletic competition at high levels of skill and existential involvement, can lift one to the heights of experience, generating a sense of profound participation transcending ordinary experiences of individual selfhood and involving a feeling of effortless, well-harmonized functioning or "flow." In this extraordinary state of mind one's sense of self and awareness of the environment flow together experientially, and one's actions, while still experienced as one's own, seem also to be given to one from beyond the narrow perimeter of ordinary intention, consciousness, and self-control. This phenomenon is not always identified as a form of religious experience; psychologists have identified and studied it over a wide range of contexts and meanings.[3] But when spiritual arts are practiced in such depth in preach-

---

3. See Mihali Csikszentmihalyi, *Flow: The Psychology of Optimal Experience* (New

ing, worship, care, acts of inspired leadership and discipleship, or in comparable professional and public practices, it seems to be gifted or "graced," carried along by a profound, unseen spiritual process. Such inspired moments seem to draw upon, liberate, and transcend the ordinary powers of self and community and their accrued practical wisdom and skill. Such, one may suppose, must be the most profound form of "ministry in depth" — a ministerial practice "in the power of the Spirit."

Developing one's ability to do ministry or any of the spiritual leadership or professional arts in depth, however, requires more than mastering finite skills. It is integrally tied to the kinds of persons and communities we are becoming or seeking to become, hence to qualities of character and spirituality. It is "existential," and one cannot have a spiritually deep practice if one is not engaged in developing an understanding of one's own life and process of growth into a richer and more profound personhood. This means that all three questions of ministry are also, and essentially, questions we must ask of ourselves and must allow and encourage others to ask of us. (1) What is going on with me — in the depths of my own "soul" — in my personal, professional, and public relationships? (2) What is God's will for me at this time, as nearly as I can tell; what may I rightly hope and pray for, for myself and my ministry and for all of us in our shared vocation? (3) By what means then can I proceed? What practical steps can I take, whether simple and obvious or subtle and profound, to more fully realize my vocation and destiny not only as a pastor but as a human being and child of God?

Concluding Reflections

What is needed today is a "ministry in depth," a ministry that hesitates before jumping to conclusions, fixing people, or managing and promoting institutional religion or moral crusades and causes. We need a spiritual practice that first searches out the less obvious and often hidden dimensions of what is going on and that searches for the divine will in relation to the deeper issues it uncovers, then works imaginatively to combine situational insight and theological direction in the concrete work of ministry.

York: Harper & Row, 1990), and Mihali Csikszentmihalyi, *Finding Flow: The Psychology of Engagement with Everyday Life* (New York: Basic Books, 1997).

Reaching toward such a creative synthesis, however, is itself a "depth" enterprise, as is all truly creative work. We integrate situation, a sense of God's direction and leading, and our own skills, histories, needs, and emerging strengths in helping bring into being the fullness of our humanity in God, as individual persons and communities, though we do so in ways we can never fully describe or control. Creative work entails both conscious intentional effort as well as unconscious fallow times of meditation and "walking away from it" that allow the unconscious workings of mind and community to move in their hidden rhythms, waiting upon the divine Wind to move across the face of the deep. In the last analysis, therefore, a creative ministry "in depth" entails participating in nothing less than the spiritual becoming of the people of God, which is finally of a piece with living more fully into the mystery and tragedy of life itself, in all its creative power and destructive possibility, and in all its hidden beauty, goodness, and Gracious Presence.

Flowers on the Altar: Initial Pastoral Visits and Communication in Depth

Russell H. Davis

In a former three-month summer interim ministry, I wanted to engage in some home visitation of parish members. Due to the limits of the interim period, I did not have time to visit every member. I wanted the visits to be significant and not simply chit-chat. How might I select which parishioners to visit? I decided to visit those parishioners who had given flowers for the church altar the previous week in order to learn of the significance of the memorial tribute. Who is being remembered, and why? In what ways was he or she significant to those now giving honor? In implementing this structure of pastoral visitation I expected to learn of the important anniversary times: times of sadness around the date of death of loved ones — times when in subsequent years a pastor might visit or send a note.

I was motivated in part by intellectual curiosity in relation to the literature on anniversary grief.[1] According to Van Gennep, mourning "is a transitional period for the survivors, and they enter it through rites of separation and emerge from it through rites of integration into society (rites of lifting the mourning)."[2] Communal rites of mourning beyond the time of the funeral and rites of "lifting" the mourning have virtually disappeared in some societies, perhaps because of an emphasis on privacy, indi-

---

1. See, for example, D. M. Moss III, "Near-Fatal Experience, Crisis Intervention and the Anniversary Reaction," *Pastoral Psychology* 28 (Winter 1979): 75-96.

2. Arnold Van Gennep, *The Rites of Passage,* trans. M. B. Vizedom and G. L. Caffee (Chicago: University of Chicago Press, 1960), 147.

This article previously appeared as "Initial Pastoral Visits and Communication in Depth," *Journal of Religion and Health* 29, no. 2 (Summer 1990): 149 66. Reprinted by permission.

vidual differences and autonomy. To give flowers for the altar may be a self-selected way of engaging in a rite of reincorporation.

I was aware also of my own anniversary feelings each year near the date of my father's death. I had in mind the many tender feelings that go with flowers: flowers that express love, say thanks, repay social debt; flowers perfunctorily given; flowers expressive of mourning; flowers given but unacknowledged; flowers that welcome or say bon voyage; flowers worn on Father's or on Mother's Day — red for the living, white for the dead; flowers that celebrate — a wedding, birthday, or anniversary; flowers for the sick or dying; flowers for the first dance, prom, or recital; flowers at the birth of a child; flowers in memory and honor, adorning an altar.

I visited each flower donor in the week following the gift. After each visit I wrote a full verbatim report from memory, including my own observations and impressions.[3] A verbatim report is one form of keeping case records in ministry. The report typically has three major sections: an introduction, which provides background on the pastoral visit, the "verbatim" section, which includes a record of what each person in the conversation said based on memory of the conversation, and a concluding section, which reflects on the encounter and assesses strengths and weaknesses of the visit. In this paper, I draw on the work of D. W. Winnicott, a British psychoanalyst and pediatrician, to augment my own assessments and reflections.

I present two of the reports below. (I have thoroughly disguised the identities of the persons involved, in order to maintain confidentiality.) I will discuss why my emphasis shifted after a few visits — from focusing on altar flowers and anniversary grief to recognizing how in-depth communication is possible in initial visits of the pastor. In the final section I shall offer some analysis and reflection in light of D. W. Winnicott's theory of communication. Winnicott may seem, at first glance, to be a strange choice as a partner in pastoral reflection. "We know Winnicott best for his descriptions of the space that grows between a mother and her infant to fa-

---

3. The verbatim pastoral report is a major tool for teaching pastoral care skills to ministers and seminarians and is best learned through taking a unit of Clinical Pastoral Education. See Charles E. Hall, *Head and Heart: The Story of the Clinical Pastoral Education Movement* (Decatur, GA: Journal of Pastoral Care Publications, 1992). For additional methods of case recording in ministry — such as diaries and journals — see David Willows and John Swinton, eds., *Spiritual Dimensions of Pastoral Care: Practical Theology in a Multi-Disciplinary Context* (London: Jessica Kingsley Publishers, 2000), and Seward Hiltner, *Preface to Pastoral Theology* (Nashville: Abingdon Press, 1958).

cilitate the infant's transition from absolute to relative dependence and eventually to independence."[4] But Winnicott also finds an analogy between childhood and maturity. An understanding of profound communication between mother and child becomes a means of understanding in-depth communication between pastor and parishioner.

Verbatim Pastoral Reports

Bob and Ann Cliff

Bob and Ann are in their late sixties. They have been members of this church nearly all their lives. Both have held prominent positions. They had given flowers in memory of a friend on the Sunday of my visit.

1. RHD: (I knocked on the screen door. To stop by unannounced was unusual but not taboo in this community. Seeing Ann come toward the door with a quizzical look, I called out.) Ann.
2. Ann: Who is it?
3. RHD: Russell Davis.
4. Ann: Who?
5. RHD: Russell Davis, from church. (Ann reached the door with Bob just behind her.)
6. Ann: Oh! Come in. How nice of you to stop by.
7. RHD: Thanks. (We all shook hands and then went into the living room.)
8. Bob: Here, have the rocking chair, if that's O.K.?
9. RHD: Fine. (Bob sat in the chair next to mine. Ann sat across on the couch, surrounded by the Sunday paper.) I was just by to see Kitty (the church member in the hospital). I phoned to see if I might come by. When your line was busy I decided to drop in anyway. (They seemed pleased.)
10. Ann: How is Kitty doing? I didn't know she was in the hospital.
11. RHD: She's O.K. Still jaundiced and hates the restriction against visitors.
12. Bob: Glad she's O.K. Her husband was one of the best mechanics in

4. Ann Belford Ulanov, *Finding Space: Winnicott, God and Psychic Reality* (Louisville: Westminster John Knox, 2001), 13.

town. It's a shame he was an alcoholic — probably caused him to die so young. Kitty, she was always cheerful though. Never seemed to let him get her down. (Pause.)

13. Ann: Where do you live?
14. RHD: Next to the college church.
15. Bob: That's a lovely area.
16. RHD: Yes, quite nice.
17. Ann: Our son, Paul, is studying to be a minister.

(For the next ten minutes Ann and Bob told in duet the story of their son quitting a good job in top management in order to go into ministry. He took his family, wife, and two children off to seminary. I put my agenda on the back burner. They kept talking. I decided that in a few minutes I would shift the conversation from the story of their son to the flowers and the friend in whose memory they were given. Before I interrupted, they shifted the conversation to their other son, Ralph. From the exchange of glances between them and the shift in the tone of their voices I sensed they had reached a tender subject. It was as if the last ten minutes had been leading to this moment. Whereas before they had more or less excluded me from their compulsively told story, now they began to draw me in. Perhaps they had been testing me. Earlier they had smiled about things of anxious concern but I had not. Now their smiles faded.)

18. Bob: Ralph, our other son, lives in Chicago. He and his wife are separated, and we don't know why. Like you said this morning, running from problems just doesn't work, and that's what he's doing. I wrote him a long letter telling him to either get things worked out with Amy or not to speak to me again.
19. Ann: One day Ralph just called up and asked if he could come see us, as if he needed to ask to come to his own home. And when he gets here he says, "I've decided to leave Amy." I couldn't believe it. We thought he was kidding. We asked him why. But we couldn't get an answer. We don't think there is anyone else involved. Amy comes up here and cries her heart out and says she will take him back at any time. And I asked him if it was because there are no children, no family to hold them together, and he said no, that the city was no fit place to raise children. Amy has a good job and Ralph does too.
20. RHD: Did they get any counseling?
21. Bob: Yes, but it didn't do any good. Ralph had his mind made up be-

fore he went. He's also been seeing a psychiatrist — but nine out of ten of them don't know what they're doing.

22. RHD: I don't know about that, but your concern is their commitment to marriage.

23. Bob: Yes. I know one who tells people to do whatever they want.

24. RHD: Sounds as if you feel the situation is out of your hands.

25. Bob: Yes. I don't know what to do. Ralph and Amy don't have a church to turn to. I don't know how they get along without prayer. Marriage and life can be awfully rough. (He looked at Ann as if she knew what he meant.) I couldn't have made it without church and prayer. Our other son talked with him one day for eight hours and he couldn't get through either. I couldn't say mine (meaning unclear) without getting torn up so I wrote him and said everything I wanted, logically and clearly. I told him to find out now why things were wrong and straighten it out.

26. RHD: Yes, that's good. I wonder, though, if Ralph will pay attention since you are so close to him. (Pause.) I will be praying for Ralph. You don't see what can be done. Yet this doesn't mean that things won't change, or that they are hopeless.

27. Bob: When this first happened, I was so torn up I couldn't even touch the piano. (Bob is known for his love of music.) Now, thank goodness, it's not that bad.

28. RHD: While I was at the hospital I took some of your beautiful flowers to Kitty. She was very appreciative. I told her they came out of your yard.

29. Ann: I'm glad she liked them. (Ann started talking of someone else, but I cut her off.)

30. RHD: I notice you gave the flowers in honor of Joan. I didn't know her. Can you tell me about her?

31. Bob: Yes, she was a grand person, a neighbor of ours for years. (Bob went on to tell of her marriage and of her divorce because of her husband's unfaithfulness. Joan was loved in the church. She was active, and taught church school.)

32. Bob: (continuing) She had a son who was an epileptic. We used to check on him while she was at work. Every Sunday we had dinner together.

33. Ann: She was like us. She didn't want gracious living to die out. Even the simplest meal was set properly — good china, silver, crystal — always a candle for dinner.

34. Bob: When she died we were taken by surprise. It must have been her heart. Even her doctor was surprised. She was in the hospital over nothing much, and suddenly she died. We never quite knew why

35. RHD: Is this about the time of her death?

36. Bob: No, this was her birthday. She died in February.

37. Ann: But we always put flowers in church at this time, and always something out of the garden. She hated stiff arrangements; she always liked something natural.

38. RHD: How long has she been gone?

39. Ann: Twelve years now.

40. RHD: You honor her quite well and devotedly, even now respecting her preferences.

41. Bob: Yes. And after she died we lost our lease and moved into her house — even have some of her things. We've only been in this house two years now.

42. Ann: Yes, I inherited this house from my uncle.

43. RHD: Thanks so much for telling me about Joan. I imagine there are other newcomers, like myself, who wondered who she was.

44. Bob: Yes, I'm sure. And they missed knowing a grand person.

45. RHD: Yes. (Brief pause) I see I must be going now.

46. Ann: Please come again. This was so good.

47. Bob: Come on, let me show you around the garden before you leave. (We walked around outside, admiring the many beautiful flowers and the new fence Bob had just built. Bob told how much the church had meant to him in the many years he had been a member. I left after good-byes.)

This verbatim report provides an example of how significant communication and a pastoral relationship can be established by suffering people despite faulty pastoral technique. I was far too rigidly preoccupied with my own agenda, especially in the early and later parts of the conversation. In the middle section (#18-26) I was able to listen and respond with care to their hurt about their youngest son's divorce. I would like to think that I did not cut Bob off as abruptly as the account makes it seem (#27). But I have not altered the way I wrote up the conversation after returning home that same day. Whether or not the transition was smoother at that point or not, the fact remains that I was somewhat preoccupied with my own agenda for the visit, and this affected my sensitivity to their need, although my basic concern came through. Fortunately, I got more than I expected from the visit and was able to learn from the experience. I came expecting to hear of their friend who had died. I left knowing that their primary concern was not the dead but the living, their son Ralph. Although I had been their interim minister for more than two months, Bob and Ann had not sought me out. But they seized the initiative once I took the first step.

I was impressed with Bob and Ann's feeling for each other. The conversation flowed easily between them without much competition or animosity. Whereas Bob had dealt with many of his feelings by means of his letter to Ralph, Ann was still struggling a great deal. She subsequently turned to me. The next month, after my interim was over, she initiated a correspondence in which she continued working on her wishes to salvage the son's marriage and to understand what went wrong. We exchanged some letters and a few phone calls. I gradually and persistently encouraged her to talk with the new pastor, which she eventually did.[5]

This visit brought home to me that my initial expectation of learning about anniversary grief was too narrow. A colleague's remark helped me clarify my already broadening perspective. My visitation project reminded him of Donald Winnicott's short-term, in-depth work with children and parents. Winnicott, a British pediatrician and psychoanalyst, holds axiomatic that: "if opportunity is given in the proper and professional way for a child or for an adult, then in a limited setting of the professional contact the client will bring and display (though at first in a tentative way) the current problem or the emotional conflict or the pattern of strain which obtains at this moment of the client's life."[6] This insight is relevant not only for counseling relationships but also for relationships in ministry and everyday life. Winnicott thinks deep communication is possible if one simply listens to the story of the person sitting next to one on a bus journey; if there is any kind of privacy the story will begin to evolve. It may be just a long tale of rheumatism or of injustice at the office, but already the material is there for a deep conversation about the deepest concerns of the person at that moment in time. "Obviously it would be irresponsible to turn

5. In addition to referral to the new pastor, I might have also referred her to a trained pastoral counselor, someone certified by the American Association of Pastoral Counselors. The AAPC membership and referral directory can be found at their web site: http://www.aapc.org/.

6. D. W. Winnicott, *Therapeutic Consultations in Child Psychiatry* (New York: Basic Books, 1971), 7.

neighbours on a bus journey into clients who would inevitably become dependent, needing further opportunities or else suffering a sense of loss at the bus stop."[7]

In the pastoral and professional context, how does one provide such an opportunity? The method involves "simply listening" and "giving yourself deliberately and in a professional way to the task of using the material offered" so that "the material becomes specific and acutely interesting since the client soon begins to feel that understanding may perhaps be available and that communications at a deep level may become possible."[8] Bob and Ann came to feel that understanding might be available, perhaps because I did not smile when they talked, anxiously but smilingly, of their son Paul (#16). Though intent on reaching my own agenda, I also had listened carefully. I had pictured their anguish over their son's separation in light of their own values and long-standing marriage. I could sense their wish to control and their yearning to understand why.

I came to see future conversations and visits with other people who donated flowers as listening opportunities in which the current concerns of the parishioners might emerge. This had already happened in the conversation with Bob and Ann. They leapt at the opportunity to share their current crisis. Someone less troubled might require a more sensitive ear, one not preoccupied with predetermined agenda. So I hoped to be open to what Winnicott calls "sacred moments,"[9] moments in which someone shows confidence and trust. My main task, as I now saw it, would be to provide, through attitude and manner, a "holding environment" in which the person's significant concerns might emerge and be understood.[10]

My emphasis, owing to the structure of the relationship, would be on communication in depth, rather than therapeutic change. By structure of relationship I mean such formal qualities as initiative, meeting (time, place, regularity), and contract. Unlike pastoral counseling, these visits were taken at my initiative; there was no agreement on further meetings, and expectations remained implicit and unclarified. The distinction be-

7. Winnicott, *Therapeutic Consultations,* 7.
8. Winnicott, *Therapeutic Consultations,* 7.
9. Winnicott, *Therapeutic Consultations,* 4.
10. By "holding environment," I mean establishing an atmosphere of reliability and trust so that the deepest concerns of the individual can come forth. See D. W. Winnicott, "Contemporary Concepts of Adolescent Development and Their Implications for Higher Education," in *Playing and Reality* (New York: Basic Books, 1971), 141.

tween counseling and visitation, however, should not be held rigidly. Even visits initiated by the pastor can shift to counseling-like conversations if there is a change in initiative from pastor to parishioner. Such a shift occurred in the visit with Bob and Ann when they took the lead in discussing their son Ralph.

Mrs. French

Mrs. French had given flowers in memory of "loved ones." After worship that Sunday, she asked me to whom the flowers she had given should be sent. I suggested two people, and she decided on a man dying of cancer. I had seen Mrs. French at church regularly but had not known her name. On this day she looked old, stooped, and tired. I estimated her age at 75 years. Before I went to see her on the following Thursday, the church secretary commented: "I don't know her very well. She's been in the church for years but is pretty much a loner." I called Mrs. French and arranged a time to see her, which allowed us about forty minutes before she had another engagement.

Mrs. French lives in the nicest section of town, although her house is among the more modest on the street, a small brick bungalow. When she greeted me at the door, she looked like a different woman from the one I had seen Sunday. Today she was fresh, rested, and wore a green Izod dress. We went inside, through a small parlor, turned left into a long, bright living room — sunlight and African violets at the far end. We sat in upholstered French provincial chairs, across from a fireplace. Between us was a small round table on which sat a few *objets d'art* and photographs of two different men displayed in a double, hinged frame. She seemed to know why I had come. After discussing the weather and learning more about where I lived, she came to her point.

1. Mrs. F: I don't get into the city much anymore. I'm alone now. My husband, brother, and mother are all dead. Now only I am left. Of course, I have friends.
2. RHD: But it's not the same.
3. Mrs. F: No. There's not the closeness, and they don't live with you.
4. RHD: I noticed the flowers on Sunday given for your loved ones.
5. Mrs. F: Yes. They're all gone now (said with a slight smile, sadly, and

somewhat pensively). I don't need this house anymore, but there's no place better to go. They all lived here with me. My husband died ten years ago, my mother five, and my brother three years ago

6. RHD: So much sadness in these last few years.

7. Mrs. F: Yes, but I had good years with them. I'm thankful for them. My husband died peacefully. One day he said, "Oh, I feel so tired," and I told him to go take a rest. He never woke up from that sleep.

8. RHD: So peaceful.

9. Mrs. F: Yes, no struggle at all. . . . We had twenty-five good years. We were married late in life. My husband was from Europe. Got his Ph.D. from Oxford. He lived in the Orient before settling here. My family is from Switzerland. My brother was the same way. He had a stroke 17 years before he died, was [partially] paralyzed, and needed us to care for him. One day I went to the store after breakfast. When I got back he was at our neighbor's. I called Dr. Fox, and he said to call the ambulance, but he was already gone. I hope I go that way.

10. RHD: Yes.

11. Mrs. F: But we never know. We have to take what the good Lord gives us. (This was said matter-of-factly. Mrs. F. has a great deal of dignity about her and a certain firmness of spirit, yet without rigidity or sentimentality.) The pictures there on the table — that's my brother, and that's my husband.

12. RHD: He was your husband? (I pointed to the man with wire-rim glasses.)

13. Mrs. F: Yes. (I thought, "Yes, he has an Oxford look." She took another frame from nearby and showed me a photo of her and her husband. They were sitting in a wooden porch swing; it was summertime. She had on a gingham plaid pinafore in the style of the late forties. I was surprised at her weight — then "pleasingly plump," now quite trim. Mrs. French was leading the way. I showed my interest with my eyes and face, but I did not say much. She continued.)

He was a member of the royal court of (she named the monarch and the country). Hitler was on the rise. And he saw that he had to get out. Then we met on a boat trip. He had been engaged to one of the ladies in the royal court. (She paused.) I don't tell most people this because . . . it seems like bragging, or they won't believe me. Anyway, I met him when I was sailing to Europe. He came to the United States for a time, and we saw each other. Then he went to the Orient. When war broke out there, I didn't hear from him for six years. After Hiroshima I got a letter from him saying he was all right and that he still loved me. I did everything I could to get him here. Finally I succeeded and he came over on a troop boat. We were married right away and immediately left the country in order to get a visa for him to remain. That took a month. Then we made it.

14. RHD: My, what a powerful story. Quite dramatic and wonderful. So you had in a sense waited for him.

15. Mrs. F: Yes. I was nearly forty-five when we married, and of course we had no children. He was the first to go, but at least I had my mother and brother. During this time I had so much to do.

16. RHD: Taking care of them.

17. Mrs. F: Yes.

18. RHD: How long have you lived here?

19. Mrs. F: Thirty-three years, and all that time in our church too. (She went on to tell how it was that her husband had changed from his faith to her church.) I wasn't very active in church organizations, but I went to worship every Sunday.

20. RHD: This was due to your responsibilities at home?

21. Mrs. F: Yes, although my brother was able to get around some. He did a small garden until his death. He was such a dear. A better brother could not be had.

22. RHD: And your mother, was she sick long?

23. Mrs. F: No, just old. She lived to be ninety-nine. Only in the last year or so was there any problem. Her mind was clear to the end. But she lost control. Many nights I was up two or three times changing her bed. Finally her doctor encouraged me to put her in the nursing home at the foot of Main Street. I did. But I still regret that to this day. You see, she lived on another eleven months. If it had only been a short time (her voice trailed off).

24. RHD: And your mother objected?

25. Mrs. F: Yes. She never said much. But she begged the nurses not to take her out to the solarium. She told me, "They're all senile out there." And they didn't call me the night she was dying — not until 5:00 A.M. when she was already dead.

26. RHD: That makes it all the harder, especially when you blame yourself.

27. Mrs. F: Yes, I still regret it. And I miss them all so much. You know I'm eighty myself.
28. RHD: Oh! (Today I was surprised. She still had a grace of movement, a lack of stiffness that belied her age.)
29. Mrs. F: Oh yes. And I'm ready to go. I only hope it is quickly.
30. RHD: You want to be with your loved ones again.
31. Mrs. F: Yes.
32. RHD: And you have a certain peacefulness and readiness about you.
33. Mrs. F: Yes. (I sensed she had finished. She had told her story, shared her guilt, and expressed her hope and wish. We wound down. She talked briefly about how her parents met and that her father died when she was eighteen. She then questioned me.) How are you liking the church?
34. RHD: Very well. I'm going to hate to leave.
35. Mrs. F: You have only a few weeks before the new minister comes.
36. RHD: Yes, that's right. (Pause.) I see that it's almost time for you to leave. I will go now and give you a few minutes to get ready.
37. Mrs. F: Thank you very much for coming. This has meant a great deal to me.
38. RHD: And to me. Thanks for sharing yourself as you did. (Mrs. French saw me to the door. We chatted a bit as I was leaving.)

This entire conversation was a sacred encounter. Mrs. French displayed trust almost from the beginning. I was touched deeply, as if I had received a great gift, which, in fact, I had. For it was almost as if she had been waiting to tell her story: "I want someone to know of my losses, my joys, my loves, my guilt, and my longing for death." She seemed to recognize that I had come wanting to be available for what was significant, and she took advantage of the opportunity provided.

Communication in Depth through Pastoral Conversations

In regard to my initial agenda, anniversary phenomena, communication in depth during home visits revealed several things. With everyone I visited, I came to know something of their loss and gained a feel for its current significance. I learned that more people give flowers at the time of the birthday of the loved one than at the anniversary of death. Does this suggest that people who give flowers are more concerned about honoring the dead than with their own experience of grief? I think so. Do most people wait until deep mourning has passed before taking the kinds of initiative involved in providing flowers for a church altar? Can such initiative be construed as a sign of integration into life after bereavement? Or does it suggest the anniversary of death is too painful? I think more the former than the latter, although both are probably true to some extent. Flowers on a birthday are more a celebration of a life, whereas flowers on the anniversary of death seem more a recollection of loss. Moreover, the public giving of flowers for the altar is, in my interpretation, one rite of passage signifying incorporation of the mourner into the church community after having been set apart by the death of a loved one.

The most significant thing to emerge out of these introductory visits was my awareness of the potentially fruitful communication first conversations offer — far too important to squander by having a rigid pastoral agenda, as happened in my visit with Bob and Ann.[11] If while visiting with people a pastor gives opportunity in the proper and professional way, the deep concerns, emotional conflicts, or patterns of strain that exist at the moment will begin to emerge. Though only two examples are provided here, this happened in varying degrees with everyone I visited. To take advantage of this opportunity, the pastor must have some awareness of the enormous potential of what Winnicott calls the "honeymoon period."[12]

The Honeymoon Period

The pastoral conversations described above took place with people I barely knew. In the beginning of any new relationship, people see each other more subjectively than objectively. Future relatedness — its tone and pattern — often receives its form and character from early encounters. The honeymoon

---

11. One of the first things I want students in Clinical Pastoral Education to learn is empathic listening. To listen empathically, one must be able to recognize and to set aside any agenda that one has for the pastoral conversation in order to discover the deepest concerns of the parishioner at that moment in time.

12. D. W. Winnicott, "Communicating and Not Communicating Leading to a Study of Certain Opposites" (1953), in *The Maturational Processes and the Facilitating Environment: Studies in the Theory of Emotional Development* (New York: International Universities Press, 1965), 185.

period exists both when the minister begins new relationships with individuals and also, on a collective level, whenever a minister begins anew in a parish. When minister and congregation are hopeful about the relationship, heightened expectation and energy characterize the honeymoon period, which provides a basis for connection. To make full use of the honeymoon period, the minister must provide opportunity for depth communication to emerge. This involves several things: establishing a holding environment constituted by genuine listening, mirroring, having empathy, and utilizing cognitive skills so that trust and significant communication can emerge.

Providing a Holding Environment

The holding environment is Winnicott's image for what is provided by a "good-enough" mother who provides a facilitating environment within which the infant's maturational process can unfold.[13] In pastoral care, the holding environment has as much to do with pastoral attitude as with ministerial action. The attitude is one of expectancy — that the significant concerns of the parishioner will develop and come forth. I carried such an attitude with me from the beginning. My error with Bob and Ann was not lack of expectant concern, but only too narrow concern.

Mirroring

Mirroring is reflecting back to another — through eyes, gesture, tone, and words — an image that corresponds, more or less, to what has come forth from the other. Mirroring is an early part of the mother-child relationship. The mirror, to begin with, is the mother's face. Winnicott describes the dynamic this way: "What does the baby see when he or she looks at the mother's face? I am suggesting that ordinarily what the baby sees is himself or herself. In other words the mother is looking at the baby and what she looks like is related to what she sees there."[14]

13. Winnicott, "The Theory of the Parent-Infant Relationship" (1960), in *The Maturational Processes*, 43-48.

14. Winnicott, "Transitional Objects and Transitional Phenomena," in *Playing and Reality*, 12.

In the early stages of any helping relationship, mirroring is an essential part of the holding environment whenever deep communication is the aim. This is so both because of what it provides and what it does not provide. Mirroring provides what Winnicott calls *cross-identification*.[15] Cross-identification involves the use of projective mechanisms which are especially significant initially. Through projection, minister and parishioner stand in each other's shoes. Such empathy is a prerequisite to trust. Particularly good examples of my use of mirroring are:

1. My comment to Bob, "Sounds as if you feel the situation is out of your hands" (#24). Bob had not actually said this, yet his feeling tone and his need to control his son suggested a desperation rooted in feeling helpless, unable to affect the outcome of his son's marriage. Also, my facial expression in the first part of that conversation, my not smiling when they smiled anxiously (#17), is another example of mirroring their deeper message.
2. Nearly all of the conversation with Mrs. French. In this visit my mirroring involved eyes and gesture (#13) as well as words (#6 and #8).

There were also times when I failed to mirror, as in the two instances previously discussed with Bob and Ann — when I shifted the focus from feeling to fact (#18) and from Bob's agenda to my own (#28). Such incidents break the holding environment and disrupt communication.

Mirroring, as part of the holding environment, is important also for what it does not provide. Mirroring is not primarily interpretation. Depth psychology has made a significant contribution to the art of helping people by demonstrating that interpretation, proclamation (of some religious message, for example), or insight do not, by themselves, effect change in a person's life. Change occurs at "teachable moments" or "in the fullness of time"; premature interpretation, that is, "interpretation outside the ripeness of the material is indoctrination and produces compliance."[16] Indoctrination is experienced by the recipient as impingement, as psychological violence, as something foreign or alien to the self. Compliance on the part of parishioners (when such occurs) may lead, in extreme cases, to the de-

---

15. Winnicott, "Interacting Apart from Instinctual Drive and in Terms of Cross-Identifications," in *Playing and Reality,* 119-37.

16. Winnicott, "Playing: A Theoretical Statement," 51.

velopment of a false self or to a diffusion of identity. We ministers, of all people, ought to avoid doing anything that encourages phoniness or diffusion in religion — that is, lack of clarity in religious identity as a result of repression or renunciation of a personal position.

An occupational expectation of ministers, one we may even believe ourselves, is that the pastor should be able to offer some words in every situation — advice, proclamation, comfort, rebuke, scripture, or prayer. However, what Winnicott noted about his work with children is true of our caregiving with people of all ages: "the significant moment is that at which the child surprises himself or herself. It is not the moment of my clever interpretation that is significant."[17] The minister or therapist who is too quick to admonish or offer analytical interpretation may steal a person's creativity. Premature proclamation in pastoral work, far from creating the desired results — deeper communication, or repentance, or personal change — may be experienced by the parishioner as either ineptness or an assault.

The crucial thing is timing and appropriateness. Winnicott's guidelines are that interpretation must await the ripeness of the material and the readiness of the person.[18] We must wait until "We become objectively perceived in the patient's [or parishioner's] own time."[19] In the honeymoon period, when projection is at a peak, interpretation in pastoral care should be kept to a minimum, as should religious proclamation. Failure to respect the readiness or lack thereof of a person to receive our point of view breaks the holding environment and threatens trust in the pastor's ability to contain his or her self, and to contain the situation at hand.

Conceptual Skills

In order for a pastor to use the opportunities of the honeymoon period to fullest advantage, he or she must bring to bear an informed point of view. My own conceptual framework and my use of Winnicott became a part of the holding environment. Through an informed conceptual perspective

17. Winnicott, "Playing: A Theoretical Statement," 51.

18. Winnicott, "Playing: A Theoretical Statement," 51.

19. Winnicott, "Communicating and Not Communicating Leading to a Study of Certain Opposites," 189.

the pastor observes the situation; through cross-identification and mirroring the pastor participates in the encounter. Conceptual skills are also tools for self-evaluation. I used the concepts "mirroring" and "holding environment" in judging the degree of helpfulness of my own work.

Such intelligent reflection also helps identify the signs for recognizing communication in depth. In my work, the signs of deep communication were different with each visit. With Bob and Ann, deeper communication became noticeable in the shift in feeling from an anxious, controlling climate (as they talked initially of their oldest son) to a more relaxed (but anguished) quality when they told of their second son's divorce. Certainly the content of their communication was also a clue. With Mrs. French, the sign was the feeling of trust: a feeling indeed of sacredness and of mystery before which I was almost silent as she told me her story. I offered her a holding environment in which she could engage in what Winnicott calls "playing," by which he means "a creative [emotional] experience taking up space and time, and intensely real."[20] For Winnicott, playing is far from frivolous. Playing is creative communication and a basic form of living. Mrs. French was "playing" in my presence and, like a good-enough parent, I mirrored her being, not through words and interpretation, but through recognition, gesture, facial expression, and feeling.

Conclusion

This essay has told the story of a summer of discovery and evolving depth in my ministry. The story began with a time when I was the part-time interim minister of a loving and lovely congregation. Due to a confluence of my desire to do home visitation with parishioners, my interest in anniversary grief, and my curiosity about the story of the altar flowers, I began a program of home visitation. After the first visit, a chance remark by a colleague led me to look at my visits in light of the work of D. W. Winnicott. In re-reading Winnicott, I shifted the reason for my visit from my agenda of anniversary grief to discovering the deepest concerns of those with whom I visited.

I found myself as a pastor wanting to give opportunity "in the proper and professional way" so that in the limited setting of the professional pas-

20. Winnicott, "Playing: A Theoretical Statement," 50.

toral contact the parishioner might be given space to "bring forth and display (though at first in a tentative way) the current problem or the emotional conflict or the pattern of strain which obtains at this moment" of their life.[21] In other words, I found myself wanting to engage in empathic listening in order to learn the deepest concerns of those with whom I visited. In order to do this, I had to follow their lead, rather than they mine.

As a result, I found the conversations to be sacred. I came to feel as if each visit took place in sacred time and on holy ground. And I gained a new appreciation of Winnicott. For me, a deeper reading of his work was evocative. What begins in Winnicott as a story of mother and child evolved, for me, into a powerful analogy of our relationship with God, and through God, with each other.

21. Winnicott, *Therapeutic Consultations*, 7.

Much Depends on the Kitchen:
Pastoral Practice in Multicultural Society

K. Samuel Lee

Ineffective knowledge is to know all about something and still to go ahead without any notion of what difference such knowledge makes in one's life. . . . Effective knowledge changes one's . . . attitude, motives, and actions.

Ann Belford Ulanov[1]

What we from our point of view call colonization, missions to the heathen, spread of civilization, etc., has another face — the face of a bird of prey seeking with cruel intentness for distant quarry — a face worthy of a race of pirates and highwaymen. All the eagles and other predatory creatures that adorn our coats of arms seem to me apt psychological representatives of our true nature.

Carl Jung[2]

---

1. Ann Belford Ulanov, "The Self as Other," *Journal of Religion and Health* 12, no. 2 (April 1973): 145.

2. Carl G. Jung, *Memories, Dreams, Reflections* (New York: Random House, 1961), 248-49; quoted in Helene Shulman Lorenz and Mary Watkins, "Depth Psychology and Colonialism: Individualism, Seeing Through, and Liberation," a paper presented at The International Symposium of Archetypal Psychology, Psychology at the Threshold, hosted by Pacifica Graduate Institute, August 31–September 4, 2000, at the University of California, Santa Barbara, CA, http://search.yahoo.com/search?p=critique+of+depth+psychology&ei=UTF-8&fr=yfp-t-501&xargs=0&pstart=1&b=11 (accessed January 11, 2008).

A friend of mine proudly shared how to prepare his new culinary invention, Mango Dessert:

A Mango Dessert
Cut up mangos.
> Prepare 2 mangos per 3 people.

Prepare 1 pint of plain yogurt.
> Add ½ teaspoon full of ground cardamom.
> Add ½ teaspoon full of syrup or sugar.
> Let it sit for a while.

Sparingly put coconut on a pan or on a cookie sheet.
> Toast in oven at 350°F for 5 minutes
> and then check.

Put mangos in dish.
> Pour yogurt over mangos.
> Sprinkle coconut on top
> and serve.[3]

Following the recipe is a bit of challenge for a non-native American like me.[4] I have to become familiar with the ingredients: mango, plain yogurt, cardamom, syrup, and coconut. I grew up in Korea, where I had no experience of tropical fruits, other than banana and canned pineapple. What makes yogurt "plain"? What is cardamom, and how is it used in cooking? Also, the recipe assumes that I know specific measuring systems. How much is a "pint" and a "teaspoon"? What temperature is 350°F in Celsius? Further, I have to be familiar with the tools used in this recipe. Do I use a regular teaspoon to measure "½ teaspoon full," or is there a special measuring spoon? What is a "cookie sheet"? How do I use an oven? So many things are assumed in this simple recipe.

As a Korean American immigrant I have now lived for thirty-four years in the United States, so I am more proficient in an American kitchen than these sentences imply. However, my questions illustrate that common activi-

---

3. The recipe was created by pastoral theologian Herbert Anderson, and this story was told elsewhere. See K. Samuel Lee, "The Teacher-Student in Multicultural Theological Education: Pedagogy of Collaborative Inquiry," *Journal of Supervision and Training in Ministry* 22 (2002): 81-99.

4. One may rightly ask who a "native American" is, since most Americans who consider themselves "native" are descendents of immigrants.

ties are actually complex cultural activities. It is easy to take for granted the things that make up our kitchens and how we go about the practice of cooking. We can barely recognize the particularity — and peculiarity — of our kitchens and our cooking. We can also easily overlook the cultural meanings attached to the kitchen as a room. Author and broadcaster Margaret Visser studies the history, anthropology, and mythology of everyday life. For her, a building, room, or any other common thing in life is a plot to be read. So she studies and writes "an account of the meanings, the culture, and the history embodied [even] in a single meal."[5] As she notes, there is more to a kitchen than "a room where food is kept, prepared and cooked and where the dishes are washed."[6] The kitchen is "a [room] that is intentionally meaningful; it reveals itself most fully to people prepared to respond to its 'language.'"[7] Consider how kitchens have been created and used to reinforce the common gender dynamic that women serve men. In Korea it has traditionally been said that "a man who enters the kitchen risks losing his penis." So even in contemporary Korea men usually stay *out* of the kitchen, happily so, while women's proper place is understood to be *in* the kitchen. A kitchen is more than a room where a meal is served. It is — and reinforces — a language, a system, a culture, a paradigm, and a way of life. Much depends on the kitchen.

What does a kitchen have to do with pastoral practice? In this chapter I will discuss how pastoral practice — like cooking, kitchens, and other common cultural activities — is a complex *cultural* activity. Likening pastoral practice to the kitchen acknowledges that there is an inherent relationship between the specific persons we are and what we do in ministry or between what we *practice* and what we *internally hold* to be true. This statement may be a truism, but the truth it conveys about our personal *cultural* specificity is not often examined. Pastoral practice is culturally conditioned, and its relevance is culturally determined. Pastoral practice takes place in a given historical time and contextual system and is governed by the grammar[8] that is embedded in that time and context. And, just as we

5. Margaret Visser, *The Geometry of Love: Space, Time, Mystery, and Meaning in an Ordinary Church* (New York: North Point Press, 2000), 2. See also Margaret Visser, *Much Depends on Dinner: The Extraordinary History and Mythology, Allure and Obsessions, Perils and Taboos, of an Ordinary Meal* (New York: Grove Press, 1986).

6. *Cambridge Advanced Learner's Dictionary,* http://dictionary.cambridge.org/define.asp?key=43829&dict-CALD (accessed November 1, 2007).

7. Visser, *The Geometry of Love,* 4.

8. For a recent example, see Joe Jones, *A Grammar of Christian Faith: Systematic Explo-*

often engage in cooking with little awareness of its cultural particularity, pastoral practitioners often engage in our work without examining the implications of our contextual systems or the cultural bases and *biases of our* practice. Or, we grow in awareness of cultural particularity, but, as Ann Ulanov suggests, we still go ahead with our practice without any notion of what difference cultural particularity ought to make in our actions. Often it is this unexamined or static cultural specificity of our pastoral practice that causes it to be judged negatively — as irrelevant, ineffective, inappropriate, imperialistic, sexist, racist, and so on.

In this chapter, my first goal is to illustrate the cultural bases and *biases* of theological education and pastoral practice. I will then discuss a few ways in which depth psychological concepts can be applied to and can increase our effectiveness in the cultural activity of pastoral practice, especially as we encounter racial-ethnic particularity and difference. Depth psychologists since Jung have generally paid little attention to race and ethnicity as dimensions of cultural experience.[9] Fortunately, there have been recent developments within depth psychology that attempt to incorporate these cultural dimensions of human experience more fully. These developments are crucial for pastoral practice in our multicultural society. I cannot emphasize enough the importance of cultural or contextual analyses of pastoral practice in our contemporary society. Population change in recent years has shown that non-European Americans number more than 22 percent of the U.S. population.[10] We live in a multicultural society, although many choose to close their eyes to the multicultural reality that surrounds our daily living. Since the events of September 11, 2001, awareness has been heightened that "ethnocultural conflicts [are] the most common source of political violence in the world."[11] Will Kymlicka, a Cana-

---

ration in *Christian Life and Doctrine*, 2 vols. (Lanham, MD: Rowman & Littlefield, 2002); theologians often speak of a grammatical analysis of theological language since theology may be viewed as "God-talk" or an analytical task to understand how religious language is used.

9. In the early years of depth psychology a "cultural school" developed, led by Karen Horney, Erich Fromm, Frieda Fromm-Reichman, Harry Stack Sullivan, and Erik Erikson. Their study of culture rarely specified or studied the dynamics of race and ethnicity.

10. U.S. Census Bureau, "Estimates of the Population by Race and Hispanic Origin for the United States and States: July 1, 2007 (SC-EST2007-04)," http://www.census.gov/popest/states/asrh/SC-EST2007-04.html (accessed July 7, 2008).

11. Will Kymlicka, *Multicultural Citizenship* (Oxford: Clarendon Press, 1995), 1.

dian scholar studying international dynamics of multiculturalism, helps us see in *Multicultural Citizenship* that grave ethnocultural conflicts have been always very much a part of human history, but human political systems have responded with "benign neglect."[12] By "benign neglect" Kymlicka refers to a general attitude in society that regards the cultural issues such as ethnic identity or religion as belonging to private life and thus not the concern of the state. In my opinion, many pastoral practitioners share this view. I will argue in this chapter that pastoral practitioners can neither afford to practice "benign neglect" nor to be anything other than competent multicultural practitioners. This is an urgent message to heed, especially for European Americans who have enjoyed a privileged status in which their "benign neglect" has rarely been challenged. Peter McLaren, a multicultural educator, argues that such neglect is never benign but represents a "predatory culture," "a field of invisibility . . . precisely because it is so obvious."[13] McLaren adds, "Its obviousness immunizes its victims against a full disclosure of its menacing capabilities."[14]

The Cultural Specificity of Theological Education

My seminary education was like learning to cook in an alien kitchen. Of course, many of my *American*[15] student colleagues were also being confronted for the first time with strange tools needed to navigate the "kitchen" of liberal theological education. We struggled to learn how to use tools for a historical-critical method of biblical interpretation — textual criticism, literary and source criticism, form criticism, tradition criticism, redaction criticism, and canonical criticism. These tools unveiled my naïve notions about the Bible and shifted my assumptions about what the Bible is and how one should read and appropriate it. For many of us seminarians, this

12. The term "benign neglect" is used by Ethan Glazer in *Affirmative Discrimination: Ethnic Inequality and Public Policy* (New York: Basic Books, 1975), 25, and cited in Kymlicka, *Multicultural Citizenship*, 3.

13. Peter McLaren, *Critical Pedagogy and Predatory Culture: Oppositional Politics in a Postmodern Era* (London and New York: Routledge, 1995), 2; also see Paulo Freire, *Pedagogy of the Oppressed* (New York: Continuum, 1992).

14. McLaren, *Critical Pedagogy and Predatory Culture*, 2.

15. Having lived in the U.S. for thirty-four years, twice as long as I lived in Korea, I consider myself American, more specifically Korean American.

shift in our view of the Bible was a fundamental shift of the ground of our being. Furthermore, we learned that logical and critical thinking was paramount in theology because that was the kind of thinking presumed to lead to truthful claims. We were taught that good theology was built with the tools of classic Western philosophy, which led to the authority of "dogmatic" theology and the internal consistency of "systematic" theology. Of course, for these truthful claims to be authoritative, they also had to be grounded in the existing tradition of the church and the Church Fathers.

Pastoral counseling classes also opened my eyes to strange new tools. Watching my psychologist-professor do role plays in class was like watching the *Iron Chef*[16] on television who, despite the surprise ingredient of the week, confidently faced down all challengers in a frenetic culinary battle. The professor seemed to know exactly when to speak, when not to speak, and, of course, what to say, using the choicest words — an impressive demonstration in my eyes, being at that time a young adult with insufficient psychological maturity. What my seminary professors taught me during my three years of M.Div. education was undoubtedly the best available in theological education at that time. Indeed I am grateful for the professors who taught me with compassion and dedication.

But there was also something that was disheartening about my experience. I experienced the "inarticulate groaning" spoken of in Romans 8:26, though I had little understanding of it until many years after I graduated from seminary. It took a long time for me to realize that my disheartened feelings were shared by many others. Consider the example of biblical interpretation. My Bible professors designed a *kitchen* in which it was my task to learn to use the tools, recipes, ingredients, and measurement systems *they made available* for me. My professors regarded these tools as universal or normative. None of the students dared to challenge our professors, who had devoted their entire lives to biblical studies and were respected around the world. After graduation, I learned other points of view. For example, I read the work of biblical scholar Kah-Jin Jeffrey Kuan, who argues that the notion "that biblical interpretation was or can ever be objective and universal" has been severely criticized.[17] Kuan forcefully makes

16. *Iron Chef* is a Japanese television program in which participating chefs weekly compete against each other. See http://www.foodnetwork.com/food/show_ic (accessed July 1, 2008).

17. Kah-Jin Jeffrey Kuan, "Reading with New Eyes: Social Location and the Bible," http://www.psr.edu/page.cfm?l=62&id=1388 (accessed February 3, 2008).

the case that "every reading and every interpretation is by nature subjective and particular. As readers and interpreters of texts, biblical and otherwise, we engage in the construction of meaning whenever we read. The meaning is never imbedded in the text; rather it is the result of the interaction between the reader and the text."[18] In this regard, the social location of the reader of the Bible matters, and it matters a great deal. Kuan quotes Fernando Segovia and Mary Tolbert:

> A number of movements in biblical criticism — such as feminist criticism, literary criticism, sociological analysis, and liberation and contextual theologies — had begun to call into question older, established exegetical and theological methods, which had often claimed for themselves universality and objectivity under the construct of an objective and scientific reader, a universal and informed reader. These newer movements all involved a shift of critical focus toward the interpreter or theologian, bringing the issue of standpoint or perspective to the forefront of the concern, with a view of the interpretive task as directly influenced by the social location of the individual in question. Thus, factors traditionally left out of consideration were now becoming areas of exploration — for example, gender, race, ethnic origins, class, sexual orientation, religious affiliation, and sociopolitical contexts — with a focus on real, flesh-and-blood readers who were always and inescapably situated both historically and culturally and whose reading and interpretation of the texts were seen as affected by their social location.[19]

R. S. Suqirtharahjah aptly summarizes the point: "[Biblical] Criticism is not an exact science, but an undertaking of social and political commitment which should not be reduced to or solidified into a dogma."[20] Suqirtharahjah's perspective could be applied to all disciplines taught in theological education. Much depends on the kitchen, and on the identity of the cook.

My inarticulate groaning was my response to what I experienced as theological education "solidified into a dogma." Although my professors

---

18. Kuan, "Reading with New Eyes."

19. Fernando F. Segovia and Mary A. Tolbert, eds., *Reading from This Place,* vol. 1: *Social Location and Biblical Interpretation in the United States* (Minneapolis: Fortress, 1995), ix.

20. R. S. Suqirtharahjah, *Postcolonial Criticism and Biblical Interpretation* (Oxford: Oxford University Press, 2002), 14.

did not intentionally practice "benign neglect," I was expected to navigate an alien kitchen that often was not conducive to my learning. I cooked with new materials in a new kitchen but often feeling as if I were "singing the Lord's song in a foreign land" (Ps. 137:4). My specific cultural experiences and identity seemed to be devalued, if they mattered at all. I did my best to follow the recipe and prepare a meal. Unfortunately, both explicitly and implicitly it was conveyed that I was not allowed to use my own recipe or the tools and the materials with which I was far more familiar. The most difficult part of cooking in a new kitchen was the unexamined and unchallenged notion that this was the *only* way the *best* cooking could be learned. It seemed the *cultural "I"* — e.g., my own taste buds, my knowledge about sesame seeds instead of cardamom, or my knowledge about other cooking processes prevalent in Korean cooking — did not matter. It seemed as if the recipe, the cooking utensils, and the cooking materials were not elements of a culture but an absolute value, and the particularity of the cook had nothing to do with interpretation of the recipe or the practice of cooking.

Postcolonial biblical scholars such as Suqirtharahjah, Kuan, Segovia, Tolbert, and many others disclose the absurdity of such a claim. They plainly disclose how all biblical interpretation and criticism is culturally conditioned, and its relevance is culturally determined. The cultural specificity of biblical criticism, and of theological education as a whole, is often hidden behind some form of authority "solidified into a dogma." What is presumed to have great value has also the potential to encapsulate one's mind. To my mind, it is an example of what Ann Belford Ulanov calls "ineffective knowledge," which makes it possible to know "all about something and still to go ahead without any notion of what difference such knowledge makes in one's life."

The Cultural Specificity of Pastoral Practice

The first pastoral assignment I received after graduating from seminary was in 1983 in a small Arizona town with a population of about five thousand. Three out of five people in that town were Mormons, one out of five Catholics, and the remaining one-fifth of the churchgoers was divided among about twenty Protestant churches. The town was literally surrounded by three Native American tribes — Navajo, Hopi, and Apache. I had a congregation of about 150 members, the largest and the oldest Protestant congregation in town. My family was the only Korean family in town. Issues of ethnicity or racism were never brought up in the church. The congregation was happy to have a young clergy*man*, having struggled for a few years with my predecessor — the church's first ever clergy*woman*. I was twenty-six years old, and the average age of the congregation was about sixty, if not older. My pastoral practice in that church was based on what the church had done for many years. I listened to the members and did my best to come up with program ideas. New Bible study programs were based on standard denominational Christian education curricula. Weekly preaching in English was an enormous challenge for a newly ordained pastor for whom English was a second language, so I based my preaching on the lectionary because I could easily buy lectionary-based preaching and worship aids. I did not work much at evangelism, but I visited elderly members who were homebound. I was invited to be a guest speaker at the high school graduation and at memorial services held at the Elks Lodge[21] and by the Masons.[22] I responded to such invitations without questioning the theological basis of or implications for doing so.[23] I did not question these pastoral practices — it was "business as usual" for a pastor.

Now looking back at this first pastoral assignment, which occurred between 1983 and 1986, I am much more struck by the multicultural reality of the time and place than I was when I served there. Psychologist Pamela Hays uses the acronym ADDRESSING to highlight the many forms of culture that make our societies multicultural: there are cultures associated with *A*ge, *D*evelopmental and acquired *D*isabilities, *R*eligion, *E*thnicity, *S*ocioeconomic status, *S*exual orientation, *I*ndigenous heritage, *N*ational origin, and *G*ender.[24] The multidimensional nature of cultural specificity that

21. The Elks Lodge is also known as The Benevolent and Protective Order of Elks (BPOE). It is an American fraternal order and social club founded in 1868 and claims over one million members.

22. "The Masons" refers to Freemasonry, an international fraternal organization that began around the late sixteenth century in England. It is estimated that there are just under two million Masons in the U.S.

23. This is an example of the "American culture Christianity" "that is not faithful to the Gospel in all its dimensions" but "inevitably becomes an instrument of the status quo"; see René Padilla, "Evangelization and the World," *Mission Trends*, vol. 2: *Evangelization*, ed. Gerald Anderson and Thomas Stransky (New York: Paulist Press, 1975), 49.

24. Pamela Hays, *Addressing Cultural Complexities in Practice: A Framework for Clinicians and Counselors* (Washington, DC: American Psychological Association, 2001).

is highlighted by ADDRESSING was, without a doubt, present in my first church assignment. To my embarrassment, however, I now realize that I was oblivious to the social and cultural context in which the church was located. It took many years after leaving that church for me to learn that something was not right. Eventually, I began to see myself and my practice of ministry during those three years as almost completely encapsulated in my own (adopted) cultural cocoon. It is mind-boggling for me now to realize that Caucasian Americans were, numerically, a minority, in that town. There were overwhelmingly more Americans of Mexican descent and Native Americans in and surrounding the town. But during my three years of service in that church I never questioned why there was only one American of Mexican descent in the membership. Why did the church or I not reach out to non-Caucasians? The church program had little to do with the homeless and transient, immigrants, gender issues, inter-religious issues, issues of aging — issues that really mattered to those who lived, moved, and had their being in that town. More than twenty years after I left the church, I question now what it was like for the members of the church to have a young Korean American man as their pastor — the first ethnic minority pastor in the church's history — who pretended to be just like them. More than twenty years after I left the church, my "benign neglect" of the persons and the issues to which I was first called does not seem so benign. What I thought to be the excellent theological education that I had received contributed very little to my ability to navigate in a multicultural society.

There were more cultures to which I was *blind*[25] when I was at that church. Living in the town was my first encounter with a significant number of Mormons. I must have believed that they had nothing to do with me and my practice of ministry. This was also my first major encounter with Native Americans and Americans of Mexican descent, but I must have believed that they too had nothing to do with me and my practice of ministry. I comfortably stayed within the cultural confines of the 150-member Caucasian church and practiced ministry that was "business as usual." I developed a neglectful blindness to persons considered not of my fold. I organized my church — my kitchen — with the only tools I had,

---

25. Some may say that I was ignorant about these cultures, which is probably true when I arrived at this church initially. But *ignorance* is too benign a word to describe one's intentional or unintentional neglect that lasted three years. Note that disability scholars and activists, e.g., Professor Kathy Black at Claremont School of Theology, critique using words (such as *blind*) that reference disability to describe inherently negative and undesirable conditions.

the ones I had been taught in my theological education and that were now somewhat familiar or comfortable for me. I must have believed at that time that these tools were more than adequate, and the basis for that belief was that I felt loved and needed by my own people. That I felt loved and needed was enough. I neglected the cultural context in which the church found itself. I was unaware of the cultural biases of my ministry. Padilla asks on my behalf, "How can I overcome culture-Christianity, when I cannot get out of my own culture?"[26] I was doubly blinded in that I denied my own Korean American culture and that I bought into the American culture-Christianity without thinking critically.

After three years at the church, I left to pursue a Ph.D. in psychology. I left the church feeling good about myself and my ministry there, in part because most church members expressed regret at my departure, saying that they wanted another pastor *just like me.* Years have passed since then, and in the interim I again began experiencing other disheartening feelings about who I was and what I did as a local pastor in that church. There are too many pastors just like me, pastors whose eyes are closed to the cross-currents and under-currents of the multicultural milieu of our time, unaware of the cultural assumptions of our practice of ministry. Consequently, the practice of ministry becomes seriously impaired, and perhaps irrelevant, for the people and the contexts we purport to serve. My experience of teaching in three theological institutions for the past thirteen years has led me to conclude that theological education in North America is still lacking the capacity to provide an education that is adequate for ministry in this multicultural society.

The Cultural Unconscious and Depth Psychology

By and large theological education as well as pastoral practice in North America may be characterized as symptomatic of the "cultural unconscious," which a number of depth psychologists in recent years have brought to our attention. One of the most important contributions of depth psychology has to

26. Padilla, "Evangelization and the World," 51. It is important to note that there are major differences between the majority's neglect of cultural contexts in pastoral practice and the minority's neglect of the same. The majority's neglect often manifests in the form of oppression while the minority's neglect takes the form of internalized oppression. This topic is too complex to deal with in this chapter.

do with the concept of *unconscious knowing* that needs to be brought to *consciousness*, so that what we hold internally and unconsciously can be more integrated with our external, conscious behaviors, practices, and intentions.

Socratic concern for the unexamined life finds a partial solution in "depth psychology."[27] A primary purpose of depth psychology is to help persons uncover what is hidden, what is unconscious, or what is avoided, presumably out of a maladaptive strategy manifesting as defense mechanisms, including what Jung called the "persona."[28] Though the persona has some necessary or even positive functions, Jung also describes it as "a complicated system of relations between individual consciousness and society, fittingly enough a kind of mask, designed on the one hand to make a definite impression upon others, and, on the other, to conceal the true nature of the individual."[29] *Persona* describes the mask I wore in my first three years of ministry as I knowingly and unknowingly pretended to be someone I was not. Ulanov characterizes depth psychology as the "study of human interiority,"[30] the purpose of which is to unmask what is hidden or to achieve a degree of transparency and communication between one's unconscious and conscious knowing. The "unmasking of the depths,"[31] which is one way to describe the goal of depth psychology, is akin to the Johannine Jesus' saying — "You shall know the truth and the truth shall set you free" (John 8:32). Depth psychologists are, of course, much more modest, acknowledging that no psychotherapy can truly set you free. Instead, Ulanov says, depth psychology serves to help you "achieve relationship" to your own persona and "shadow," so that you can become a more integrated person.[32]

27. The term *depth psychology,* from a German term *Tiefenpsychologie,* coined by Eugen Bleuler (1857-1940), refers to what is below the surface of conscious or visible human functioning. See S. Freud, "On the History of the Psychoanalytic Movement," in *The Standard Edition of the Complete Psychological Works of Sigmund Freud,* vol. 14, ed. J. Strachey (London: Hogarth Press, 1914), 41.

28. What may be considered "maladaptive" is culturally based and also a matter of degree within socially acceptable conventions.

29. C. G. Jung, Gerhard Adler, and R. F. C. Hull, "The Relations between the Ego and the Unconscious," in *Collected Works of C. G. Jung,* vol. 7: *Two Essays on Analytical Psychology* (New York: Pantheon Books, 1966), 305.

30. Ann Belford Ulanov, "The Christian Fear of the Psyche," *Union Seminary Quarterly Review. The Daniel Day Williams Festschrift* (Spring 1975): 140.

31. Daniel Day Williams, "What Psychiatry Means to Theological Education," *Pastoral Psychiatry* 7 (October 1965): 4, quoted in Ulanov, "The Christian Fear of the Psyche," 146.

32. Ulanov, "The Christian Fear of the Psyche," 143.

The shadow is collectively or universally present in all persons and is everything in one's interior that is hidden and underdeveloped, thus preventing persons from achieving their full potential. "Achieving relationship" to our own shadow therefore means that we *work through* our shadow to uncover what is hidden, to bring what is unconscious to consciousness, and to take responsibility for who we are, both the good and the bad.

As we work through our own shadow, we learn about the unconscious processes operative in our pastoral practice. In my case, I learned to uncover my unconscious need to be liked by others as a form of self-validation in my pastoral practice. Seeking others' validation was also a means to compensate for what I felt at that time to be the sacrifice I had made when I changed my career goal from science to pastoral ministry. I also learned how my own shadow could get in the way in my pastoral practice. Seeking approval from others sometimes functioned as a shadow, "not me" way of being in ministry, causing me to forget the fundamental reason for my being in ministry — to be of service for God and others rather than to be served by others. I came to see that my unmet needs from early childhood and the dynamics in my family of origin were manifest as unhealthy *masks* that led me toward self-indulgent or self-aggrandizing tendencies. I worked very hard to understand the underpinnings of my emotions. All in all, in my early years of pastoral ministry, depth psychology taught me in significant ways to achieve a certain level of transparency between my interiority and exteriority. These insights undoubtedly contributed to my personal and professional maturity. Such insights strengthen our vocation because ours is not the vocation of "self service" but of service to Self. Ulanov articulates the point:

> At one extreme lies the use of others to serve our own needs. At some unconscious level we treat them like a gas tank; they are there to service us, to give energy to our self. At the other extreme lies service to something beyond us — to the Self, to a meaning which gathers and constructs itself as we find and create it, which we find ourselves experiencing in a devotional way.[33]

How is the *cultural unconscious* related to these crucial issues conceptualized by Jung as belonging to the shadow and the persona? The way I

33. Ann Belford Ulanov, "Self Service," in *The Functioning Transcendent: A Study in Analytical Psychology* (Wilmette, IL: Chiron Publications, 1979), 143.

have spoken thus far about my learnings from depth psychology, i.e., focused on individual insight but largely a-cultural and a-contextual, characterizes the historical tendency of depth psychology that did not adequately address the importance of the *cultural unconscious.* Depth psychologists Thomas Singer and Samuel Kimbles note that by rarely dealing with the *cultural unconscious* depth psychology as a whole has "done a great disservice to our tradition and its potential to contribute to a better understanding of group [or cultural] forces in the psyche."[34] Singer and Kimbles state that depth psychology is an open system with the capacity to account for new concepts such as the *cultural unconscious.* They offer explanations as to why depth psychology by and large failed to deal with the *cultural unconscious.* First, Jung's witness of the twentieth-century horror of collectivity "bathed in blood, violence, and terror through two world wars," coupled with the later "nightmare horror of imagining nuclear holocaust," resulted in Jung's "dread of the psyche's falling into possession by collective and archetypal forces."[35] Furthermore,

> collective life as a whole, more often than not, has slipped into the Jungian shadow — so much so that it is easy to feel within the Jungian tradition as if the life of the group and the individuals' participation in it exist in no man's land, suspended in the ether somewhere between the much more important and meaningful individual and/or archetypal realms.[36]

Singer and Kimbles also state that "Jung's natural introversion . . . and his fundamental focus on individuation had an unacknowledged tendency to set the individual up against or in opposition to the life of the group."[37] In doing so, "group life was left to the shadow." Singer and Kimbles summarize:

> Jungian psychology — with its theory of complexes — was well positioned in its earliest theoretical conceptions to understand these cultural, collective, and group phenomena. But, with its own anti-group bias and preference for understanding such material in terms of archetypal pos-

34. Thomas Singer and Samuel Kimbles, "The Emerging Theory of Cultural Complexes," in *Analytical Psychology: Contemporary Perspectives in Jungian Analysis,* ed. Joseph Cambray and Linda Carter (New York: Brunner-Routledge, 2004), 178.

35. Singer and Kimbles, "The Emerging Theory of Cultural Complexes," 177.

36. Singer and Kimbles, "The Emerging Theory of Cultural Complexes," 177.

37. Singer and Kimbles, "The Emerging Theory of Cultural Complexes," 178.

session, analytical psychology has not lived up to its promise and potential. Our tendency to archetypal reductionism, our fear and distaste for the collective, and our primary and legitimate focus on individuation are all factors that have not lent themselves to a careful, objective consideration of group phenomena within the individual and collective psyche.[38]

How, then, does the idea of the *cultural unconscious* fit into Jungian depth psychology? For Jung, the collective unconscious is a pool of mental patterns shared universally by all persons. It manifests as archetypes of patterns and symbols — as in dreams, mythologies, and fairy tales. Jung differentiated the personal unconscious from the *collective* unconscious and assumed whatever was *cultural* was also *collective*. Singer and Kimbles explain the traditional Jungian approach to cultural issues:

> First, [Jung] was sensitive to how Eurocentric, rationalistic attitudes alienated many Westerners from their primal, instinctual roots. Second, in his conceptualization of the collective unconscious he made a series of assumptions that had implicit within them a privileging of Western attitudes and values but also a derogation of traditional cultures. Finally, the concept of the collective unconscious was defined in a way that did not allow room for the cultural matrix to have its own field of action coexistent with personal and archetypal layers.[39]

In general, Jung's aim was to search for human universality. As Singer and Kimbles state, for Jung, "the archetypal took precedence over issues of human diversity. . . . But we observe much more variety and see more diversity than the homogeneity implied in the concept of the collective unconscious."[40] Another depth psychologist, Michael Vannoy Adams, also states that "one of the most dynamic contemporary disciplines is 'Cultural Studies' but that . . . Jungian psychoanalysts have remained 'more or less inattentive' to culture."[41]

---

38. Singer and Kimbles, "The Emerging Theory of Cultural Complexes," 178.

39. Singer and Kimbles, "The Emerging Theory of Cultural Complexes," 181.

40. Singer and Kimbles, "The Emerging Theory of Cultural Complexes," 182.

41. Michael Adams, *The Fantasy Principle: Psychoanalysis of the Imagination* (New York: Brunner-Routledge, 2004), 134. See also an interesting application of the cultural unconscious to a Muslim man in Michael Adams, "The Islamic Cultural Unconscious in the Dreams of a Contemporary Muslim Man," a paper presented at the 2nd International Academic Conference of Analytical Psychology and Jungian Studies at Texas A&M University, July 8, 2005, http://www.jungnewyork.com/islamic.shtml (accessed July 7, 2008).

Jung's implied connection between the individual and the collective is also expressed by Ulanov: "To go deep within the life of our own psyche really unites us with every other psyche. To touch the deep unconscious dimensions of our own personal problems introduces us to that level of association that is really communal."[42] In a similar vein, my seminary professor Henri Nouwen[43] used to say that when one delves into one's own psyche, the deeper one travels, the more universal (or collective) connection one finds with the rest of humanity. The need to state more clearly that such a progressive movement from one's personal psyche to a communal or universal association — or in Jungian terminology, a movement from a psychological ego complex to a more collective Self — must take into account the cultural and contextual matrices is clearly a growing edge in both depth psychology and Christian spirituality. Only in recent years has a corrective to this theory of human universality thought to exist within the cultural unconscious been proposed by Joseph Henderson.

Henderson defines the cultural unconscious as

> an area of historical memory that lies between the collective unconscious and the manifest pattern of the culture. It may include both these modalities, conscious and unconscious, but it has some kind of identity arising from the archetypes of the collective unconscious, which assists in the formation of myth and ritual and also promotes the process of development in individuals.[44]

Henderson goes on to say that "what Jung called personal was actually culturally conditioned."[45] As we speak of *cultural unconscious,* then, we can also speak of *cultural shadow,* including cultural and national prejudice, ethnoculturalism, racism, heterosexism, monoculturalism, ageism, and so on. This addition of the cultural matrix in depth psychology is an extremely important contribution because depth psychology can now more fully account for the diversity of human functioning in our multicultural society without having to resort to archetypal reductionism.

42. Ulanov, "The Christian Fear of the Psyche," 149.

43. Nouwen was my teacher at Yale Divinity School when I was a student there (1980-83).

44. Joseph Henderson, "The Cultural Unconscious," in *Shadow and Self* (Wilmette, IL: Chiron Publications, 1990), 102.

45. Henderson, "The Cultural Unconscious," 104.

K. *Samuel Lee*

Cultural Unconscious and Carl Jung

Jung was a world traveler with interests in other cultures and religions. Based upon insights he garnered from non-European cultures and other religions, he modified his theories of depth psychology. His goal, however, included the development of universal theories despite the reality and limiting influence of his own cultural unconscious. Our reading of Jung's discovery process with respect to his own cultural unconscious reveals that the *cultural unconscious* is a theoretical and psychic entity different from the *collective unconscious*. Depth psychology's more recent explicit attention to the cultural unconscious is an important advance in our understanding as we become more aware of what it means to live in a multicultural society.

Depth psychologists Helene Schulman Lorenz and Mary Watkins recount a story about Carl Jung's visit, at the age of fifty, to Taos Pueblo in New Mexico:

> Ochwiay Biano, the chief, shared that his Pueblo people felt whites were "mad," "uneasy and restless," always wanting something. Jung inquired further about why he thought they were mad. The chief replied that white people say they think with their heads — a sign of illness in his tribe. "Why of course," said Jung, "what do you think with?" Ochwiay Biano indicated his heart.[46]

Lorenz and Watkins note that after this experience Jung fell into a "long meditation" and "grasped for the first time how deeply colonialism had affected his character and psyche." Jung himself wrote:

> Someone had drawn for me a picture of the real white man. It was as though until now I had seen nothing but sentimental, prettified color prints. This Indian had struck our vulnerable spot, unveiled a truth to which we are blind. I felt rising within me like a shapeless mist something unknown and yet deeply familiar. And out of this mist, image

46. Helene Shulman Lorenz and Mary Watkins, "Depth Psychology and Colonialism: Individuation, Seeing Through, and Liberation," a paper presented at The International Symposium of Archetypal Psychology, Psychology at the Threshold, hosted by Pacifica Graduate Institute, August 31–September 4, 2000, at the University of California, Santa Barbara, CA, 1.

upon image detached itself: first Roman legions smashing into the cities of Gaul, and the keenly incised features of Julius Caesar, Scipio Africanus, and Pompey. I saw the Roman eagle on the North Sea and on the banks of the White Nile. Then I saw St. Augustine transmitting the Christian creed to the Britons on the tips of Roman lances, and Charlemagne's most glorious forced conversion of the heathen; then the pillaging and murdering bands of the Crusading armies. With a secret stab I realized the hollowness of that old romanticism about the Crusades. Then followed Columbus, Cortes, and the other conquistadors who with fire, sword, torture, and Christianity came down upon even these remote pueblos dreaming peacefully in the Sun, their Father. I saw, too, the people of the Pacific islands decimated by firewater, syphilis, and scarlet fever carried in the clothes the missionaries forced on them.[47]

Lorenz and Watkins point out that in this experience Jung's eyes were opened to his *cultural unconscious* and that "Jung did not access these insights into the cultural unconscious while alone in his tower at Bollingen."[48] This awakening happened as a result of "being in deep enough relationship and dialogue with" a cross-cultural teacher. They further argue that although depth psychology developed a century ago as "a social critique of the narrowed vision of the dominant aspects of Euro-American culture," it contains "many of the same dichotomizing and hierarchizing structures that are critiqued in post-colonial theory." Lorenz and Watkins explain:

Colonialism, which created the material basis and wealth that gave rise to the technologies of the twentieth century, is based on two kinds of power. The first is the power of one group or individual to appropriate the resources, labor, and territory of another group or individual, creating hierarchy and inequality. The second power is the capacity to deny responsibility for having done so, to silence resistance and opposition, and to normalize the outcome. By normalization we mean that the resultant inequities and suffering are made to appear as if they are completely natural through mythologies of scientific racism, gender role, ethnic identity, national destiny, and social Darwinism. In "official cul-

---

47. Jung, *Memories, Dreams, and Reflections*, 248. Cited by Lorenz and Watkins, "Depth Psychology and Colonialism," 1-2.

48. Lorenz and Watkins, "Depth Psychology and Colonialism," 2.

ture," the supposed superiority of some is taken as fate, while the imagined inferiority of others is taken as fact. Beneath this tear in the social and psychic fabric, we each carry the uneasy feeling-sense that there is much about our experience of self, other, and community that can not be said, indeed, even formulated into thoughts.[49]

Lorenz and Watkins conclude that "the psychic structures and contents that depth psychologists describe reflect the psychic corollaries of colonialism, despite the fact that the context of colonialism is hardly ever named."[50] Lorenz and Watkins point out the sobering cultural assumptions deeply embedded in depth psychology. Depth psychology, too, is a cultural practice which is culturally conditioned, and the relevance of which is culturally determined. Examining the cultural context of ministry in practice is a critical step toward broadening its relevance in a multicultural society.

Pastoral Practice in Multicultural Society

Universalizing any theory about clinical or pastoral practice is a strenuous task at best. A progressive movement in theory building from one's personal psyche to a communal association risks archetypal reductionism and potential cultural violence to the powerless. It has been noted in social science that what holds true in a given system with a high level of internal validity (or internal coherence) does not necessarily hold a high level of external validity (or generalizability across different contexts). In fact, the increased internal validity can actually lead to decreased external validity in some situations.[51] It is important to point out that the *cultural unconscious* is not identical to the *collective unconscious,* nor made conscious in the same way. The *collective unconscious* is a universal phenomenon (e.g., since all human beings have mothers, they also all have a *mother archetype* that resides in their unconscious). The *cultural unconscious* modifies this collective according to the specific time and place of those living in a par-

---

49. Lorenz and Watkins, "Depth Psychology and Colonialism," 3-4.

50. Lorenz and Watkins, "Depth Psychology and Colonialism," 2.

51. See the classic book on the topic: Donald T. Campbell and Julian C. Stanley, *Experimental and Quasi-Experimental Designs for Research* (Chicago: Rand McNally & Company, 1963).

ticular culture (e.g., what are the particular attitudes toward motherhood that exist in any given subculture?). Jung delved in depth into his own psyche "while alone at his tower in Bollingen,"[52] but his capacity to delve into the cultural unconscious did not happen there. His emancipation from the cultural unconscious did begin when he left his context and "crossed over" to another cultural context.[53] In order to achieve an adequate relationship between one's interiority and exteriority — an important goal in depth psychology — one must also pay attention to the relationship between one's intention and practice. Our practices often betray unconscious and culturally bound assumptions and values that contradict our consciously held intentions to be practitioners for all peoples.

In Romans 7:19-24, Paul declared about his own experience: "For I do not do the good I want, but the evil I do not want is what I do. . . . Wretched man that I am!" Depth psychologists may argue that Paul's struggle had to do with his inner, hidden, unconscious conflicts between his motives and actions. Paul's lament may also stem from his discovery that his intentions are often betrayed by his practices. Consider my own experience in my first three years of ministry. I had believed that I was a pastoral practitioner of the all-inclusive message of the gospel for all peoples. In retrospect, I can see how limited and limiting my cultural encapsulation was. I had believed that who I was culturally had a unique theological value, but I did not live out that belief or my cultural particularity because of my own cultural unconsciousness. I was so culturally unconscious, merely seeking personal validation, that I did not see the relevance of the gospel I preached to issues of racism, sexism, homelessness, homophobia, ageism, to name a few. (One might also consider the precise cultural specificity of the very concerns I am now highlighting, e.g. racism, sexism, homelessness, etc. as particular concerns arising in particular cultures of contemporary liberal Protestantism.)

For these reasons, Charles Ridley challenges us to examine the relationship between our practice and intentions, and our "unintentions."[54] Rarely do pastoral practitioners intentionally practice racism. But is it pos-

52. Lorenz and Watkins, "Depth Psychology and Colonialism," 2.

53. The phrase "crossed over" is used by John Dunne in *The Way of All the Earth: Experiments in Truth and Religion* (New York: Macmillan, 1972).

54. Charles Ridley, *Overcoming Unintentional Racism in Counseling and Therapy: A Practitioner's Guide to Intentional Intervention* (Thousand Oaks, CA: Sage Publications, 2005).

sible, as we saw through the story of Jung's discovery of his cultural unconsciousness, that our well-intentioned caregiving practices are a manifestation of our own cultural encapsulation? Is it possible that such practices
are not benign, that others suffer because of what we do, even unintention-
ally?[55]

How I wish I could go back to my first three years of ministry in a
wonderful small town in Arizona! If I could go back, I would listen more
deeply, without fear, to the messages of my heart and embrace the insecu-
rity, the need for validation, and the difficult upbringing I experienced in a
post–Korean War era in Korea. I would not mind as much my accented
English, and I would find words to preach more genuine for me than those
I found in monthly preaching aid subscriptions. I would spend more time
with Mormons, Native Americans, Hispanic Americans, and Catholics
and, if they would be willing, ask them to be my cross-cultural teachers. I
would have used their stories more in my sermons and Bible study groups.
I would have considered other cultural aspects more carefully: What could
I do to help congregation members just after their struggle with their first
clergywoman? How could I bring up the issues of racism and homophobia,
which were so clearly present in the life of the congregation? What words
could I speak at the high school commencement that would be more in
line with my theological convictions? What could this church have done to
address the issues and needs related to homelessness in their town? Now,
at the age of fifty, my eyes have been opened to these and many more questions.

Perhaps such limitation in vision is simply part of the human life cycle. We see things differently at fifty than we do at twenty-five. Yet because
I believe in the value of education, I can't help but hope that my personal
lament will be heard as one with wide-ranging implications for our cultural pastoral practices. And so I hope that the next time you begin to
cook, you will think about the implications of your practice — all the assumptions you bring to your cooking, the cultural context of your practice,
and its relationship to all you hold dear, internally. As you cook, note how
much depends on the kitchen, and on the cook, and maybe you, like Jung,
will fall into a long meditation about your pastoral practices in multicultural society.

---

55. See also K. Samuel Lee, "Becoming Multicultural Dancers: The Pastoral Practitioner in a Multicultural Society," *Journal of Pastoral Care* 55, no. 4 (Winter 2001).

Healing Wisdom for Human Flourishing

The Ministry of Everyday Life:
Psychological and Spiritual Development

Ana-María Rizzuto

According to the Bible, God created Adam and Eve as fully formed adults. That is not the case with us, their descendants. Human beings are born with the *potential* to become mature individuals. The development of such potential into the adult capacity to relate to others, to the world, and to the divine is conditioned by the provision of environmental requirements adequate for each developmental moment.

The growth of living creatures, including humans, orchestrates a sequential emergence of capabilities, each with its own specific need for a response from the environment. When each emergent process finds its necessary response, the creature activates its potentials with the aid of external supplies to form biological, neural, and psychic structures as established modes of functioning and relating. The resulting structures condition and color the organization of the new functions that continue the developmental process.

With respect to human beings, the earliest established integration of the physical and human milieu leaves profound marks on the individual. It may facilitate or limit the optimal organization of later functions and developmental moments. Biologically, we know that an embryo becomes a fetus that becomes a baby that will eventually become an adult, given adequate physical care. Psychically, psychoanalysis has demonstrated that the emotional development necessary to become an adult depends on our involvement with others. Freud discovered that we need the emotional investment of others, relating to us as ourselves, to become mature adults. In this, Freud saw the great importance of early life:

> For psycho-analysis has taught us that the individual's emotional attitudes to other people, which are of such extreme importance to his later behaviour, are already established at an unexpectedly early age. The nature and quality of the human child's relations to people of his own and the opposite sex have already been laid down in the first six years of his life. He may afterwards develop and transform them in certain directions but he can no longer get rid of them. The people to whom he is in this way fixed are his parents and his brothers and sisters. All those whom he gets to know later become substitute figures for these first objects of his feelings.[1]

Other factors of normal development such as nutrition, physical care, adequate sensory and cognitive stimulation, are no less essential. Yet, they are all delivered to children by their own parents or primary caregivers as components of their relationship. Every exchange between them is a meaningful emotional event.

A newborn child is a mystery and an enigma. For people of faith, who value religion or spirituality, a new child points to a mystery that transcends our perceptions. It calls for contemplative reverence and humility because we really do not know who he or she might become in the broader order of life. As a biological being, the child is a unique enigma of genetic inheritance endowed with specific temperamental dispositions. No baby is ever a *tabula rasa*. Psychoanalysts, infant observers, and child development scholars have demonstrated that a new baby requires specific responses to attach to the mother and father and to recognize itself. When the parents and other adults accurately perceive the child's bodily and psychic needs, the baby's satisfaction and feeling of being responded to establish his or her capacity to receive and to give love. Such capacity is inscribed in the infant's bodily and affective non-conscious memories. Progressive relational experiences with others along the different moments of development condition the mature capacity for intimacy with another, the conscious desire for psychical communion with a beloved person, and even the capacity to relate to God.

---

1. Sigmund Freud, "Some Reflections on Schoolboy Psychology," in *Standard Edition*, vol. 13 (London: The Hogarth Press, 1914), 243.

Developing the Capacity for Intimacy: Beginning in Infancy

Biological functions, environmental factors, and human relationships con
verge to bring about an adult capable of intimate relationships. Of all
these, none is of greater significance than the affective interaction with
others from birth to death. A hungry child needs not only good food but
also a parent or caregiver who offers that child an expression of personalized care. The caregiving one, in turn, needs to see that the baby welcomes
both food and care as a meaningful exchange of mutual acceptance. Each
stage of the child's development depends upon the presence of an adult
that offers age-appropriate emotional involvement, helping the youngster
to achieve the sense of being recognized and accepted. In this chapter, I
will describe the interactions that are of paramount importance to the
child's sense of being a self in relation to others, in particular his or her
mother and father.

Winnicott describes the maternal face as the essential mirror for the
earliest emotional development and organization of the sense of self. He
suggests that "[W]hat the baby sees is himself or herself. In other words
the mother is looking at the baby and *what she looks like is related to what
she sees there*."[2] If the mother (or mothering one) is in contact, the baby
sees himself or herself. If she is depressed and removed, the baby either
does not see himself or herself or perceives that something is wrong between them. Of course, mirroring needs only to be "good enough," not
perfect, to make room for the infant's initiative to do his or her part in the
process of becoming a self. We must add to the mother's gaze the mirroring function of the maternal voice with its affective potential to establish,
before language proper, emotional contact through tone, melody, rhythm,
and pitch. Voice and gaze must be complemented by physical handling
and touching exchanges that integrate the whole body of the child into the
sense of being itself in the safety of the parental hands. These foundational
experiences remain unconscious and cannot be consciously remembered.

The maternal and paternal ministrations of the newborn become for
Christians part of the ministry of everyday life. Ministration and ministry
have the same root and belong to the same category of service to others, be
it your child or your congregation. The ministry of parents *is* the founda-

2. D. W. Winnicott, "Mirror-Role of Mother and Family in Child Development," in
Playing and Reality (New York: Basic Books, 1971), 112.

tion of all other ministries and the indispensable psychic grounding for the later development of the capacity to love God, neighbor, and self, the basic commandments of the Gospel.

Most parents receive neither formal information nor education to be prepared to welcome and relate to their child as the unique new being he or she is. All they have to go by is their experience with their own parents. Congregations can open up parents' minds and hearts by organizing informal discussion groups for expectant and new parents centered around the importance of knowing the parents' feelings about the new baby and the need to relate to him or her as God's new creation lovingly entrusted to them. This ministry of the faith community not only helps the parents express their hopes and fears about their new task as guardians of the next generation but also connects the couple to other couples involved in a similar experience.

The Function of Representation:
Beginning with Toddlers and Preschoolers

Involvement with others engages the older baby's representational capacity to form internal models of others, the self, and their interaction. Between fifteen and eighteen months, the child becomes consciously aware of himself or herself, recognizes its image in the mirror, learns the first words, and begins to develop a sense of "I." Fantasizing becomes conscious and the child gets invested in ascertaining the intention of others in relation to himself or herself. The emotional assessment of the adult's intention becomes the measure the youngster uses to evaluate his or her stance in front of others. In a very short time the infant has become a very complex being. He or she lives now not only in the perceivable world of relationships with caregivers but also in the *representational world,* in which fantasies about and subtle perceptions of the intentions of others combine to create an internal reality of *believed interactions.* A young woman said: "My mother fed her daughter, but not me." Now suffering from anorexia, the young woman was convinced that the mother only attended to that aspect of her that was a daughter and neglected her as herself. Once the representational world between self and parents has been formed it remains with us, with some modifications, to the end of our lives. We all unconsciously live in an internal world where we *feel* how our parents have seen and responded to us. This internal world becomes the lens we have to approach all other encounters in life, including the God of our understanding. We live life with one foot in our internal world and the other in what we like to call perceived reality.

The three-year-old child develops a *core gender identity* linked to the recognition of its body and identification with the parent of the same gender.[3] The child proclaims: "I am a girl," "I am a boy." The declaration announces gender as a lasting component of that individual's identity. The parents, in turn, contribute to the organization of the *gender-role identity* by favoring behaviors that best suit a boy or a girl. A conflict may arise for a parent who had wished for a child of another gender. Subtle interactions may convey to the child that he or she is not what the parent wanted. A parent may also see in the child traits of a beloved or despised relative and find it impossible to separate the child from that person. One mother said: "I can't help myself. Tony is identical to my uncle Tom, whom I despised." These tragedies of everyday life contribute to the establishment of conflicts in the child's identity and sense of being a person of value.

The child, aware of personal desires, wants to be the agent of actions, to find some autonomy while being dependent on the parents. External and internal conflicts ensue. They contribute to the formation of his conscience, as the representative of the parents and of his appraisal of what is good or bad. The child has to find a manner to remain himself or herself, while striving to be acceptable and lovable to the parents. These are conflicts about "being the right child," conflicts of self-esteem, and doubts about being physically adequate, belonging to the right gender, being smart enough, in short, being able to please the parents. The foundation is now laid for the character traits and conflicts that would mark the individual's relationships to others and to the divine.

In the third year, children enter into a period of great excitement about themselves and the world. They unabashedly insist "Look at me! I can . . . I have . . ." indicating how splendid they find themselves to be. Something similar occurs with people, objects, and unseemly things. This is a critical moment. The child must be permitted to be excited, surprised, enchanted. This excitement lays the foundations for the capacity for awe, reverence, and religious ponderings later in life. The youngster's capacity

3. Phyllis Tyson and Robert L. Tyson, *Psychoanalytic Theories of Development: An Integration* (New Haven and London: Yale University Press, 1990), 250-54.

to be engaged with reality as enticing and mysterious begins with experiencing his or her own self as exciting and deserving of adoration during this developmental moment. This transient situation makes room for the child's more realistic valuation in the context of others. Yet, if the girl's or boy's excitement is ignored or crushed with moralistic attitudes, the moment will be lost forever, leaving behind an inhibited individual. For example, a preschooler's impulse to "play doctor" out of innocent curiosity about the bodies of others could be met with punishment when discovered by adults who see such mutual play between peers as inappropriate or even abusive. The fact that "private places" should be kept private in public does not make private places bad. On the contrary, the play is an opportunity for the adult to talk with the child about the mysterious genitals.

In the midst of this excitement the child notices that the parents have a private involvement with each other from which he or she is excluded. The small person tries to understand what goes on between parents, in particular in the bedroom. The manner in which children appraise the sexual relationship between their parents will become an unconscious organizer of their future relations to people of either gender and of their future sexual relations. The child with a heterosexual orientation identifies with the parent of the same gender and wishes to have with the parent of the opposite gender the privileged relationship that the same-gender parent has with their spouse. Yet, gender identity is more complex. Freud discovered that there is a constitutional bisexuality in the articulation of desire and of the sexual role we want to display with others. Early in life, children desire intimate relations with both parents even if one parent remains the most favored. We have no knowledge about the factors that would predispose a child for a later homosexual partner preference. Some youngsters do give early indications that they favor their own gender. For some children this may be a transient phase while for others it might be the early manifestation of a permanent homosexual partner role identity. The early indication of a homosexual preference requires a most delicate handling. The child must be accepted and loved as he or she is, but it may also need some professional help to ascertain if the observed behavior represents a transient symptom to resolve some conflict with one of the parents. In any case, in its self-exaltation, the child ignores the generational difference and its bodily immaturity. The way in which the child accepts the generational difference and the need to wait for a partner until maturity will mark his or her relational life and motives for selecting a sexual partner.

The manner in which children are helped to reorganize their desires to share in the parental intimacy is echoed in children's religious conception of God. Earlier, at the beginning of the conscious awareness of his or her representational world, the youngster may have pondered about the invisible being his parents called "God." Unable to find any sensory information about such an elusive character, yet impressed by the reverence of others toward God, the child solved the problem by linking the imperceptible divinity to the being he or she considered the greatest, most frequently the mother.[4] Later interactions with the father, relatives, religious persons, and educators will add other dimensions to the child's private representation of God. The way in which the child resolves the conflict with his parents will further modify his or her conception of God. Accepting himself or herself as an offspring unequal to the parents in age and hierarchy helps the child understand what it means to be a creature of God. Postponing the finding of a life partner facilitates the understanding of waiting for the heavenly encounter with a loving God.

The small child is part of a broader community. The congregation may help parents by offering educational and other services. Early stimulation and play opportunities with peers are significant components of a child's emotional, cognitive, and social development. The congregation can support parents and children by providing affordable age-appropriate learning and play opportunities for infants, toddlers, and school-age children. The church environment and socialization with other children and parents convey to the child in a spontaneous manner that God and the church are invested in the child becoming fully himself or herself. Such participation is a significant part of Christian education carried out not only in words but in actions and personal encounters that become part of the child's personal history. Later formal Christian education will then find receptive soil when the child has experienced a community that welcomes and accepts him or her.

When church services and Sunday school classes are suited to the developmental needs of children, in particular their freedom to be spontaneous, playful, and acceptably mischievous in the context of a caring envi-

---

4. Ana-María Rizzuto, *The Birth of the Living God: A Psychoanalytic Study* (Chicago and London: University of Chicago Press, 1979); Ana-María Rizzuto, "The Father and the Child's Representation of God," in *Father and Child: Developmental and Clinical Perspectives,* ed. S. Cath, A. R. Gurwitt, and J. M. Ross (Boston: Little, Brown, 1982).

ronment that requests social integration, the child, even as a toddler, may develop a positive feeling for the church.[5] When activities intended for children are constraining and the atmosphere is dominated by discipline and strong injunctions that inhibit the child's ebullient self-assertiveness, the child may develop an aversion to church participation.

I have described how the child forms an internal representational world, a psychic reality. It holds representations of the child's self, parents, God, other people, and the interactions with them, as well as the fantasies and narratives the child has created to make sense of them. Early in life, the youngster finds it difficult to separate psychic reality from external relational and other events. In the third year of life the child starts recognizing what belongs to his or her subjective experience and what is there, in reality. The child is able to notice the connection between internal and external realities while knowing that they are different and belong to different realms of perception and appear in his or her mind as differentiated *representations*. The adult must assist the youngster to recognize them. Adults need to capture the child's mental states and reflect them back to him or her in words. The reflection has to be accurate, but it must add the adult's point of view, which, through some affectionate but differentiating angle of vision connects the child's representation to reality. The task is difficult, and yet most adults know spontaneously how it works and how important it is that the adult engages the child with respectful seriousness. The youngster realizes that what he thinks and feels are *representations* of what he finds in himself or herself, in others, and in external reality and that the minds of others function like his or her own. This achievement inserts the child into the symbolic realities of other minds, culture, and religion.

The child's knowledge of his or her mind is urgent during preschool years when wild fantasies dominate the youngster's inner life, as fairy tales and movies for children illustrate. Parents need to be prepared to *believe* the wild fantasies of the child and at the same time provide a meaningful and playful distance from them. In short, parents and adult caregivers need to know how to play the indispensable game of make-believe. The child's make-believe world should be entered into with seriousness and respect; the parent's attitude is neither solemn nor somber but simply playful.

---

5. Karen-Marie Yust, "The Toddler and the Community," in *Human Development and Faith,* ed. F. Kelcourse (St. Louis: Chalice Press, 2004), 147-64.

Dialogue is essential when the child poses the big questions. Where did I come from? Do you love me? Do girls have a wee-wee? Where is God? May I marry Daddy? How can I have a baby? Can you have two mothers? and many others. These questions need the parents' full attention to grasp accurately the child's representations and desires prompting the question. The boy's or girl's concerns must be fully attended to, while the adult keeps emotional contact with the child and does his or her best to remain at the level of the child's question. Yet parents must gently add reality dimensions to the child's concern. The verbal dialogue between parent and child has profound and life-lasting benefits. It names the child's internal representations, welcomes them, and makes them acceptable to the youngster; it offers in the parental answer a way of enlarging and modifying the scope and meaning of the representation; it creates a common vocabulary for their exchanges in the future; it connects the child's internal world to the language of the culture; it demonstrates that it makes sense to talk to parents; it makes possible the child's "conversation" with God. Finally, dialogue becomes an internally available tool for the child to talk to himself or herself when he or she wants to understand some confusing experiences. Obviously, the parents will need to continually change the level of dialogue to keep pace with the new stages of the child's development. Once this function of internal dialogue has been established, the child is gifted with the basic tools to participate in interpersonal exchanges, join the culture, and attend school.

What holds true for parents also applies to ministers. When the occasion arises the minister needs to be psychologically prepared to dialogue with the child at the child's level. Sometimes, when parents lack the ability to truly hear and respond to their child, a trusting dialogue with a minister or lay leader may open new panoramas for a youngster. Most children readily place ministers in the same psychic space where parents belong.

The Educational Role of Teachers, Pastors, and Authority Figures: The School Age Child

Children will judge their teachers and their offerings by their competence, their capacity to establish emotional contact with the class, the aptness and genuineness of their responses, and, in particular, by the coherence between their words and behavior. We cannot fool children. They detect if the person is saying something because they are convinced or because, being a teacher or a pastor, the person feels obliged to say and do the right thing. Schools and religious education programs offer the child enough knowledge to bring them to the threshold of adult life equipped with what they need to live in the world. Yet, their task is incomplete if the young person has not taken into his internal reality the type of obligations and laws of human and divine relatedness that are indispensable for an adult's committed life. The person of the educator or pastor offers the means for integrating a manner of becoming adult. Wexler sums up the great significance of the personal *being* of the caregiver saying: "One person's nature is another person's nurture."[6] The quality of *being* of the educator stimulates the integration of patterns of learning and modes of relating to oneself and to others.

If their religious message reaches the youngster as coming from a person whose emotional contact with the child's self is convincing and if the teacher's attitude appears genuine and compatible with the content of the teaching, the conditions are given for the possibility of believing it. It is not until late adolescence and early adulthood that a person acquires the capacity to separate the truth of the teaching from the person of the teacher and even then only to a point. Only personal, loving, respectful witnessing is convincing to young people.[7]

Between birth and puberty a child gains the capacity to become a fully functioning adult, able to love and to work, through the nurture offered by parents, adults, teachers, and the faith community. Through mirroring, attunement to their inner reality, and genuine affective and verbal exchanges, adults must offer young people an open invitation to became adults themselves in due time. Becoming human depends upon intimate acts of shared communication between adults and children. The perceived and felt communication between the minds of the child and the adult engaged in respectful and emotionally responsive exchanges is the cornerstone of becoming an adult and of wanting to become one.

6. Bruce E. Wexler, *Brain and Culture: Neurobiology, Ideology, and Social Change* (Cambridge, MA: MIT Press, 2006), 16.

7. Ana-María Rizzuto, "Development: From Conception to Death: Reflections of a Contemporary Psychoanalyst," in *Formation and the Person: Essays in Theory and Practice*, ed. Alessandro Manenti, Stefano Guarinelli, and Hans Zollner (Leuven and Dudley, MA: Peters, 2007), 39-40.

Self-definition: Puberty, Adolescence, and Late Adolescence

The pubertal body is suddenly suffused with sexual hormones and grows exponentially, while the genitals transform into mature organs that make themselves obvious by menstrual blood or ejaculations. New abstract thinking and formal logical operations call for moral judgments and build theories about the universe, society, religion, and the meaning of life. These changes bring about a new crisis of self-definition. Sexual urges call for a partner and for the definition of sexual orientation because pubertal development includes the emergence of some homosexual components. No adolescent may avoid the encounter with such aspects of himself or herself. Tyson and Tyson conclude that

> The coming to terms with the homosexual component of pubertal sexuality is an implicit development task for all adolescents. The ultimate sexual-partner orientation will be determined largely by the resolution made at this time.[8]

The resolution of the sexual-partner orientation in the second part of adolescence can deeply affect the individual's identity. It raises social concerns about fitting in at school and in the social group and feeling that one is becoming an adequate member of one's gender. It awakens painful questions about the adequacy of the sexual organs and body in the view of the person selected as a partner.

The biological and psychical changes have consequences for the relationship with the parents. Adult wishes for physical closeness with adolescents must be dealt with carefully because actual sexual behavior is possible. Unfortunately, this is the moment when incest between father and daughter, and much less frequently mother and son, occurs in disturbed families where psychical and generational boundaries are poorly established. The time has arrived for the adolescent to moderate their closeness with parents and find members of the same generation as the objects of their affections and sexual interest. Nonetheless, the parents are still there, and the adolescent must resort to defensive maneuvers to deal with his or her attachment to them and dependency needs. The best defense is to find the parents wanting. Finding them inadequate facilitates the adolescent's

8. Phyllis Tyson and Robert L. Tyson, *Psychoanalytic Theories of Development: An Integration* (New Haven and London: Yale University Press, 1990), 291.

separation from them. The capacity to evaluate an adult reaches an acute point in adolescence, when all adults are harshly scrutinized against newly developed standards of perfection.

That said, it is not uncommon to find young adolescents greatly idealizing some teachers, frequently of the same sex. The homosexual component of this experience has more to do with erotically idealized feelings and the search for models for identification than with actual sexual desires. The adult must remain unshakably a teacher that maintains generational distance, accepts the adolescent's exaltation of himself or herself, and supports the adolescent search for identity. Any sexual enactment on the teacher's part creates a life-lasting disruption of the sexual and personal identity of the student.

Most adolescents are now deeply involved with peers in school, sports, social, and religious activities. He or she is also hooked on television, the internet, iPod music, and the cell phone as part of the peer culture. This virtual world simultaneously connects and isolates the adolescents from others. How can parents and teachers remain relevant to adolescents immersed in virtual reality? Dialogue, open, accepting, respectful, inviting dialogue, is the only avenue left open. The dialogue has a very different aim from that intended to help the child mentalize representations and the inner world of others. The adolescent, with his highly developed cognitive operations, needs adults capable of helping him or her wrestle with the issues of becoming a sexual being, a person concerned with social, moral, and religious issues. This wrestling must include a solid intellectual respect for the adolescent's thinking, honest questioning on the adult's part that precludes the superiority of knowing the answer beforehand, and regard for the laws of debate. The atmosphere of the dialogue must include the paradox of playful seriousness, solid critical thinking, and the subdued affection appropriate to a parent, a teacher, or a minister. Dialogue with a respected grown-up is the greatest gift adults have to offer to an adolescent. It is not an easy gift to make. The adult has to *be* a truly genuine person, flexible enough to accept losing a debate, solid enough to continue at the service of the young person, enthusiastic enough to be passionate about truth, beauty, God, and the world. Who among us is apt for the task?

During this most difficult period of growing up the congregation may offer youngsters the peer forums they need to vent their ruminations, complaints, fears, doubts, religious concerns, and need for identification with their age group. Outings, camping, nature exploration, and all kinds of group activities under the guidance of adults capable of maintaining discipline and freedom simultaneously are memorable experiences that frequently open the door to lasting friendships between members of the congregation. They facilitate the formation and consolidation of individual and group ideals and foster the sense of "we" as a distinctive group that can sustain and facilitate the individuation and self-definition process of this period of life.

Late adolescence brings about the consolidation of character structure and the final definition of identity. The adolescent must revise the internal representation of the parents, de-idealizing them and himself or herself, in order to enter adult life. The vicissitudes of the relationship to God — as Freud suggested — evolves together with the relationship to the parents that provided the initial source for a divine representation The painful emotional separation from the parents profoundly affects the transformation of the representation of God and actual relationship with the divinity. The complexity and subtlety of the processes involved in the transformation allow few generalizations and call for a personalized approach to the faith of each individual adolescent. An image of God whose primary source is a united parental couple that the child has accepted as his parents with a life of their own offers the best possibility for an acceptable representation of a divinity that can be worshiped. A God representation that includes in its transformation in late adolescence the parental couple indicates that the young person has successfully accepted the difference between generations, the impossibility of relating sexually to the parents, and the son's or daughter's origin in the sexual relation of the parental couple. Such psychological transformation facilitates the adolescent's relationship to a divinity who is the creator as well as the Great Mystery that exceeds our smallness.

The sexually mature adolescent searches for a soul mate. In early adolescence a soul mate contributes to the consolidation of identity. In late adolescence wishes for future lasting commitment to a partner appear as anticipations of becoming an adult. The adolescent now searches for an intimate partner with whom to share his or her innermost being. He or she must make explicit a sexual-partner orientation by choosing a partner. The majority of adolescents have consolidated a heterosexual orientation. A certain number of adolescents cannot help but feel an intense emotional and sexual attraction to persons of the same gender. No adolescent chooses to be homosexual. To this day, no one knows what psychic or biological factors contribute to a homosexual orientation. The homosexual adolescent needs all the respect and understanding that adults are capable of offering in honest and direct dialogue, emotional support, and educational information. The consolidation of a heterosexual identity is difficult enough. Sorting out a homosexual identification is harder because it includes social disapproval, peer pressures, and moral and religious issues that exceed the competence of a young person. Parents, teachers, and pastors need to clarify in all honesty their own stance to be able to help an adolescent who is convinced that he or she is homosexual. As always, open, honest, and caring dialogue is what the homosexual adolescent desperately needs from all the adults around him or her during this painful process of gender partner identity development. The point made above bears repeating: dialogue with a respected grown-up is the greatest gift adults have to offer to an adolescent. It is not an easy gift to make.

Present-day peer pressure insists that sexual activity confirms one's sexual orientation, one's value to the group as a male or female, and one's status as a "cool" person. The pressure is unrelenting. I still remember my own disbelief twenty-five years ago when a twenty-year-old attractive female student arrived at my consulting room complaining that she was a virgin. She was one of the most normal adolescents I had met. Her problem was the conflict of generations: her peers insisted that she had to have sex; her devout parents enjoined her to remain a virgin. She wanted to be a "normal" college student and a good daughter, and she did not know how to solve the contradiction. A therapeutic dialogue in which I remained uncommitted to one position or the other helped her to clarify her wishes and her moral commitments to find her own way out of the conundrum.

In middle and late adolescence self-esteem is measured by the boyfriend or girlfriend the young person has. Peers "certify" adequate femaleness or maleness as well as social status. Those who cannot find a boyfriend or girlfriend often consider themselves losers, social misfits. Adults are rarely privy to the convolutions of the adolescent's falling in and out of love. But, if the young person opens up his or her secret life to the adult, the latter needs to be prepared to be a good and patient listener who speaks only when requested to do so. Most adolescents only need a sympathetic ear to elaborate their losses and gains in matters of love.

Late adolescents must decide what to do with their lives. The multitude of options available nowadays may confuse the young person who may require a period of rehearsals and transient jobs before committing to a particular field. The capacity for commitment consolidates all the trends that converge in the final stage of entering adult life. The psychic structure of the young adult integrates silently and efficiently in the service of committed activities and relationships all that he or she has collected during the growing up years: the affectionate relationship and dialogues with the parents, the fantasized ideal adult he or she desires to be as the result of dialogues with admired teachers and religious figures, the sense of being himself or herself. The integration of all these human encounters and the fantasies and desires emerging from them bring the late adolescent to the threshold of committed adult life, where the wish for a permanent relationship leads most young adults to the search for a partner suitable for a committed relationship and, perhaps, the creation of a family. When children are born to the new couple, the life cycle of becoming human starts anew.

Becoming Human in Community:
The Ministry of Everyday Life

Becoming human is not a matter of educational techniques. It results from the adults' nonconscious and conscious offering of modes of relatedness, recognition, affection, respect, and stimulation to the new child to assist him or her to become a self. In the end, it is true that "One person's nature is another person's nurture." If the adult's "nature" is loving, respectful, open to dialogue, inviting the child to meet the world, and open to the awe of all that exists, we have reason to expect that the child will become an adult capable of love and compassionate dialogue, aware of the transcendent dimensions of being human.

Assisting a child to become a socially and spiritually responsive human being results from our ministry of everyday life. Preparing for that ministry is something we have frequently neglected. We all need to learn more about the needs of children at each developmental moment to be able to offer them the emotional and actual nutrients they need at that moment. This is not only a matter of knowledge of the sequences of child development. It also requires each individual's preparation to have those nutrients available as part of his or her personal commitment when children need them. Then, recognizing that children are a mystery entrusted to our care, we will be ready to offer them our own being to help them become adults.

Sacred Space and the Psyche:
Reflections on Potential Space
and the Sacred Built Environment

Pamela Cooper-White

Maria-Teresa[1] strides purposefully into the nave of the San Fernando Cathedral in San Antonio, Texas. It is early on a Friday afternoon. Noon Mass is over. Parishioners and tourists have eaten lunch on the adjoining plaza outside, and the sanctuary is now dark, cool, and quiet. A handful of people are scattered throughout the pews — homeless men and women nodding in sleep or in prayer, a few camera-laden tourists sitting briefly to get their bearings and absorb the sense of calm here, a handful of "regulars" who live or work in the neighborhood and stop in to say a rosary or light a candle, and today, me, a visitor, researcher, and spiritual pilgrim. I am praying, too, after having thoroughly absorbed as much of the visual richness of this historic place as I can through sight (with my own eyes and the lens of my camera), touch, smell, and hearing; I have listened to the stories of several people who graciously shared with me what this place means to them.

It is out of the corner of my eye, while praying, that I first catch sight of her as she enters the church — not tall, but powerfully built, with brown shoulder-length hair streaked with white, and a weathered, round, dark brown face. She appears to be "Latina," but the particularities of her story and her people are unknown to me. Like so many of the "regulars" here at San Fernando, her appearance (as, no doubt, her life story) defies simple classification but is part of the colorful, hybrid texture of cultures and ethnicities that is known as *mestizaje*[2] (a mixture of people descended from

---

1. Not her real name.
2. Virgilio Elizondo and Timothy Matovina, *San Fernando Cathedral: Soul of the City*

many peoples over many centuries on a contested, often re-boundaried land). San Antonio is thus a liminal place itself, a place of thresholds and shifting cultural identities where it is easy to perceive the Spirit blowing like the wind among the movements, songs, cries, and struggles of many peoples as they blend, negotiate, fight, and come together again. San Fernando Cathedral, containing within it the oldest church building from colonial times, is often referred to as the heart of the city, and within its walls and outside on its plazas beats the restless rhythm of a *mestizo* Spirit. It is a place of *Ruach* (breath-wind-spirit) — a place of dynamic power.

In the heart of this liminal city, this seemingly hard-working *mestiza* woman crosses the threshold of the Cathedral, and the sight of her determined stride literally takes my breath away. She powers through the main door, briefly blocking the brilliant light from the sunlit Plaza de las Islas, her work shoes swift but quiet on the old tile floor. Most people, including myself, have entered shyly, somewhat hesitantly, mindful of proprieties we have been taught and now imagine about ancient, holy places. But this person knows exactly where she is headed, and without hesitation marches over to one of the many *santos* (carved saint statues) lined up along the side aisles of the church. She matter-of-factly reaches up, shoulder height, to grasp one of her saint's feet with her left hand. She plants both feet firmly on the floor, places her right hand on her hip, and stands beside the saint whose foot is now beneath her grip, facing the nave. She closes her eyes and begins to move her lips silently in what appears to be confident, ferociously faithful prayer. I avert my gaze quickly, not wanting to intrude on her intimate exchange with God, but I realize as I continue to be aware of her presence in my peripheral vision that she is not in the least troubled by my presence, or by any of the other people here. She is utterly, securely at home — both in this space and in her practiced faith.

Our Relationship with Sacred Space

The purpose of this chapter is to open a conversation about the "depth dimension" of sacred space.[3] It is assumed that the readers of this anthology

---

(Maryknoll: Orbis, 1998); cf. Nestor Medina, "The Religious Psychology of Mestizaje," paper presented to the American Academy of Religion, San Diego, CA, November 2007.

3. Sacred space has generated a vast scholarly literature in Christian theology and be-

are students of religion, church leaders, or otherwise have at least some significant experience in religious buildings and congregations. But how often do we enter into our religious buildings without giving a second thought to the structure of the place itself, let alone how that structure speaks to us, invites us into a relationship with it? Buildings speak.[4] But if we remain too preoccupied with the words we read, the choreographies we enact in our rituals, or the programs we design while we are bent on fulfilling our mission as religious leaders, we may miss the more subtle and *sensual* ways in which the church itself — its bricks and mortar, the "bones" of its structure, the interplay of concrete and steel and wood and glass and paint — also speaks to us.

Our buildings themselves originally were designed by someone to convey a message. If we do not take time to be still and quietly engage the space, we may miss all that there is in this space to take in through our senses. We may miss not only the messages intended by the original planners, but also all that *we* and others are bringing to this space — our expectations about what constitutes "holiness," how we should or should not behave here, what parts of ourselves we may allow to come in and what parts we may try to hide or exclude from view, our desires for what such a holy place might be able to do for us, give us, feed us, heal in us, or strengthen us to go back out and undertake.

Like all relationships that engage us at both conscious and uncon-

---

yond, e.g., Alejandro Garcia-Rivera, *The Community of the Beautiful* (Collegeville, MN: Liturgical Press, 1999); Richard Giles, *Re-pitching the Tent: Re-ordering the Church Building for Worship and Mission* (Minneapolis: Augsburg Fortress, 1999); Timothy Gorringe, *A Theology of the Built Environment: Justice, Empowerment, Redemption* (Cambridge: Cambridge University Press, 2002); Robert M. Hamma, *Landscapes of the Soul: A Spirituality of Place* (Notre Dame, IN: Ave Maria Press, 1999); Leslie King-Hammond, *The Bible and the Aesthetics of Sacred Space in Twentieth-Century African American Experience* (New York: Continuum, 2000); Belden Lane, *The Solace of Fierce Landscapes: Exploring Desert and Mountain Spirituality* (Oxford: Oxford University Press, 1998); Jon Pahl, *Shopping Malls and Other Sacred Spaces: Putting God in Place* (Grand Rapids: Brazos Press, 2007); R. Kevin Seasoltz, *A Sense of the Sacred: Theological Foundations of Christian Architecture and Art* (New York: Continuum, 2006); Philip Sheldrake, *Spaces for the Sacred: Place, Memory, and Identity* (Baltimore: Johns Hopkins University Press, 1991); Mark A. Torgerson, *An Architecture of Immanence: Architecture for Worship and Ministry Today* (Grand Rapids: Eerdmans, 2007); and R. J. Werblowsky, ed., *Sacred Space* (New York: New York University Press, 1998). However, there has been little specifically addressing its psycho-spiritual dimension and its relation to persons.

4. Giles, *Re-pitching the Tent,* 61-67.

scious levels, the relationship we have with our sacred spaces is an *intersubjective* relationship,[5] characterized not so much by what "belongs" on each side of the relationship (the separate domains of the "I" and the "Thou," or in this case, the space and the person) but by the meaning that is co-constructed in the *between* — in the interplay of the one who gazes and what is gazed-upon. Because a building is inanimate, this is not equivalent to a human-to-human face-to-face encounter. However, because human persons first designed and constructed each church building, and through "revelation, ritual, remembrance, and recognition"[6] set it apart and named it as sacred, we can perceive at least dimly a human attempt to speak to us — sometimes directly, sometimes indirectly, down through the ages, as to persons yet unknown. The older and more actively inhabited the place with others' holy and deeply personal intentions, the more perhaps we may feel that this building speaks to us. Layers of mystery and the lives of other people — their griefs and joys, burdens and sorrows — may come to feel almost palpable in this place as we contemplate the lives that have passed through these walls.

What, then, exactly, *is* "sacred space"? Jesuit philosopher and psychoanalytic writer Michel de Certeau made an important contribution to the study of sacred space by distinguishing between "place" and "space."[7] For Certeau, "place" *(lieu)* refers to an actual physical location, a fixed point on a map, characterized by its stability.[8] A "space" *(espace),* by contrast, is dynamic. It encompasses how the place functions and is used by the people who move within it. It is not so much inscribed on a map as described, as Certeau states, by taking a "tour"[9] — a narrative journey in which the social relations of the space are entwined with its physical features. *"Space is a practiced place"* (emphasis added).[10]

The sacred space with which we are most concerned in this chapter, then, is the space as it is inhabited by people — by their experiences, ritu-

---

5. On intersubjectivity, see Pamela Cooper-White, *Shared Wisdom: Use of the Self in Pastoral Care and Counseling* (Minneapolis: Fortress Press, 2004), 35-60.

6. Hamma, *Landscapes of the Soul,* 43-53.

7. Michel de Certeau, *The Practice of Everyday Life,* trans. Steven Rendall (Berkeley: University of California Press, 1984), 115-30.

8. Certeau, *The Practice of Everyday Life,* 117.

9. Certeau, *The Practice of Everyday Life,* 119.

10. Certeau, *The Practice of Everyday Life,* 117. For Certeau, "every story is a travel story — a spatial practice," 115.

als, cultural practices, creative movements, conflicts, and narratives. We can "read" a space as a source of multiple meanings. "Sacred space" is more than just the bricks and mortar or the precise location of a building in terms of longitude and latitude; it is the sum of the stories the space has to tell, the energy of its inhabitants that has saturated its structural bones, and the living relationships we may yet encounter when we cross the threshold and enter there.[11] Moreover, anthropologists who study space and ritual now take it as axiomatic that sacred space is always *contested space*.[12] The Gettysburg battlefield, for example, has become a site of both spiritual and commercial pilgrimage because of the harrowing actions that took place there and the multiple layers of cultural meaning invested there by subsequent generations.

Place is also therefore political. As Jesuit philosopher Philip Sheldrake has written, "We need to become aware of what might be called "a longer narrative" in which "the others" who have been made absent by those who control public or institutional histories are now being restored as people who are fully present.[13] Ground Zero in lower Manhattan is a good example of the evolution of such a complex, multivalent, and contested "sacred space." Such understandings of a site as sacred are never abstract but always incarnational — "mediated through the cultural and contextual overlays we inevitably bring to nature and to our understandings of the sacred."[14] In this sense, then, every space can be understood as a text with an "excess of meaning" that "persistently overflows any attempt at final definition."[15]

All this, however, is still only one side of the continuum of relationship — the side the space itself conveys to us when we enter it. We also bring the multiply layered mystery of our own selves, both our outward person-

11. Cf. Sheldrake, *Spaces for the Sacred*, 1, 4, 7.

12. John Eade and Michael Sallnow, "Introduction," in *Contesting the Sacred: The Anthropology of Christian Pilgrimage*, ed. Eade and Sallnow (London: Routledge, 1990); Sheldrake, *Spaces for the Sacred*, 20-22; cf. Mircea Eliade, *Patterns in Comparative Religion* (New York: World Publishing, 1963); and Victor and Edith Turner, *Image and Pilgrimage in Christian Culture* (New York: Columbia University Press, 1978).

13. Sheldrake, *Spaces for the Sacred*, 20-21, 26-29; also citing Henri Lefebvre, *The Production of Space* (Oxford: Blackwell, 1991) and Gustavo Gutiérrez, *We Drink from Our Own Wells* (Maryknoll: Orbis, 1984).

14. Sheldrake, *Spaces for the Sacred*, 16.

15. Sheldrake, *Spaces for the Sacred*, 19.

alities and our innermost realms of thoughts, feelings, fantasies, sensations, memories, and desires, and our own incarnate practices.[16] While we may only initially be aware of fleeting impressions at the conscious level — whether the place feels "friendly" or "closed off," "warm" or "cold," too bright, too dark, too hard, or too soft. When we first enter an unfamiliar sacred space, we tend to behave like the fairy-tale character Goldilocks, wandering into a bear family's home in search of comfort, sampling their food, and trying out all their beds until she found the one "just right" for a nap: we try out the pews, the chairs in the parish hall, the porridge at the soup suppers, to find a place for ourselves within the larger space that seems "just right." Often, as visitors, we fail to move beyond this initial stage of testing. We fear the bears that are a hidden part of our own psyches, and we run when we spot a stern, critical bear or a too-gushy, potentially invasive or engulfing bear or a baby bear that might ask too much of us. But if we linger, we may acknowledge that the bears in this place are all pretty much just like ourselves — sniffing the air, testing the cushions, and growling at others occasionally to feel safe.

Potential Space and Transitional Experience

A concept I have found to be most helpful in illuminating the "depth dimension" of sacred space is the idea, from D. W. Winnicott, of "facilitative space" or "potential space," [17] and the closely related idea of the "transitional object" or "transitional experience."[18] Winnicott, a British analyst in the first generation after Freud, was first a pediatrician. His work therefore always bears the marks of an unusual respect for the mother-infant relationship.

As the infant develops, in Winnicott's understanding, he or she must begin early on to differentiate between "me" and "not-me,"[19] and this inevitable realization of separateness leads to a primal experience of loss. The

16. Simon Schama, *Landscape and Memory* (London: HarperCollins, 1995), cited in Sheldrake, *Spaces for the Sacred,* 16.

17. D. W. Winnicott, *Playing and Reality* (New York: Basic Books, 1971), 41.

18. See also F. Robert Rodman, "Architecture and the True Self," in *Psychoanalysis and Architecture,* ed. Jerome Winer, James William Anderson, and Elizabeth Danze (Catskill, NY: Mental Health Resources, 2005), 57-66.

19. Winnicott, *Playing and Reality,* 1.

extent to which the "good enough" mother[20] is able to *hold* the child, both literally and figuratively (with her gaze, her emotional presence, her reliability in feeding, bathing, and soothing), is the extent to which this growing awareness of separateness is allowed to be non-traumatic, even growth-producing. The child who is securely held develops the capacity to "be alone in the presence of the mother,"[21] and then "gradually, the ego-supportive environment is introjected and built into the individual's personality, so that there comes about a capacity actually to be alone."[22] Winnicott describes the entire arena of this give-and-take between the infant's and toddler's developing needs and the mother's sensitive response as a "holding environment,"[23] which is both the maternal provision itself and the atmosphere created around the nursing couple.

Out of this understanding of the "facilitative" or "holding environment," Winnicott developed the concept of "transitional phenomena,"[24] through observation of very young children and their mothers. At first, Winnicott identified the role of the "transitional object,"[25] well known to anyone familiar with small children as the scruffy beloved blanket or stuffed animal toward which many children form an intense attachment. This well-used and abused creature functions as a stand-in for the mother in her absence. The blankie or bunny is cuddled, dragged, pummeled, and sucked in a fierce oral embrace that echoes the passionate avarice the child has for the mother's breast and body. In the small child's still uncertain sorting out of "me" and "not-me," the transitional object belongs simultaneously to both domains. In one of Winnicott's most perceptive, paradoxical descriptions, he states that the power of the transitional object lies precisely in that the child simultaneously "discovers" the object (as coming from outside himself or herself) and senses that he or she has "created" it (it is immediately recognized as a part of one's internal self).[26]

20. Winnicott, *The Maturational Processes and the Facilitating Environment: Studies in the Theory of Emotional Development* (London: Hogarth Press, 1965).

21. Winnicott, "The Capacity to Be Alone," in *The Maturational Processes,* 30.

22. Winnicott, "The Capacity to Be Alone," 36.

23. Winnicott, *The Maturational Processes.*

24. Winnicott, "Transitional Objects and Transitional Phenomena," in *Playing and Reality,* 1-25.

25. Winnicott, "Transitional Objects and Transitional Phenomena."

26. Winnicott, "The Use of an Object and Relating through Identifications," in *Playing*

Winnicott went on to theorize that the function of the specific transitional object also pertains to a wider arena of transitional phenomena, in which a space opens up in the holding environment that shares the same paradox of "discovered" and "created" as the transitional object itself. Now it is not only the blanket or the teddy bear that bridges the gap between "me" and "not-me," "me" and "mother," but there is an entire *space* that characterizes that intermediate realm. Again, if the mother's holding is "good enough," her presence and provision reliable enough, the child will feel safe setting out to explore. The growing infant or toddler will engage in a healthy cycle of "separation" and "rapprochement."[27]

Within the holding environment, then, a transitional arena develops, in which the child is safe to paddle around mentally, emotionally, and physically in a *space* that is not wholly "me" or "not-me," where fantasy, play, and real relating with the primary caretaker join together and *take place*. It is the arena of creative potential, a sacred and embodied aliveness, as Ann Ulanov beautifully elaborated in *Finding Space: Winnicott, God, and Psychic Reality*.[28] For Winnicott, the capacity to play in childhood is the direct outcome of this fecund "potential space," and it is the direct antecedent to adult creativity, including the production of culture, the arts, and religion.[29]

Sacred Space as Maternal Matrix and Potential Space

Sacred space can be understood both as a "holding environment" in the Winnicottian sense — including specifically as a *maternal* holding environment or *matrix* (womb)[30] — and as a transitional or "potential space" where

---

and Reality, 89; see also "Communicating and Not Communicating, Leading to a Study of Certain Opposites" (1963), in *The Maturational Processes,* 180-81.

27. Margaret Mahler, *The Psychological Birth of the Human Infant: Symbiosis and Individuation* (New York: Basic Books, 2000; orig. 1975).

28. Ann Belford Ulanov, *Finding Space: Winnicott, God, and Psychic Reality* (Louisville: Westminster John Knox Press, 2001). From a Jungian perspective, see also Ann and Barry Ulanov, *The Healing Imagination: The Meeting of Psyche and Soul* (Einsiedeln, Switzerland: Daimon Verlag, 2000).

29. Winnicott, "Transitional Objects and Transitional Phenomena," in *Playing and Reality,* 14; "Communicating and Not Communicating," in *The Maturational Processes,* 184.

30. Cf. Robert F. Harris, "Encountering Architecture: Subjective Responses to the Basilica of the Mission Dolores," in Winer et al., eds., *Psychoanalysis and Architecture,* 17; Seasoltz on "mother church" in *A Sense of the Sacred,* 139.

imagination, creativity, play, and reality meet. Why specifically maternal? Much of Winnicott's theory has been helpfully revised to include fathers and other primary caretakers in the role of providing the infant's earliest "holding environment." My own view of gender is that it is at least as much a social and cultural construct as a fixed biological entity or essence.[31] However, in this case, I also believe that there is something primal (in the Jungian sense, even archetypal — that is, a symbol resonating at conscious and unconscious levels with universal human experience[32]) about the maternal aspect of sacred space, because we all began life in a very particular space, the space of a mother's womb. The "good enough" provisions of fathers and other primary caretakers, even from the moment of birth, may add to the infant's sense of ongoing security and warmth and nurture. But we are all held initially in that floating, recumbent state, tied by an umbilical cord to a mother's own flesh and blood, surrounded by her heartbeat and bodily noises, and contained in a space that holds us — until we are squeezed and expelled into a new cosmos of sound and air and sudden touch and light.

The security of the womb and the relative ease or difficulty (even trauma[33]) of our own births constitutes our earliest felt experiences. Regardless of our gender-identity now or the gender-identity of our primary parent(s), we all were formed in an amniotic paradise and expelled from it through an amniotic rupture. This imprint will resonate with every experience we have of both "mother" and "space."

For this reason, the interior of a church building holds a certain primal resonance to that first space. Some buildings by their shape, their lighting, the colors of their furnishings, may be more primally reminiscent of our unconscious first memories than others. For example, the Chartres Cathedral labyrinth that is now being replicated throughout many North American churches[34] might be seen as a fairly explicit symbol for the spiral of life in and out of the maternal matrix. But in any sacred interior, we are held and contained, by design, and this holding recalls our first experience of being held in the womb. Moreover, because this space is specifically set

31. Cooper-White, *Shared Wisdom*, 52-54; Judith Butler, *Gender Trouble: Feminism and the Subversion of Identity* (New York: Routledge, 1990).

32. C. G. Jung, "The Archetypes and the Collective Unconscious," in *The Collected Works* (Princeton: Princeton University Press, 1954-71), 9:1.

33. Otto Rank, *The Trauma of Birth*, 2nd ed. (New York: Dover, 1994; orig. 1929).

34. Beginning with Grace Cathedral, San Francisco — see Lauren Artress, *Walking a Sacred Path: Rediscovering the Labyrinth* (New York: Riverhead/Penguin Putnam, 1996), 67.

apart *as sacred* space, it functions with a very particular, heightened intensity in relation to the inner space of our psyches. We are more likely to project onto the "sacred" whatever we have come to associate with the "spiritual" — perhaps those aspects of our inner life that we hold most precious, tender, even most "core" or secret — our most primal needs and desires, and even dreads and fears.

Just as the psyches of mother and infant originally meet and form a unique intermediary space between them, which is internalized in the unconscious life of the infant and then "exists" both internally and in the actual relationship with the mother and the environment, prior experiences of "mothering," both by actual parental figures and by the church, will enter into the way we now perceive the church we are in (both as "place" — physical building and as "space" — the social community it houses). This interaction will create a unique intersubjective reality between this sacred building and each individual that will be "like all others" who enter there (sharing a common human condition), "like some others" (conditioned, for example, by our race, culture, gender, and economic situation), and "like no others" (carrying our unique history and personal experience, at both conscious and unconscious levels).[35]

Sacred Space as Paradox

If we understand our sacred spaces in some sense, then, to be both maternal holding environments, matrices of our ever-growing psyches, and also transitional or "potential" spaces in which our souls are invited to play in the holy realm of "me/not-me" "me/the divine," we should expect to find places of light and shadow, plain meaning and mystery — in short, places of *paradox*.[36] Church buildings, as both "places" (brick and mortar) and as social "spaces," visually represent and serve as a perpetual reminder of a series of overlapping paradoxes. By recognizing the church as a place of

35. Pamela Cooper-White, *Many Voices: Pastoral Psychotherapy in Relational and Theological Perspective* (Minneapolis: Fortress, 2006), 45-50, also citing Emmanuel Lartey, *In Living Color: An Intercultural Approach to Pastoral Care and Counseling*, 2nd ed. (London: Jessica Kingsley, 2003), 26.

36. Winnicott placed a high value on maintaining the creative tension inherent in paradox and ambiguity: Introduction, in *Playing and Reality*, xii; see also Emmanuel Ghent, "Paradox and Process," *Psychoanalytic Dialogues* 2, no. 2 (1992): 135-59.

paradox, the container of the church building can then be that "potential space" in which imagination and creativity can blossom — a matrix where both healing rest and explosive, dynamic birthing can *take place.*

The paradoxes that constitute church life are made visible in what I would call "honest" church buildings — that is, buildings that attempt to show and not cover up the inherent tensions and ambiguities of a living *ekklesia.* In Jungian terms, each church embodies elements of both "ego" and "Shadow" — that is, both what is desired consciously and what is unconsciously split-off or disavowed. Sensitivity to the paradoxical elements of sacred space may help us as church leaders and congregants to find ways in which we can help our buildings speak more complexly (including the narratives of those whose stories may have been previously muted or excluded) to those who inhabit its walls.

Paradoxes include: inside/outside; familiar/strange; past-present/present-future; and reflecting both immanence and transcendence.

1. Inside/Outside

Every interior, however solidly enclosed, is also penetrated by openings to the outside. The impression of interiority can be heightened or diminished by the porousness of its walls, the amount of exterior light and views, and the acoustical quality incorporated in its design. Just limiting our survey to Western architecture, consider the feeling of a Gothic cathedral: interior sources of light are muted and flickering, exterior light is filtered through colored glass, which may also reiterate in images the stories that are read and told inside the space; sound reverberates, mystifying its point of origin; there are no immediate views to the outside world. With its soaring arches and ribs, it replicates the feeling of being deep inside a forest[37] — some of the most stunning gothic carvings even include shapes of leaves and vines and woodland creatures. Yet it is an entirely artificial space — a product of culture that replicates but also embellishes nature with its fantastic creatures and images, while actually remaining insulated from the actual forces of the out-of-doors. Depending on the beauty of this artifice, it can even serve to heighten the sense of awe experienced in nature, to

37. Sir James Hall, *Essays on the Origins, History and Principles of Gothic Architecture* (London, 1813), cf. http://witcombe.sbc.edu/sacredplaces/chartres.html.

concentrate it, and to foster an atmosphere conducive to the psychic meeting of nature and imagination.

Other church buildings have an opposite aesthetic. Light, clarity, and transparency to the outside world are evident in the serenely proportioned, white-walled interiors of eighteenth-century Enlightenment churches with large, clear-glass windows opening onto views of either natural scenery or town (the prototype for which was the architecture of Christopher Wren). Some contemporary structures are designed deliberately to point the worshiper's gaze outside, beyond the sanctuary, for example, Christ Chapel at the Episcopal Seminary of the Southwest in Austin, Texas, where the cross is situated *outside* a clear-glass window.[38] In the Salvadoran *campo* (countryside), an unwalled tin-roofed structure barely encloses a row of benches. As children and chickens scamper underfoot, the people listen in the open air to the Word proclaimed and receive the Sacraments of Baptism and Eucharist to strengthen them for acts of mercy, justice, and resistance to the powers of evil.[39]

Maintaining this paradox is important for the health of the congregation and its members. Too much interiority can replicate Luther's "self curved in on self"[40] — a womb that holds but cannot give birth; a place of rest and containment but not of creative release. Too much exteriority can lead to mission fatigue and burnout; a barren, dry womb with no placenta for nourishment. Liturgical theologian Gordon Lathrop argues theologically for an orientation of the church grounded in baptism, that "always balances 'here' and 'away from here,' a "reoriented map in which the cardinal directions are toward God, toward the assembly toward the poor, and toward the earth itself."[41]

The threshold of the space also becomes an important mediator of this paradox — I would argue that it does so at both the conscious and unconscious levels. "A threshold is a sacred thing."[42] The threshold or *limen* has

38. Christ Chapel, Episcopal Seminary of the Southwest, Austin, TX, www.etss.edu/tour6.shtml (accessed July 2007).

39. Personal visit to El Salvador, January 1985.

40. Martin Luther, "Lectures on Romans" (1515-16), in *Luther's Works*, vol. 25, ed. Hilton Oswald, trans. Jacob Preus (St. Louis: Concordia, 1972), 291-92.

41. Gordon Lathrop, *Holy Ground: A Liturgical Cosmology* (Minneapolis: Fortress, 2003), 172.

42. Porphyrus, third century, *The Nymph's Cave*, cited in Gaston Bachelard, *The Poetics of Space*, trans. Maria Jolas (Boston: Beacon Press, 1994; orig. 1958), 223.

been recognized in Jungian psychology as having archetypal resonance with the soul's journey.⁴³ As we stand in a particular church building, we might ask: what is the quality of the door or doorways in and out of this particular sacred space?⁴⁴ Is it usually open, closed, even locked or gated? Does it look like an inviting opening, or a heavy fortress barrier? The contemporary trend in church architecture, inspired by the liturgical renewal movement, has been toward more transparent doors that let in views of the street and conveys welcome to those outside.⁴⁵ This can be a healthy symbol that, even within this containing matrix, there is a place for the liminal. There is room to move in and out, like the breath of Spirit that expands and contracts the lungs. The womb, to be fertile, must be able to be penetrated by the Other, to be able to give nurture at its center, and then to release new life again beyond its walls.

In many churches, the intermediate area around the entrance is widened to include both a plaza-like space or porch outside the door and a narthex inside. Such spaces may function as a kind of bridge, an expanded liminal space leading into the deeper "potential space" of the interior. It is worth paying attention to the relative size and shape of plaza or porch and narthex, and to what they convey. Is the door fully accessible to people of varying physical abilities? Does a narthex become so wide as to eclipse the function of bridging between the outside world and the mysterious confines of the interior, sacrificing an approach to mystery for the sake of an enlarged social space? Or is it so narrow that there is really no bridge effect possible, but the sojourner is immediately squeezed through and pushed into the nave?

Lathrop has offered one image for this paradox in liturgical space as a "juxtaposition" between "strong center and open door."⁴⁶ I would suggest pushing this image even further, however, to suggest that the center itself must not be identified too much with any one thing — one tradition, or doctrine, or interpretation of truth. The very notion of "center" is always being impacted, energized, and changed by the stranger who enters through the threshold. The door is not only open to let the Other in, but also to set the inhabitants free to go forth and live into newly imagined fu-

43. E.g., Nathan Schwarz-Salant and Murray Stein, eds., *Liminality and Transitional Phenomena* (Wilmette, IL: Chiron, 1991).

44. On doors, see Certeau, *The Practice of Everyday Life*, 211-31.

45. Giles, *Re-pitching the Tent*, 155-59.

46. Lathrop, *Holy Ground*, 173.

tures that even Christian tradition alone may not be able fully to envision: "Unless a grain of wheat falls into the earth and dies, it remains just a single grain; but if it dies, it bears much fruit" (John 12:24). Thus, the paradox of inside/outside parallels as well the paradox of setting limits and transgressing limits.[47]

The symbolism of both door and threshold points toward a restlessness that already exists in the psyche, a dynamic movement that does not allow us ever to settle, as if congealed, in one place. "We are *'spiral beings.'*"[48] We are continually moved by imagination and newness, "an unsettled being which all expression unsettles."[49] As Adam Phillips in his biography of Winnicott writes, *"Playing stops when one of the participants becomes dogmatic."*[50]

2. Familiar/Strange

The image of the threshold and the relationship to the Other lead us to the second paradox of familiar and strange. Maria-Teresa is thoroughly at home in the San Fernando Cathedral as she prays at the feet of her favorite *santo.* Yet it is also clear that whatever spiritual encounter takes place for her in this nave is not the same as the spirituality she practices in her personal home, even among the shrines and altars she has set up there. To speak of our "church home" is commonplace, and in churches where we feel "at home" we expect to find something both comforting and familiar. But the very nature of religion is also to mediate the transcendent to us, so we also expect (at least theoretically) to be met in our communal sacred spaces by the Holy that is wholly Other — the sense of the "numinous" — a *mysterium tremendens*[51] that, if we allow ourselves to be open to it, could overshadow our everyday consciousness with an experience of ineffable awe.[52]

---

47. Certeau, *The Practice of Everyday Life,* 127; Dirk Lange, "Worship at the Edges: Redefining Evangelism," in *Centripetal Worship: The Evangelical Heart of Lutheran Worship,* ed. Timothy Wengert (Minneapolis: Fortress, 2007), 69-70.

48. Bachelard, *The Poetics of Space,* 214.

49. Bachelard, *The Poetics of Space,* 214; Sheldrake, *Spaces for the Sacred,* 67-68.

50. Adam Phillips, *Winnicott* (Cambridge, MA: Harvard University Press, 1988), 142.

51. Rudolph Otto, *The Idea of the Holy,* 2nd ed. (Oxford: Oxford University Press, 1958).

52. Robert A. Scott, *The Gothic Enterprise: A Guide to Understanding the Medieval Cathedral* (Berkeley: University of California Press, 2003), 153-54.

This paradox of a space that is simultaneously familiar and strange resonates with Freud's discussions of "the uncanny"[53] (*das Unheimlich* — the unhomelike) in which the familiar (homelike) and the unfamiliar are closely intertwined at the level of the psyche. Because the word *Heimlich* can mean both familiar/homelike and private/secret, what is comfortably familiar can also slide over into what is hidden, even mysterious. Conversely, the *Unheimlich* produces an eerie feeling precisely because it involves an encounter with something familiar that has been repressed and then returns unexpectedly in an inexplicable or mysterious way: "the frightening which leads us back to what is known of old and long familiar."[54] Freud links this process to several infantile anxieties, but perhaps most intriguing in relation to this essay on *sacred* space as a womb or matrix, he links the uncanny with the mother's genitals, or her body more generally: "This *unheimlich* place . . . is the entrance to the former *Heim* [home] of all human beings, to the place where each one of us lived once upon a time and in the beginning."[55]

Not everyone of course enters into a sacred space to seek an overpowering sense of Otherness and mystery. Alan Jones, Dean of Grace Cathedral in San Francisco, has suggested that sometimes people go to church on Sunday precisely to get just a little *bit* of religion and thus inoculate themselves against a true encounter with the divine![56] However, the extent to which a sacred space is by definition a *practiced space,* full of paradox and multiple layers of storied meaning, we cannot avoid the otherness that will meet us there — even if we try only to remain attached to what is familiar and known within it.

Otherness is also mediated to us by the extent to which we make room for the Other as it is incarnated in the actual human stranger in our midst. Ethicist Thomas Ogletree, drawing on the philosopher Immanuel Levinas, has placed hospitality to the stranger at the center of the Christian moral

---

53. Sigmund Freud, "The Uncanny" (1919), in *Standard Edition* 17:217-56.

54. Sigmund Freud, "The Uncanny," 220.

55. Sigmund Freud, "The Uncanny," 245; see also Madelon Sprengnether, *The Spectral Mother: Freud, Feminism and Psychoanalysis* (Ithaca: Cornell University Press, 1992), 230-32; Diane Jonte-Pace, *Speaking the Unspeakable: Religion, Misogyny, and the Uncanny Mother in Freud's Cultural Texts* (Berkeley: University of California Press, 2001); Ana-María Rizzuto, *Why Did Freud Reject God? A Psychodynamic Interpretation* (New Haven: Yale University Press, 1998).

56. Alan Jones, personal interview, April 10, 2006.

life, calling for the embracing of otherness that the stranger represents, and welcoming the transforming power of the stranger's story in our own lives.[57] New Testament scholar John Koenig has described the tradition of hospitality in New Testament times as "one of the pillars of morality upon which the universe stands."[58] Theologian Kosuke Koyama has further asserted the Christian principle of hospitality to strangers as a missiology of *theologia crucis,* in which the suffering of the marginalized is embraced and the otherness of the stranger can be a vehicle for *metanoia,* as it is an invitation to critique all of one's own idolatries.[59]

Furthermore, a depth-psychological sensibility reminds us that the stranger to be welcomed in our sacred spaces is also the stranger within *ourselves,* and in the psyches of the people who are already here. We are multiply constituted beings with complex identities.[60] We embody a whole landscape of "inner objects," some of whom we know, and some of whom we do not consciously recognize. One of the greatest dangers, of course, as psychoanalysts of various schools of thought have taught us over the past century, is that we may project our inner unknown self-states and aspects onto others — particularly those parts of ourselves we most wish to disavow — and then regard as the enemy those onto whom we have projected these inner "others."

So as we spend time in our particular sacred spaces, we might also ask ourselves the question: What is here that is home-like, familiar, and safe? And at the same time, where is a welcome given in this space to mystery — to the *Unheimlich,* the uncanny, the strange — not only in the form of the newcomer who might come through the door, but the stranger seeking hospitality among and within the people I know, and even here *within me?*

57. Thomas Ogletree, *Hospitality to the Stranger: Dimensions of Moral Understanding* (Philadelphia: Fortress Press, 1985), 3ff., also citing Immanuel Levinas, *Totality and Infinity: An Essay on Exteriority* (Pittsburgh: Duquesne University Press, 1969).

58. John Koenig, *New Testament Hospitality: Partnership with Strangers as Promise and Mission* (Philadelphia: Fortress Press, 1985), 2.

59. Kosuke Koyama, "Extending Hospitality to Strangers: A Missiology of Theologia Crucis," *Currents* 20, no. 3 (June 1993): 165-76.

60. Cooper-White, *Many Voices,* 35-66.

3. Past-present/Present-future

One of the facts about any building, including sacred structures, is that as soon as it is constructed, it has already become a monument to the past. One of the sociological perils of sacred space, in fact, can be the veneration of a building's history, long after the shell of the place itself has ceased to house a living community or to serve a living purpose.[61] At its most creative, however, the older a building becomes, the more narrative tensions and dynamic movements it can contain. The best and most creative renovations — while often greatly contested during the planning process — will lovingly preserve the sacred relics and monuments from a church's past, while opening up aesthetically beautiful spaces that are hospitable and serviceable to new practices.[62] Thus sacred spaces maintain a living paradox between the church's past as it is remembered in the present; and the hopes, dreams, and sense of vocation and mission that are discerned in the present as a trajectory into the future. Here the living and the dead can truly come together as a "cloud of witnesses," sustained by tradition and story, in order to perceive the ways in which God might be saying "Behold, I am doing a new thing!" (Isa. 43:19).

One of the important sacred functions of remembering the past is to provide a space for mourning and grief.[63] Particular concerns are also given visible space for prayer and contemplation — for example, the AIDS chapel in Grace Cathedral and the Genocide Bay in the Cathedral of St. John the Divine in New York. Many churches, moreover, actually house tombs and relics of departed saints and provide burial places for ordinary members. This trend is returning, as many parishes are installing *columbaria* (indoor vaults with niches for ashes of the departed), in addition to outdoor gravesites.[64]

---

61. Richard Vosko, *Designing Future Worship Spaces,* Meeting House Essays No. 8 (Chicago: Liturgy Training Publications, 1996), 6ff.; Giles, *Re-pitching the Tent.*

62. E.g., compare descriptions of the renovations of the Philadelphia Cathedral and the Episcopal Church of St. Martin-in-the-Fields, Philadelphia, in Roger W. Moss, *Historic Sacred Places of Philadelphia* (Philadelphia: University of Pennsylvania Press, 2005), 216-21, 282-87.

63. On the relationship between the sacred and burial spaces, see Philippe Aries, *The Hour of Our Death* (Oxford: Oxford University Press 1981); Sheldrake, *Spaces for the Sacred,* 48-51; Scott, *The Gothic Enterprise,* 183-208.

64. E.g., Richard Vosko, *God's House Is Our House: Re-imagining the Environment for Worship* (Collegeville, MN: Liturgical Press, 2006), 160-66.

From a psychoanalytic perspective, this is deeply appropriate. One of the most important aspects of pastoral care or the "cure of souls" is the care of bereaved and dying persons, accompanied by the proclamation of resurrection, the perpetuation of faith and meaning that transcends individual death. All buildings, from the moment of their completion, are historical buildings, and all historical buildings are memorials. Monuments, statuary, and even church buildings themselves function as the externalization of loved ones who are gone but still invested with continuing intense love and attachment internally. Freud in his *Mourning and Melancholia*[65] stressed the importance of the process of turning inward for a time during grief, until the reality of loss can be accepted and the inner representation of the lost loved one can be integrated into the experience of life beyond the beloved's death. These inner love objects live on, after a time of healthy grieving, in the form of inspiration for new loves and creative work. External memorials serve to strengthen the inner power and presence of these loved ones, who are lost in the external world but live on in the collective interior landscape. Church buildings function often in just this way, as a powerful witness to the collective memory of the faithful departed, as well as the beliefs and values that motivated the building of a memorial work of art or architecture, such as the statue of Martin Luther King Jr. in the National Cathedral. These beliefs, which continue on in a living legacy of social and political movements for change, are mirrored in the representations of these tangible memorials.

They also provide spaces *within* them that mirror the inner space of the psyche in which mourning and healing take place. Chapels set apart along the sides of the nave or in the apse, cloister gardens, and spaces dedicated for meditation may function as particular "potential spaces," a womb within a womb, in which the inner life of the believer can meet the outer world in a protected liminal space that invites the conscious, rational mind to be at rest and facilitates the healing emergence of the symbolic realm, deep feelings, fantasies, fears, inner images, dreams, and prayers without words.

Church buildings are not just preservationist monuments to the past, however. They do not function only as sacred inscriptions of the collective

---

65. Sigmund Freud, "Mourning and Melancholia" (1917), in *Standard Edition* 14:239-57; see also Peter Homans and Diane Jonte-Pace, "Tracking the Emotion in Stone," in Winer et al., eds., *Psychoanalysis and Architecture,* 261-84.

memory of the people or as places for mourning and recollection. They are also places of both "memory and imagination,"[66] where the values and forward-looking hopes and dreams of the people can be collected in the form of word and symbol. In a creative and masterful planning process, the leadership of Ebenezer Baptist Church in Atlanta built a new church building, named the "Horizon Sanctuary," across the street from the original Ebenezer church. While the old church continues to function as a shrine to the past and a place of pilgrimage and contemplation where one can listen to powerful sermons of Dr. King being broadcast from the small, humble pulpit, the new building is a spectacular architectural gesture toward the future. With a wing-like exterior structure and a contemporary wood-paneled interior that echoes themes of an African meeting house with African symbols and natural materials,[67] the new building rises up out of the grounds of the Martin Luther King Jr. Memorial site as a kind of exhortation for the uplifting of the black community in the present and future.

In this way, church buildings function to articulate the values of the community, and these in turn cohere around the sacramental objects and enactments of liturgy. So the font at the entrance and the altar in a central location toward the eastern end become more than architectural features, serving as reminders of the central promises of the faith and the commitments of the faithful themselves — reminders of the daily rhythms of the sacramental life of the community and the individuals who sojourn within it.

4. Immanence/Transcendence

Finally, there is the paradox that God is both here in the spaces we cordon off as holy, and yet God is never contained in them. This is the biblical paradox of the God of the tabernacle and cloud and fiery pillar who wanders with the people and tents among them as an itinerant and who also becomes the God of the temple who dwells among them in a central holy

66. Vosko, *Designing Future Worship Spaces,* 14, 39-56, and *God's House Is Our House,* 3-17.

67. Designed by the Rev. Joseph Roberts Jr., Senior Pastor, and architects William Stanley III and Ivenue Love-Stanley, http://www.stanleylove-stanleypc.com/videoPBS.htm. Joseph Roberts Jr., personal interview, February 22, 2006.

place. Because of the multiple stories that come to be housed in certain places, or even because of a quality of light or a feature of the landscape that has spoken to pilgrims over the ages of a certain simplicity or grandeur that tells something of God, humans do seems to sense certain "thin places," as the Celtic tradition has named them — places where the veil of separation between humans and the divine seems more permeable. But God's presence is surely not limited to such places. And many people have found themselves feeling closest to God in the midst of the most abject wastelands of poverty, disease, or despair.

"God is that reality whose centre is everywhere and whose circumference is nowhere."[68] Sacred spaces are sacramental — as buildings made by human hands, they are "outward and visible signs of an inward and spiritual grace" and perhaps even at times "the means by which we receive that grace."[69] Theologian Marianne Micks likens a sacrament to a magnifying glass: the light of the sun is all around, diffuse and available, and the magnifying glass can focus that light so intensely that it could even burn a piece of paper.[70] We do not control the light of God with our sacramental rites (that would be magic), but through these human ritual activities, we catch a more focused glimpse of God's healing energy and experience it in a more concentrated way. So a church building may serve to set apart a place where we may focus our intentions to meet God through prayer and community life, but it never can capture or domesticate God within its walls.[71]

The paradox of inner and outer, and the liminal spaces between, help to convey the mystery that God is simultaneously here (immanent) and beyond (transcendent), God-with-us *(emmanu-el)* and God as wholly Other. As the Spirit moves in and out of our sacred spaces, so we move in and out in the rhythm of contemplation and action. Sacred space does not finally contain us but becomes a living "potential space" that we enter and then take with us when we leave. We internalize these spaces, and they

68. Blaise Pascal, *Pensées,* cited in Martin Laird, *Into the Silent Land: A Guide to the Christian Practice of Contemplation* (Oxford: Oxford University Press, 2006), 12; see also Giles, *Re-pitching the Tent,* 9-52.

69. Catechism, *The Book of Common Prayer* (Episcopal) (New York: Seabury, 1979), 857.

70. Marianne Micks, *Loving the Questions* (New York: Seabury Classics, 2005; orig. 1993), 106.

71. Sheldrake, *Spaces for the Sacred,* 67.

may continue to make room within our psyches for the play of imagination and creativity they first opened up for us. No matter where we may physically be, "God does not know how to be absent."[72]

Finally, as the early church fathers and mothers knew,[73] the *people* are the space of God. To quote Sheldrake once more,

> The primary sacred place is, singly or collectively, described as the temple of the Spirit in women and men of faith. The locus of the sacred transgresses former boundaries and is to be found particularly where people seek to be a community in Christ, distinguished by the destruction of traditional separations and by a quality of common life. Christ is to be met in those who are rejected or excluded in the old religious and cultural dispensation — the hungry, thirsty, naked, imprisoned, women, Samaritans, Romans, publicans, sinners (Matt. 1:23; 25:31ff).[74]

Maria-Teresa's spiritual life is certainly not wholly contained or circumscribed by the interior of the San Fernando Cathedral. Some congregations, like San Fernando, facilitate the linkage explicitly from church "home" to personal home. Festivals observed by the San Fernando community, such as the *Levantada* ceremony in which the Christ child is solemnly taken up from the nativity scene at the end of Christmastide,[75] are properly celebrated by the church community in the homes of its members. Other rituals, quite famously, are celebrated publicly, as in the neighborhood parades, the *Posadas,* re-creating the journey of Joseph and Mary during Advent,[76] the public processions to celebrate the Feast of the *Virgen de Guadalupe* (a strong Mexican symbol of *mestizaje* and indigenous resistance),[77] and the highly dramatic *Viernes Santo* (Good Friday) re-enactment of the Passion of Christ on the Plaza.[78] The spirituality of San Fernando is not contained within the church but spills out into the city

---

72. Laird, *Into the Silent Land,* 15.

73. E.g., Minucius Felix, Origen, and John Chrysostom, cited in Vosko, *God's House Is Our House,* 25.

74. Sheldrake, *Spaces for the Sacred,* 37-38.

75. Elizondo and Matovina, *San Fernando Cathedral,* 2-7.

76. Elizondo and Matovina, *San Fernando Cathedral,* 86.

77. Elizondo and Matovina, *San Fernando Cathedral,* 34-37, 82-85.

78. Elizondo and Matovina, *San Fernando Cathedral,* 90-96; Adán Medrano, Producer, *Soul of the City*/Alma del Pueblo (videotape) (Houston: JM Communications, [n.d.]), audio excerpt at http://www.jmcommunications.com/english/soul.html (accessed July 2007).

streets, mingling with the everyday life of pedestrians, merchants, and tourists and pouring healing, encouragement, and political resistance into the homes and the hearts of its members.

Conclusion

In conclusion, whenever we dwell within our "sacred spaces," wherever they may physically be, we might consider what "depth dimension" we can discover there. For the "potential space" that we encounter in the matrix of sacred places is also *in us:* "Immensity is within ourselves."[79] We might consider how this space functions for us as a sacred matrix, filled with multiple layers of meaning, accessible at both conscious and unconscious levels, the paradoxical relations of inside/outside; familiar/strange; past-present/present-future; immanent/transcendent. How might such spaces become true "potential spaces" in which we can discover/create the loving, holding presence of the Holy and in which all that we are — light and shadow, known and unknown, familiar and strange, self and Other (even the Other within) — can be embraced, healed, and empowered by God's unfailing love?

79. Bachelard, *The Poetics of Space,* 184.

A Wisdom Model for Pastoral Counseling

Daniel S. Schipani

For the past several years I have sought to serve with a non-medical model of pastoral counseling, both in the congregation and in the medical setting of a community health center where I volunteer. In my view, pastoral counseling can be best understood as a specialized form of caregiving ministry centering on spiritual wisdom rather than mental health as its ground metaphor.[1] In pastoral counseling practiced from a Christian perspective, *human emergence*[2] is uniquely sponsored through a distinctive way of walking with others — individuals, couples, family members, or small groups — as they face life's challenges and struggles. The overall goal, simply stated, is that they may live more wisely in the light of God.[3]

---

1. See Daniel S. Schipani, *The Way of Wisdom in Pastoral Counseling* (Elkhart, IN: Institute of Mennonite Studies, 2003).

2. The expression "human emergence" in this context denotes a process of humanization viewed primarily in theological perspective. It is about becoming "more human" in terms of (our understanding of) God's gift and promise of authentic freedom and wholeness; further, it connotes human becoming according to the wider ethical-political and eschatological framework biblically symbolized as the reign of God, that is, the normative commonwealth of love, peace, and justice. Hence the process of "emerging" involves the kinds of formation and transformation in people's lives that is associated with Christomorphic moral and spiritual growth. Therefore, human emergence must not be merely equated with psychological notions of development and maturation, even though connections with "natural" human development and with psychological understandings of human flourishing must be adequately established in the theory and practice of pastoral counseling.

3. This characterization is thoroughly explicated in Schipani, *The Way of Wisdom*, 91-114. To be sure, wise living in the light of God is not an exclusively Christian counseling

My practice is aimed fundamentally, although not exclusively, at awakening, nurturing, and developing counselees' moral and spiritual intelligence. Simply put, moral and spiritual intelligence is about how to live well, especially in the face of conflict, crisis, difficult decisions, disorientation, suffering, and loss.[4] Therefore, this ministry may be viewed as one dimension of the larger work of caring toward health and wellness.

This chapter presents such an understanding of pastoral counseling as a ministry of the Christian church. It illustrates the contours of a new paradigm for the field of pastoral care and the discipline of pastoral theology, one that is centered on wisdom in the light of God. I will describe a case from my pastoral counseling practice and, in relation to the case, offer a systematic discussion of the key components of the wisdom model.[5] I have chosen to discuss my work with a "non-Christian" counselee because both in counseling practices and in hospital chaplaincies, Christian pastoral caregivers must learn to care well for increasing numbers of "other-than-Christian" care-seekers. I believe that I have been called to care *pastorally* as well as *Christianly.* The pastoral nature of my work is determined, first of all, by my pastoral identity, including some form of ministerial accountability to the church regardless of the setting within which pastoral counseling is practiced. Second, my caregiving is pastoral to the extent that it is consistently practiced with a pastoral-theological frame of reference.[6] By "caring Christianly" I mean the kind of spiritual care that stems from three interrelated dimensions of the Christian faith: a particular vision of reality and the good life; a disposition to care as a form of love of neighbor (and, especially, the care-seeking stranger) in-

---

goal. Within my pastoral theological framework, the normative content implied in such goal is supplied by the life, faith, and ministry of Jesus.

4. The notion of moral intelligence is sometimes used as a present-day equivalent to practical wisdom (*phronesis,* which in Aristotle's ethical writings meant the intelligence or wisdom of the good person, closely associated with virtue and good character). My use of moral intelligence includes a holistic consideration of virtue and character in spiritually grounded and theologically defined moral formation. Further, I use the term "spiritual intelligence" specifically in reference to wisdom in the light of God, which necessarily includes and transforms moral intelligence.

5. The following illustration is based on a real pastoral counseling situation. I have changed several pieces of information, however, in order to preserve confidentiality.

6. For a systematic discussion of such a frame of reference, see Daniel S. Schipani, "The Pastoral-theological Nature of Pastoral Counseling," in *Mennonite Perspectives on Pastoral Counseling,* ed. Schipani (Elkhart, IN: Institute of Mennonite Studies 2007), 7-29.

spired by Jesus Christ; and a sense of vocation to serve in partnership with the Spirit of God.

Case Illustration

Annelies was a single woman, thirty-seven years of age, who had recently become chief executive officer of a major company. During the year prior to the counseling she had begun to wonder whether she should discontinue a close friendship with her former boyfriend, thirty-nine-year-old Matt. Matt had married somebody else and become the father of two children, but he had been separated from his wife for a couple of years. From time to time, Annelies had entertained the idea of reuniting with Matt. She recognized, however, that even though they could have fun together, they were two very different people and not really compatible as a couple. For several weeks before pastoral counseling started, Annelies had had what she called "strange dreams" involving angels trying to communicate something to her. Her need to understand what was going on in her life and a deeply felt desire to resolve her existential crisis became the occasion for counseling. She was referred to me by a mutual acquaintance, and she knew that I am a Christian pastoral counselor.

Annelies had been raised in a Catholic family, but she considered herself a non-religious person with deep spiritual sensitivities. From time to time she had enjoyed practicing diverse expressions of Eastern spirituality and "new age" activities aimed at holistic cleansing, enlightenment, enhanced appreciation of beauty, and the freedom to create and to love.

In the first pastoral counseling session, while sharing her life story, Annelies confided that during the time she was originally involved with Matt, she had had an abortion, about eight years earlier. Now, at thirty-seven, she deeply regretted the decision, which Matt had encouraged, and felt sorry about it. She indicated that she was sure that the child would have been a girl and, in fact, started to call "her" Naomi (the actual name of a dear, close relative). After clarifying mutual expectations, we agreed to meet for a short-term pastoral counseling process.

Annelies received as a hopeful sign my observation that the name "Naomi" means "pleasant." She also realized that we would need to revisit painful memories and to find ways to deal constructively with her sense of loss and guilt. I encouraged her to welcome her dreams and, as much as possible, write down their content so that, by considering them together in the counseling setting, we might be able to find meaning and a sense of direction.[7] We also agreed that angels may symbolize "messengers" as well as "guardian spirits."

In addition to the attempt to reconcile and integrate unconscious material by attending to her dreams, Annelies found it especially helpful to engage her imagination in the manner of writing letters to "Naomi" and sharing them with me, including the possible response that she might have received from her child. As a therapeutic method, that activity became a fruitful way of processing both her grief and her guilt. It also made it possible for her to begin to visualize a way forward opened by a unique experience of forgiveness. No longer inhibited by the power of a buried secret, she decided to tell her mother and siblings about the abortion, as well as about her work in therapy. Not surprisingly, she began to experience new freedom from bondage to the past, as well as a sense of hope.

From the beginning, I encouraged Annelies to consider her experience of loss and distress both as an emotional trauma and as a spiritual struggle. At one point I told her that I always pray that I may be the best possible conversation partner in counseling, and I also pray for the counselees, whether they know it or not.[8] She indicated appreciation for my praying in her behalf. Interestingly, by the end of the counseling process, Annelies had come to perceive me not only as a guide and as a witness to her ongoing healing process but as a messenger (or "angel") as well.

The wisdom model of pastoral counseling that I have developed has four interrelated components, which are (1) a four-dimensional view of reality and knowing; (2) interdisciplinary assessment and agenda; (3) complementary goals for care-seekers and caregivers; and (4) an overarching purpose and fundamental approach.

---

7. In depth psychology dreams are deemed meaningful and subject to interpretation. Sigmund Freud was one of the great pioneers in dream interpretation (see his *The Interpretation of Dreams* [New York: The Modern Library, 1950]); so was C. G. Jung (*Memories, Dreams, Reflections* [New York: Random House, 1963]; and *Dreams* [Princeton: Princeton University Press, 1974]). There are many popular publications on dreams including, among others, Morton Kelsey's *Dreams: A Way to Listen to God* (New York: Paulist Press, 1978).

8. The decision to tell or not to tell counselees that I privately pray for myself and for them of course depends, first of all, on whether the subject of prayer is a pertinent focus of conversation, even as a passing reference. It also depends on my spiritual assessment of the care-receivers, especially as I explore the nature of their needs, hopes, and emotional and spiritual resourcefulness from their perspective and in their own terms.

A Four-Dimensional View

As a bright, energetic, socially popular, and fun-loving woman, Annelies had been enjoying life surrounded by many friends and co-workers. She had accomplished much, yet she had begun to experience increased restlessness associated in part with her complex relationship with Matt, her long-time former companion, and the demands and opportunities of a successful professional career. Annelies was actually entering a new chapter in her life that presented serious challenges, including a changing sense of identity and conflicting desires regarding sexuality and the possibility of motherhood, as well as an increasing wish somehow to "get settled" in life. Her distress and disorientation involved several dimensions of her self and her lived world. Therefore, pastoral counseling would need to address a number of biological, emotional, and relational issues.

Our model, however, calls for an analytic framework and counseling strategy larger than the two dimensions — *the self* and *the lived world* — implied in the previous paragraph. We must also include two existential-spiritual dimensions — *the Void* and *the Holy*, as James E. Loder describes them. Loder writes that "being human entails environment, selfhood, the possibility of not being, and the possibility of new being. All four dimensions are essential, and none of them can be ignored without decisive loss to our understanding of what is essentially human."[9] These dimensions were also part of Annelies's experience and potential for healing and growth. The faces of the Void, the implicit threat of nonbeing, was experienced with existential anxiety connected with a deeply felt sense of loss — the loss of the opportunity to give birth to a child. Her choice to have an abortion, which she now regretted, was accompanied by the lingering effects of suppressed grief. Another face of the Void for Annelies was the fear that she might not be able ever to love and be loved again. That multidimensional threat had to be confronted in the counseling setting as I sought to guide her through a process by which she might experience the gifts of grace and freedom. Annelies's distress might thus be transformed into a new experience of light and love — that is, a negation of the negation — resulting in some degree of growth into "new being" or "being more" (the

---

9. I allude here to James Loder's notion of "the fourfold knowing event" — which involves the lived world, the self, the Void, and the Holy. See *The Transforming Moment*, 2nd ed. (Colorado Springs: Helmers & Howard, 1989), 69.

lure of the Holy, so to speak). Her spiritual sensitivities and wholehearted search for reorientation and renewal were, of course, indispensable resources which elicited hope.

I seek to address the existential-spiritual dimensions in all counseling situations. I believe it is essential to evaluate those situations four-dimensionally, along the lines proposed by Loder. We must not only consider transactions between self and lived world, which is the limited horizon normally addressed in other forms of counseling and psychotherapy.[10] We must also work within a larger framework that includes the threat of nonbeing — the Void — and the possibility and invitation to new being — the Holy.

Interdisciplinary Perspectives and Assessment

The application of interdisciplinary perspectives and assessment is the second component of the wisdom model of pastoral counseling. We can state this guideline as follows: it is indispensable to identify the pertinent issues of the counseling agenda both from a psychological and a theological perspective, even as we work with an integrated understanding of those seeking care and of the very setting and process of pastoral counseling. Therefore, we must affirm the integrity of the disciplines of psychology and theology. We must avoid reducing either to the terms of the other, even as we maximize the potential for complementarity between their unique contributions. At the same time, we must give priority to the pastoral and theological nature of our ministry work, including systematic reflection on the practice of pastoral counseling itself.[11] This priority is worth empha-

10. Excluded from this generalization are counseling and psychotherapy that intentionally address spirituality issues and practices in a non-reductionistic manner. See Scott Richards and Allen E. Bergin, *A Spiritual Strategy for Counseling and Psychotherapy* (Washington, DC: American Psychological Association, 1997); and William R. Miller, ed., *Integrating Spirituality into Treatment: Resources for Practitioners* (Washington, DC: American Psychological Association, 1999). These contributions address spirituality both as a subject matter in its own right (including, for example, issues of acceptance, forgiveness, and hope) and as a resource for therapeutic intervention (meditation and prayer, for example). For an explicitly Christian perspective, see Mark R. McMinn, *Psychology, Theology, and Spirituality in Christian Counseling* (Wheaton: Tyndale House Publishers, 1996).

11. These three methodological and epistemological principles are viewed and explicated in detail by pastoral theologian Deborah van Deusen Hunsinger as the threefold

sizing, because of the ways in which theology addresses fundamental questions of life and thus distinctly informs the normative dimensions of pastoral counseling. What does it mean to live well in the light of God's reign and to seek wisdom in the midst of our life's challenges and struggles? What is the shape of human completion and wholeness? How do we understand and foster maturity, and how do we know which is the way forward in human emergence?[12] Theology is uniquely suited to address such questions, always in creative conversation with the human sciences. By helping people like Annelies to make choices oriented to a more wholesome life, pastoral counseling can foster spiritual intelligence and moral and spiritual growth in wise living.

In light of this component of the wisdom model, Annelies and I agreed that we needed to address interrelated issues. We needed to address her sense of loss, guilt, and depression, while keeping in mind systemic dynamics related to her family background, as well as her current interpersonal, social, and professional situation. Specifics of the pastoral counseling agenda that we identified included the following:

- Annelies's image of herself as a woman, in connection with her roles as a professional, friend, and lover; this agenda included an understanding of the nature and the dynamics of her *false self*[13] nurtured by mul-

---

"Chalcedonian pattern" applicable to the relationship between psychology and theology in pastoral counseling theory and practice. See van Deusen Hunsinger's *Theology and Pastoral Counseling: A New Interdisciplinary Approach* (Grand Rapids: Eerdmans, 1995), especially chapter 3. See also, by the same author, "An Interdisciplinary Map for Christian Counselors: Theology and Psychology in Christian Counseling," in *Care for the Soul: Exploring the Intersection of Psychology and Theology,* ed. Mark R. McMinn and Timothy R. Phillips (Downers Grove: InterVarsity Press, 2001), 218-40.

12. These questions are explicitly addressed by, among others, the following: James W. Fowler, *Becoming Adult, Becoming Christian: Human Development and Christian Faith,* rev. ed. (San Francisco: Jossey-Bass, 2000); James E. Loder, *The Logic of the Spirit: Human Development in Theological Perspective* (San Francisco: Jossey-Bass, 1998); Neil Pembroke, *Moving Toward Spiritual Maturity: Psychological, Contemplative, and Moral Challenges in Christian Living* (New York: Haworth Press, 2007).

13. The notion of "false self" refers to a person's interaction with her world when it is determined more by the demands and expectations of others than by her own needs and desires. The concept comes from pediatrician and psychoanalyst D. W. Winnicott and his study of the psychodynamics of early self-development (see *The Maturational Process and the Facilitating Environment* [Madison, CT: International Universities Press, 1965]). As

tiple superficial relationships, a number of sexual affairs, and professional overachievement.

- Relationships with significant people in her life, especially her former lovers, friends, and family, and the challenge of facing and dealing with suppressed anger, guilt feelings, and unresolved inner conflict about intimate relationships and vocation.

- Appropriate identification of present needs as well as hopes, including her vocational sense of direction and projections concerning professional work.

- Availability of internal and external resources that would potentially contribute to the healing process.

In addition to these and related issues, the explicitly pastoral theological approach that I brought to the counseling process elicited for both of us a number of concerns, such as these:

- An appropriation of grace and care in connection with hurtful experiences in the past and inadequate processing and resolution (especially regarding poor choices and assuming responsibility for them[14]), which might be characterized in terms of moral failure, and the possibility of transformation and healing.

- Views of shame and guilt as well as acceptance, forgiveness, and reconciliation in light of Annelies's own sense of moral integrity and responsibility, possibly connected in some way with a reconstructed memory of her early Christian views and practices.

---

pastoral theologian Gordon Lynch helpfully notes, two significant implications stem from Winnicott's idea of the false self: "First, this concept indicates that attending to the needs of others can, for some involved in caring work, have a compulsive and pathological dimension to it. Second, Winnicott believed that individuals can recover more of their true selves in adult life through being in relationship with others who demonstrated reliability, attentiveness, responsiveness, recollection and durability. This highlights qualities which might usefully be embodied in pastoral relationships." See Gordon Lynch, "False Self," in *The New Dictionary of Pastoral Studies,* ed. Wesley Carr (Grand Rapids: Eerdmans, 2002), 124.

14. One of my concerns in counseling is to help care-receivers evaluate and make good choices by keeping in mind both psychological and ethical-theological criteria. I agree with Christine Cozad Neuger that the goal of pastoral counselors is to help people make choices "that open up a preferred direction that is healthy, moral and hopeful." *Counseling Women: A Narrative, Pastoral Approach* (Minneapolis: Fortress Press, 2001), 188.

- The meaning and function of Annelies's unique spirituality and its possible role in reshaping her life story, identity, and sense of life vocation.
- The overall potential for spiritual growth as the core of human flourishing to be uniquely experienced in a more wholesome life and in fashioning a better future.

Complementary Goals

The third indispensable component of the wisdom model of pastoral counseling consists of identifying and integrating two distinct sets of pastoral counseling goals. On the one hand, goals (in the sense of desired outcomes) must be selected from the perspective of the person seeking care, in consultation with the pastoral caregiver, as they emerge from the counselee's felt needs, hopes, and resources. On the other hand, pastoral counselors must also seek clarity about goals for their work as they guide the counseling process. Further, Christian pastoral counselors must seek to honor their call to mediate divine grace and wisdom as representatives of the caring church and the healing Christ without discriminating or proselytizing, regardless of the nature of the care seekers' spirituality and (religious or nonreligious) faith.[15] The character of pastoral counselors must reflect their ongoing participation in faith communities attuned to the reign of God in the world[16] and their commitment to minister not only as competent clinicians or therapists but also as moral and spiritual guides.[17] In fact, these personal characteristics — call, character, compe-

15. The term "spirituality" is meant here as the overarching construct, connoting a fundamental human need for meaning and value and the disposition for relationship with a transcendent power. Following the contribution of James W. Fowler, I use "faith" as denoting developmentally patterned ways of being "spiritual."

16. For an illuminating discussion of the relationship between the reign of God as ethical culture, the church as an ethical community, and the therapist as an ethical character, see Alvin C. Dueck, *Between Jerusalem and Athens: Ethical Perspectives on Culture, Religion, and Psychotherapy* (Grand Rapids: Baker Books, 1995).

17. Rebekah L. Miles notes that good guides have distinctive knowledge and wisdom, and as practical pilgrims they are constantly training and preparing themselves for their art. Further, good guides are confident leaders who know their limits and temptations, know when they need help and are willing to seek advice, remember that others are free and responsible, teach others the lessons of pilgrimage and guidance, and develop excellent capacities for dis-

tence, and commitment — along with explicit formal accountability to the church, are essential elements of counseling that is truly pastoral.

I set for myself, and regularly review, goals that serve not only to provide overall orientation to my pastoral counseling ministry but also to evaluate that practice. These goals are indispensable to keep in mind as I remain accountable to care-seekers, colleagues with whom I work, and the church I represent, which validates my ministry. Some of the general goals that apply to all kinds of counseling situations are:

- To welcome care-seekers in a safe and caring space where they can express themselves freely, clarify the nature of their challenges and struggles, make wise choices, and be empowered to move on.
- To faithfully represent the healing Christ and the church as a community of wisdom and healing, as an implicit, non-verbalized role that includes the attempt to mediate grace in compassionate and generous ways.
- To become a temporary companion in people's journeys toward (re)orientation, transformation, reconciliation, and healing.
- To minister as a caregiving sage who practices counseling with clinical and therapeutic competence, especially by adequately employing the manifold resources provided by psychology and psychotherapy as a practical human science.

I needed to keep in focus these general goals as I tried to help Annelies face the crisis precipitated by her current existential disorientation and distress. At the same time, however, I also had to identify pastoral counseling objectives in light of her need for support and guidance. These specific objectives, which at the risk of oversimplification may also be considered desired outcomes of the counseling process, included the following:

- For Annelies to experience emotional relief through catharsis.
- For Annelies to begin to understand the nature of the crisis she was experiencing and to appreciate and integrate the reality of her pain and sense of loss and disorientation.

---

cernment. They not only know the rules but also know that the rules must sometimes be bent or even changed, and they remember the most important things — the shared destination and the source of power. *The Pastor as Moral Guide* (Minneapolis: Fortress Press, 1999), 6-7.

- For both Annelies and me to identify and activate available resources, both internal and external, to help her cope in healthy ways with the crisis and its ramifications.
- For both Annelies and me to strengthen — emotionally and spiritually — her sense of personal identity and integrity.
- For both Annelies and me to develop a plan of action for her, beyond the counseling setting.

I needed to apply therapeutic methods and resources commonly associated with the strategies of crisis, supportive, and narrative pastoral care and counseling.[18] Therefore, specific objectives for my caregiving endeavors with this counselee included the following:

- To be carefully hospitable to Annelies while keeping in mind that she had a spiritual and theological background, and a moral and ethical framework different from my own. So not only did I need to be consistently respectful of her unique spirituality and worldview, I would also have to practice *language care*[19] in order for us to find common ground and to be able to communicate in meaningful and helpful ways.
- To become a supportive pastoral presence and a source of emotional and spiritual comfort by listening responsively to Annelies, helping her find her voice, and making available resources from diverse sources (the human sciences, the Christian faith tradition, and the local faith community) in order to sustain her process of painful recalling, lamenting, and grieving.
- To help Annelies clarify her own feelings and articulate her ways of understanding her experience of disorientation and loss in her own terms.
- To encourage Annelies to make healthy new choices in the face of the

18. For descriptions and illustrations of supportive, crisis, and bereavement pastoral care and counseling, see the following: Howard Clinebell, *Basic Types of Pastoral Care and Counseling* (Nashville: Abingdon Press, 1984), chapters 7, 8, and 9, respectively; Howard W. Stone, *Crisis Counseling*, rev. ed. (Minneapolis: Fortress Press, 1993); and, especially, Christie Cozad Neuger, *Counseling Women: A Narrative, Pastoral Approach* (Minneapolis: Fortress Press, 2001).

19. For a discussion of "language care," see Leah Dawn Bueckert and Daniel S. Schipani, "Interfaith Spiritual Caregiving: The Case for Language Care," in Leah Dawn Bueckert and Daniel S. Schipani, *Spiritual Caregiving in the Hospital: Windows to Chaplaincy Ministry* (Kitchener: Pandora Press, 2006), 245-63.

new realities in her life, and to guide her in reality testing in terms of her chosen path to restoration and healing.

- To sponsor Annelies's spiritual growth by exploring ways to nurture life-giving practices, both individual and communal, including new forms and disciplines such as meditation, journaling, and prayer.
- To encourage Annelies to reach out to other people who might extend responsible support and gentle accountability beyond our short-term pastoral counseling.
- To convey my openness to be available for further counseling in the coming days or in the future, while exploring where she could turn for caring support among her family and friends.

An Overarching Purpose and Fundamental Approach

Each pastoral counseling situation calls for specific objectives, however we may articulate them. Each situation also requires the application of pertinent strategies to reach those objectives. At the same time, all pastoral counseling situations have much in common. I believe that those commonalities center on issues of overall purpose and fundamental process, the fourth component that points to wisdom in the light of God as a fitting, heart-of-the-matter metaphor for pastoral counseling.

Annelies had voluntarily entered a pastoral counseling relationship because she was experiencing disorientation and distress. In the course of our short-term counseling process, she was invited — implicitly rather than explicitly, to be sure — to become a wiser person in the light of God as we worked together in the face of the challenges and struggles she was encountering at this particular juncture in her life journey. The overarching purpose of becoming wiser included three inseparable aspects of her search for relief and resolution. As pastoral counselor, I needed to keep in mind that each of these aspects integrates psychological as well as theological and spiritual perspectives on the self. In the following paragraphs I succinctly articulate a threefold normative understanding of growth in wisdom that I keep in mind as a Christian pastoral caregiver. This way of conceptualizing purpose is part of my pastoral-theological frame of reference but is not necessarily made explicit as such in the counseling situation, especially with non-Christian care-receivers.[20]

20. Readers should keep in mind that there is no such thing as philosophically and eth-

Daniel S. Schipani

Growth in Vision

First, the counseling experience was meant to help the counselee find new and better — more holistic — ways of knowing and understanding reality, including the dimensions of self, the lived or social world, the threatening Void, and the gracious, embracing Holy. From a Christian formation viewpoint, Annelies needed to grow in her ways of seeing, so that she would be increasingly able to perceive reality (especially herself and other people) with the eyes of God, metaphorically speaking. Such growth in vision would entail the practice and development of dispositions and behaviors such as heightened awareness, attentiveness, admiration and contemplation, critical thinking, creative imagination, and spiritual discernment.

Growth in Virtue

Second, the counseling experience encouraged the care-seeker to discover more fulfilling and faithful ways of being and loving, with specific focus on her relationships with others — friends, family, and co-workers, especially — with the gracious Spirit, and with herself. In Christian formation terms, I would say that Annelies's heart needed to be increasingly conformed to the heart of Christ. Such growth in virtue entails an ongoing process of formation and transformation, shaping the inmost affections and passions, dispositions, and attitudes — habits of the heart — and defining the content of her moral and spiritual character. In short, in and through the counseling process, God was calling her to become a unique expression of human love.

Growth in Vocation

Third, the counseling experience sought to empower Annelies to make sound choices and to invest fresh energies in relationships, work, leisure,

---

ically "neutral" counselors or psychotherapists. We all hold certain views of reality and the "good life" that inform and guide our practice. For an insightful systematic treatment of the implicit deep metaphors and principles of obligation embedded in and around the conceptual systems of contemporary psychotherapeutic psychologies, see Don S. Browning, *Religious Thought and the Modern Psychologies: A Critical Conversation in the Theology of Culture* (Philadelphia: Fortress, 1987).

spiritual nurture, and service, and to find ways to sustain those choices with integrity. She needed to find a freer and more hopeful orientation toward life, especially her social situation. Such growth in vocation may be viewed theologically as participating increasingly in the life of the Spirit in the world. For the counselee, it could open the possibility of a fruitful and joyful response to the invitation to collaborate with God in creative, liberating, sustaining, and renewing purpose and activity. As her ways of being and living became increasingly consistent with a wisdom understanding of divine purpose and activity, I anticipated that her life would receive the gifts of further meaning, value, hope, and courage.

In summary, the overarching purpose of pastoral counseling was to help Annelies to know how to live a more hopeful, moral, and wholesome life. In order to realize its potential as a ministry of care, pastoral counseling would need to awaken, nurture, and empower her moral and spiritual intelligence, as characterized above. Understood as wisdom in the light of God, spiritual intelligence transforms emotional and other forms of intelligence, whenever the latter have merely promoted adaptive or conforming aims and means of conventional and pragmatic wisdom in any given social and cultural milieu.

Though in each pastoral counseling situation we need to select diverse, appropriate counseling strategies and methods, nevertheless, our collaborative work in all cases must always involve the fundamental approach and pivotal practice of discernment as an essential aspect of pastoral counseling. Viewed from my perspective as pastoral counselor and theologian, a multi-directional critical conversation must always take place. The conversation includes the counselee's personal stories and hopes, located in family and sociocultural contexts; human science viewpoints, insights, and tools (especially from personality theory, psychodynamic and cognitive therapy, narrative, and family systems theory and therapy); and theological, spiritual, and pastoral resources.[21] Stated in

---

21. To say that a critical conversation took place means that the resources of the human sciences and theology, together with my personal and professional experience and expertise, were also subject to evaluation, correction, and improvement, even as they illuminated the counselee's life challenges and struggles and suggested ways to resolve them satisfactorily and wisely. In other words, the uniquely hermeneutical work characterizing the process of pastoral counseling that occurred in the counseling situation must be viewed dialectically. The implication, in this light, is that pastoral counseling is a way of doing practical theology, and must always be practiced as a dialectical-hermeneutical process.

other terms, this hermeneutical activity of discernment leads us, first, to ascertain what a particular situation calls for; second, to search for alternatives and to develop a course of action; and third, to evaluate ongoing responses to the challenges and struggles the counselee is facing.

From a theological perspective, the setting and the process of pastoral counseling encompasses more than counselors and psychotherapists usually recognize (at least explicitly). The four-dimensional understanding of reality — and of knowing, in particular — determines the nature of the overall approach and the discerning activity we are discussing here. Counseling that is truly pastoral occurs not only in a safe therapeutic space but also in a sacred place where the presence and activity of the Spirit is acknowledged (at least by the pastoral counselor). Further, we seek to minister in partnership with the Spirit in the process of our endeavoring to know the real nature of the problems and the best ways creatively to confront and transform them.

Comprehensively viewed, therefore, the activity of discernment conditions the process (the *how* — approaches, methods, and techniques) as well as the content (the *what* — agenda, themes, and issues) of pastoral counseling in significant ways. Further, learning the very practice of discernment, especially as a collaborative, dialogical, and even prayerful endeavor, also becomes a distinct and overarching objective, a desired outcome for counselees in all cases. Indeed, an indicator of growth and progress for Annelies and countless other care-receivers is their willingness and ability to engage in discernment. In other words, growth in wisdom always entails discerning and choosing wisely, as well as learning to act and to relate to other people wisely in a consistent manner. *Wisdom in the light of God* thus supplies the guiding principle and the master metaphor, because the way of wisdom thus understood and appropriated is a process of knowing how to live a better life in the midst of our existential and social circumstances.

That is how the wisdom model of pastoral counseling seems to have affected Annelies. After we had completed the counseling process by mutual agreement, she wrote several e-mail messages telling me about helpful conversations with Matt and with key family members concerning her experiences of loss and grieving and her commitment to grow. She also reported that she felt she was making good decisions in different areas of her life, even as she continued to heal. Counseling had helped her to address key struggles and to set in motion a process of their resolution with a recovered sense of hope.

Knowing and Unknowing God:
A Psychoanalytic Meditation
on Spiritual Transformation

James W. Jones

Toward the end of high school, Samuel underwent a dramatic conversion at a concert of contemporary Christian music sponsored by a church in his town that he attended at the urging of friends. Samuel had spent most of high school feeling he could never live up to his parents' expectations nor match their successes. He dabbled at soccer, poetry writing, and the science club but he could never commit himself vigorously enough to anything to be able to succeed at it. Instead he floundered. That warm spring night under the stars, with country-rock songs of Jesus' love echoing in his ears and embraced by the current of fellowship that ran through the assembled, hand-holding group, Samuel felt an acceptance he never thought possible. He opened his heart to the experience and, without a second thought, gave his life over to following Jesus. What he called "the sense of a Presence" engulfed him there. When he began his studies at the State University, the Christian student fellowship was the center of his world. The support and direction he received there enabled him to complete his studies and become certified as a high school history teacher.

After ten years of teaching history, Samuel became increasingly dissatisfied. He wished for something more challenging intellectually. He enrolled in philosophy classes at the nearby state college. In one of them, the professor took obvious relish in pointing out the flaws he saw in the teachings of the various religions and what he took as the logical contradictions in religious doctrines. The professor never missed a chance to argue that religious beliefs lacked proof. These lectures unnerved Samuel because he did not know how to refute them. At the same time, the responsibilities of teaching and being a graduate student left less and less time in Samuel's life for church activities. Gradually the sense of presence and conviction that marked his conversion experience began to wane.

When confronted in class one night about whether or not he believed in God, Samuel was shocked to hear himself say that he didn't know. Previously he would have said, "yes," without a second thought. The convictions about which he had felt so certain were shaken by the professor's rhetorical pounding. It was simpler just to say, "I don't know," than to engage in an argument and be ridiculed in front of the class.

But it certainly didn't feel right to say that he was an atheist. Samuel still felt that "sense of presence" — sometimes in church or out in nature. But whenever he tried to put words to it, he realized immediately that the words would sound like nonsense to his professor and classmates; they even sounded that way to Samuel himself sometimes. Often he would wonder, "Am I a believer or a non-believer?" Neither term seemed to fit him.

In desperation he went to see his pastor.

If you were his pastor, what would you want to communicate to Samuel?

Encountering the Depths

Like all human relationships, pastoral encounters are always multi-dimensional. Obviously, the personal characters and styles of the pastor and his visitor shape the event. But this involves not only their overt and conscious behavior, affect, and cognitive statements; it also involves unconscious expectations, wishes, and emotions that each one carries with them into their meeting. For example, why does Samuel bring this problem to a pastor, rather than to a close friend, relative, or the family doctor? Samuel goes to see his pastor rather than his philosophy professor because consciously he thinks of this as a religious problem. Unconsciously, he may be looking for permission from a religious authority to question his beliefs. Or, unconsciously he may be looking for an authoritative hand to forbid and constrain him from starting down the road of doubt out of fear of losing the sense of meaning and direction his beliefs give him. The pastor, in turn, consciously recognizes Samuel's concerns as relevant to his profession. Unconsciously, he may be struggling with doubts himself and so may either feel threatened by Samuel's questioning and so distance himself from the young man or may subtly encourage Samuel in his doubting and so act out his religious struggles through his visitor.

Then there is the dimension of culture and difference. Does it matter to Samuel if his pastor is a man or a woman? If he had gone to a woman pastor, he might have done so feeling a woman would understand him better because "that's how women are." Or perhaps he went to the male pastor expecting that a man would understand him better because they are both male. How much difference can Samuel tolerate in this close encounter? Is he looking for a twin — someone of the same race, ethnicity, gender, and theological outlook? Is there some fantasy here that the hard work of making himself understood will be vitiated by someone who appears to share his background, experiences, and outlook? Or is he looking for an older person who carries the patina of wisdom and life experience? It matters whether Samuel wants advice from a wise elder, constraint from an authority figure, or understanding from a compassionate fellow-pilgrim. And how might the pastor regard these possible differences? Would an older male pastor see in this energetic young man a symbol of his own past youthfulness now long gone? Would a female pastor unconsciously regard this young man as the son she never had? Or as another chance to be a mother? Or are they close enough in age for her to regard him as the brother she always competed with or even as a male to seduce in fantasy if not in reality? Would a male pastor see Samuel as a younger brother in need of guidance and initiation into manhood? Or as the son *he* never had? Must the pastor and his visitor agree on matters of faith and doctrine? Again, is difference a problem and the appearance of twinship necessary for either Samuel or his pastor? Or are both open and skillful enough to forge a working alliance across a chasm of difference?

There is the additional element of theology here. "Bidden or unbidden, God is present" is the motto Carl Jung carved over his doorway.[1] Does Samuel seek out a pastor rather than a secular psychotherapist because he wants, consciously or unconsciously, for God or the gods to be bidden to enter? Will the experience of God be bracketed out in an intellectual debate between the pastor and the questioning young man? Or will the presence of the Spirit be recognized in the corners and interstices of their discourse?

---

1. *Vocatus atque non vocatus, Deus aderit* is a statement that Jung discovered among the Latin writings of Desiderius Erasmus, who declared the statement had been an ancient Spartan proverb. Jung inscribed this statement over the doorway of his house and upon his tomb.

James W. Jones

Out of the Depths

Every pastoral encounter is a relational moment. It involves not only the relationship of the pastor and her visitor but also their relationships with the concepts, ideas, and experiences under discussion. From a contemporary psychodynamic perspective, the ideas we find convincing, the experiences we undergo, as well as the behaviors we act out all express deeper, often unconscious, relational templates.[2]

Psychological theories about religion reveal the theorist's model of human nature. All psychoanalytic theories agree that our beliefs, feelings, and behaviors are expressions of deeper, more basic psychological forces. Freud, for example, envisioned human nature as a system of antisocial drives that must be channeled, sublimated, or defended against. Within this framework, religion was seen as a way of relating to these drives through repression, projection, and other defenses.[3] Jung thought of human nature as rooted in a transpersonal or collective psychological reality, and for him the function of religion was to give access to that deeper psychological stratum of the personality. Psychological theories of the origin and function of religion, then, carry within them distinctive models of human nature.

Contemporary relational theory represents a fundamental revision of earlier psychoanalytic views of human nature. Phenomena that Freud attributed to biological instincts is seen by the relational theorist as the consequence of interpersonal experience. Human relationships are not, as Freud thought, the product of anti-social impulses gradually modified into socially accepted forms out of a compromise between fear and desire. Rather, human experience is structured around the establishment and maintenance of connections with others. The nature of these connections

2. James W. Jones, *Contemporary Psychoanalysis and Religion* (New Haven: Yale University Press, 1991).

3. According to classical Freudian theory, individuals defend themselves against threatening, anxiety-provoking, or otherwise unwelcome thoughts and feelings through a series of unconscious psychological maneuvers that serve to keep these unwanted thoughts and feelings out of awareness. These "defense mechanisms" include "repression," which keeps the unwanted experiences hidden in the unconscious, and "projection," whereby they are projected onto some outside real or imaginary object. According to Freud, feelings such as guilt, fear of the father, or the need for protection were projected onto an imaginary figure called "god."

— pleasurable, frustrating, or distant — and not their instinctual motivation is what influences the quality of our interpersonal experiences. The self develops from the *internalization* of infant-caregiver interactions. If these episodes carry sufficient parental attunement, they contribute to positive self formation. Their psychological import comes from the meaning they acquire in the context of early interpersonal encounters. Such a view theorizes the unconscious as neither the container of biological drives and defenses against them, nor as the carrier of universal archetypal forms, but as the internalization of relational episodes laid down in the course of our development. These relational themes echo and reecho through our devotional practices, spiritual disciplines, and cherished philosophical and theological convictions.[4]

An important implication of all psychoanalytic psychologies is that theological beliefs and claims are never purely cognitive but rather express potent affects, strongly held sensibilities about self and world, deeply felt wishes and fears, all of which are often unconscious. Theological beliefs and convictions (like all beliefs and convictions) are carriers of profound, early experiences and developmental processes. To understand them fully involves comprehending more than their cognitive content. We need also to understand what inner relational patterns are expressed in our philosophical theologies, our devotional practices, our moral stances, our meditational disciplines, our social crusades.[5] What relational complexes resonate in the *koans* of Zen Buddhism, the syntheses of Aquinas and Barth, the speculations of the Upanishads, the ecclesiastical platforms for social transformation? And what in you attracts you to them or is repelled by them?

In addition, from this psychodynamic perspective, since our private images of God, moral outlooks, and basic convictions about self and world carry deep unconscious affects, wishes, and fears, they are not easily changed. Given their deep roots in the unconscious, attempting to transform a person's theological convictions by purely conscious means (preaching, theological lecturing, reading, or debating) might appear slightly naïve.

---

4. Jones, *Contemporary Psychoanalysis and Religion*.
5. Jones, *Contemporary Psychoanalysis and Religion*.

Into the Depths

Where would you start to help Samuel discover or rediscover an experience of God?

An English monastic and spiritual guide from the late fourteenth century recommends that we begin the search for God from what is nearest to us, the awareness of our own existence. "Come down into the deepest point of your mind . . . and consider in the simplest way not what your self is but that your self is," he recommends.[6] The writer suggests that the sense of our own existence is the doorway to the experience of God. The first step in experiencing or re-experiencing God is therefore to "keep focused on the central core of your spirit, which is your being" (138). Therefore, "the most important point of your spiritual awareness is the naked perception and blind consciousness of your own being" (141). Because we are self-reflexive creatures, we not only know that we exist but, by focusing our attention, we can plumb the depths of that experience of existence to its source. "There is no name, no feeling, and no contemplation that so corresponds to the everlastingness that is God than what can be possessed, seen, and felt in the blind loving awareness of this word IS" (143).

Implicit here is a specific understanding of God: "God is your being" (159). God's most basic nature is to bestow being, "for the first gift to each creature is only the being of that individual creature" (141). Thus "God is your being and in him you are that you are, not only because he is the cause and being of all that exists but because he is your cause and your being" (136). This is not to equate God with everything that exists, for God's mode of being transcends the created world; the world is dependent on God, God is not dependent on the world. "He is our being and source but we are not God's being and source." Still,

> All things exist in God as their cause and their being, and God is in all things as their cause and their being, but he alone is his own cause and source of his own being, for nothing can exist without God and he exists because he is the only source of existence. He is the source of existence both for himself and for everything else. (136)

6. Phyllis Hodgson, ed., *The Cloud of Unknowing* and *The Book of Privy Counselling* (London: Oxford University Press, 1944), 138. The Hodgson text is a critical edition of the text in medieval English, which I have rendered into contemporary English. Hereafter, page references will be given parenthetically in the text.

So for this late medieval spiritual guide, the first step in experiencing or re-experiencing God is this simple reflexive awareness of our own existence. That reflexive consciousness is both a solution and a problem in our knowledge of God. It is both the door to such knowledge and the final hindrance to it. The awareness of our own being can come between us and the simple, direct, "blind" awareness of God as the ground and source of our existence. So the final step is to let go even of that awareness of self, to "remove, spoil, and utterly unclothe your self of all awareness of your self so that you might be able to be clothed with the gracious awareness of God's self" (156). The goal of this spiritual practice is finally to let go of the awareness of self and be aware only of God.

When all discursive thought has been left behind and only a direct, "blind" awareness of God remains, the result is what our ancestral spiritual guide calls, in the title of his most famous work, *The Cloud of Unknowing*.

> It is usual to find nothing but a darkness around your mind, or, as it were, a cloud of unknowing. You will know nothing and feel nothing except a naked intention toward God in the depths of your being. No matter what you do, this darkness and this cloud will remain between you and your God. You will feel frustrated, you will not be able to see God clearly by the light of rational understanding, nor feel God with the sweetness of deep affection. Make yourself remain in this darkness as long as you can. . . . If in this life you feel and see God at all, it must be within this darkness and this cloud. (17)

As the source of everything that exists, God is not another physical object among all the other physical objects. So, God cannot be discussed in the categories used to describe physical objects, that is, the categories of our everyday speech. Discursive thinking leads us nowhere. But as the ultimate subject of our longing and desiring, God can be loved.

> How shall I think about God in himself, and what is he? And to this I can only answer thus, I do not know. For with your question you have brought me into the same darkness and into that same cloud of unknowing that I wish you were in yourself. . . . Of God himself no one can think. Therefore I will leave behind everything that I can think and choose for my love that which I cannot think. For why: God may well be loved but not thought. He can be taken and held by love but not by thought. (26)

Longing and love reach where reasoning, analyzing, and moralizing cannot go. Thinking can only take us so far. Then desire and love must take over. "Reject every brilliant, subtle thought and cover it with a thick cloud of forgetting, no matter how intense or holy it is, it will be no help to you. In this life love may reach to God but not knowledge" (33). God attracts, God does not coerce. Our natural longing for a loving union with our Source lures us forward. The spiritual life comes to us not primarily as duty or argument but as desire and love. Human desire is not the enemy of the spiritual life but just the reverse. Desire is the wellspring and motivation for taking up a spiritual practice. Through the disciplines of the spiritual journey, our deepest desires are not repressed or denied but are rather facilitated and allowed to expand infinitely.

This is a practice: to immerse yourself in that darkness and renounce all discursive activities of the mind, to "keep on working in this nothingness which is nowhere" (124). This is a hard task, to persevere in this darkness, this emptiness, in which the mind has nothing to hold onto. This is a kind of purification: not a moral purification but intellectual purification, purifying the mind of all thoughts and feelings and memories, and, eventually even of the awareness of one's own existence. For the author, this is the most advanced state of the spiritual life, in which "everything depends on this darkness and on this cloud of unknowing which one enters with a loving stirring and a blind beholding of the naked being of God himself alone" (50). Arising out of the disciplines of the Christian life, the cloud of unknowing itself constitutes a further discipline. "Make yourself remain in this darkness as long as you can" — this speaks of a practice, not an episodic event.

Earlier in our spiritual journey we may have felt that we understood about God. Now we realize we did not and cannot. "You will feel frustrated," the author of *The Cloud of Unknowing* assures us, because our minds are unable to grasp the divine reality. This deeper spiritual journey begins with traditional creeds, texts, rituals, and symbols. Gradually, after a time of living and working with them, these forms may begin to lose their former profundity. Part of the power of a spiritual practice is that when done consistently, it pushes us to the limits of that very practice itself. Liturgical worship may become too familiar and grow stale. Sitting and meditating may eventually become dull. Intellectual activity may lose its attraction after many years in the library. Rather than signaling a loss of faith, such dark moments may indicate that the Christian seeker is coming to the limits of any finite formula in the face of the ultimate. Every liturgy, every word, every symbol, every practice is finite and limited and eventually loses its meaning in the face of the infinity of God.

The Cloud of Unknowing arises out of traditional religious practices taken to their limit. Entering the cloud of unknowing means that all other ideas and practices, no matter how devout, are put aside (24). No matter how truthful or pious a thought or image or object is, it is to be lovingly but firmly put under foot as a distraction from the experience of that divine reality that is beyond all words and images and forms. In order "to feel and see God as he is in himself" it is necessary to enter "this darkness and this cloud" in which everything else fades into the background and God is known as God by not being known (in a conventional sense) at all.

Entering the cloud of unknowing, the Christian seeker goes beyond all religious forms, "casting them down and covering them over with a cloud of forgetting, stepping above them stalwartly but lovingly" (26). While no longer identified with the divine reality, which is beyond all possible identifications, prayers and texts and symbols are still valued as part of the larger context of practice in which the spiritual seeker lives. In classical texts like *The Cloud,* the traditional objects of belief are not lost, rejected, or given up, but rather given a new context.

No doubt this is a very difficult stance to maintain: to value the forms of religion without making them into absolutes. Those who confuse fanaticism with devotion refuse to do this, preferring instead to demand submission to what they see as absolute. Likewise, those who reject all religious beliefs and practices refuse to look beyond them to their more encompassing Source. But among those who can maintain this difficult stance, religious texts and teachings are no longer seen as divine themselves; but they are still cherished as parts of the life of Christian practice.

Depths Speak to Depths

What kind of discourse is this? Is it simply abstract, philosophical discourse? No! Rather, such discourse is a spiritual practice, a spiritual discipline. The purpose of this discourse is not to prove a point, to win an argument. Rather, as our fourteenth-century author makes clear in his book of spiritual counsel, it is to evoke a vision, an experience, a realization. It is to facilitate our being awestruck at the miracle of existence, shocked that anything is here at all. Nothing had to be here; everything is contingent, not necessary. There was time when it wasn't here and there will come a time when it won't be. "Awesome," as my students say.

Being awestruck is a close cousin to the experience of wonder. Wonder at the reality of existence brings us to a fundamental question: "Why existence, why anything, why not sheer, terrifying emptiness and non-existing?" For our fourteenth-century guide and for some contemporary theologians, "being" is the answer: that most basic, most fundamental, most ultimate reality, the one thing everything cannot do without. For example, Paul Tillich expands the category of "being" into "God as the ground of being."[7] John Macquarrie expands it even further into "God as Holy Being — an object of worship and devotion."[8] Like Tillich and Macquarrie, the medieval writer equates "being" or the "source of being" with "God."

Using an abstract philosophical term, "being," to denote what in scripture is a personal being, "father," "creator," etc., does not seem to bother this medieval spiritual guide. But the medieval author must confront the same problem as the more contemporary theologians: how to reframe religious language? If God's true nature is to be the "being of everything," then the personalistic language of scripture and devotion must be understood as (in some sense) symbolic, not literal or even descriptive. The author of *The Cloud* has prepared the way for this move by his insistence that finite language cannot literally, directly apply to the transcendental source of the finite world. Human language is limited, finite; the transcendental source of everything is not. In *The Cloud* we have God as "being" — the transcendental source beyond space, time, and language, that cannot be described, that is essentially unknowable, that can only be experienced as an abyss, an emptiness, in other words, a Cloud of Unknowing.[9]

7. Paul Tillich, *Systematic Theology,* vol. 1, part 2 (Chicago: University of Chicago Press, 1951).

8. John Macquarrie, *Principles of Christian Theology* (New York: Charles Scribner's Sons, 1966); see chap. 5.

9. A brief historical footnote: this understanding of God as the transcendental source from beyond all speech and the correlated understanding of authentic religious language as symbolic rather than literal or descriptive is the traditional view. This view of God and of religious language, indebted to Neo-Platonism, is central to all the first Christian theologians: Justin, Irenaeus, Clement, Origen, Augustine (at least his early writings), and the Cappadocian Fathers, who gave us the Doctrine of the Trinity. The idea that religious lan-

However, this is not religiously sufficient, this unknowable God. For God also manifests God's reality. In the period directly before the beginnings of Christianity, when answering the question of how the transcendental, un-namable source described in Exodus 3 could be known, intertestamental Hebraic thinkers claimed that in the beginning was God's *logos* (a Greek, Stoic term meaning "reason" or "fundamental pattern/ structure") and God's *Sophia* (the Greek term for "wisdom"). The transcendental God created the world, revealed God's self, interacted with humankind, presided over the redemptive history by means of the Divine Logos and/or the Divine Wisdom (see, for example, the Book of Wisdom). In the second and third centuries, when the early Christian theologians wrestled with the same problem, they had recourse to the same categories: the Christ was easily identified with the Logos (e.g., John 1) and the Holy Spirit with Sophia.[10] Thus was born the doctrine of the Trinity.

The point is practice, not speculation. Like the language of "being" in *The Cloud,* the doctrine of the Trinity is not a philosophical abstraction but what I have called elsewhere a "contemplative strategy."

> The doctrine of the Trinity is not about intellectual debate. The doctrine of the Trinity is a contemplative strategy, the contemplation of which can take us deep into the heart of the divine mystery. The contemplation of this mystery strikes us dumb with amazement before the reality that from an unnamable Source comes forth compassion and wisdom — the Son and the Holy Spirit — and everything we see around us. To *speak* of such a mystery creates only words and concepts — reifications that easily become idols that separate us from each other and from our Source. The God beyond affirmation and negation is a mystery that cannot be comprehended. The amazement at an Abyss from which comes forth the cosmos we see and the compassion and wisdom that can redeem it,

---

guage should be concrete and literal is a purely modern, post-Enlightenment claim. It would have appalled the orthodox Christian theologians of the first several centuries. Also, it is post-Reformation individualism and the modern philosophy of personalism that gave us the idea of God as a person. That was not the vision of the Church Fathers. See James W. Jones, *The Mirror of God: Christian Faith as Spiritual Practice — Lessons from Buddhism and Psychotherapy* (New York: Palgrave, 2003).

10. In Greek, *Sophia* or wisdom is feminine. The Book of Wisdom often speaks of her in ways reminiscent of the divine feminine and some early Middle Eastern liturgies recite the section of the Christian creed dealing with the Holy Spirit as "she spoke through the prophets." This, too, is part of the greater Christian tradition.

such amazement connects us to the mystery at the heart of reality. Such amazement strikes us dumb and renders us silent with contemplation.[11]

What our fourteenth-century predecessor calls "being" is not an object, is not a thing, does not exist within world of space and time. So why then speak at all? Not for the purpose of speculative intellectualization. The author continually ridicules philosophical and theological intellectualization done for its own sake. This author, whose writings are devoted to the care of souls, speaks the language of "being" in order to evoke an experience, not to describe an object called "being." The purpose is not speculation, but practice. Not intellectualizing, but bringing to mind a vision, an experience: that our individual life is grounded in, sourced by, an eternal reality continually overcoming the threat of nothingness, continually bringing being out of nothingness, life out of death.

Conclusion

To return to Samuel and the question we began with, what might a pastor or spiritual director wish to communicate to Samuel? That God is the source of our existence. We live and move and have our being in God. As the *source* of the finite world, God is transcendent, beyond the finite world. So it is not surprising that a life of faithful devotion has led Samuel to a place where ordinary theological categories are losing their meaning, for none of the finite, contingent categories of human language can apply directly to God. This is not an abstract claim to be believed or not believed, it is rather a profound and transforming experience. It is the Cloud of Unknowing. Religious language, even the category of "being," points beyond descriptive speech; it is language that cannot be objectified or reified. Many discourses about God, about "being," can be understood as spiritual practices, contemplative strategies, not speculations. Their purpose is to induce an experience, a state of awareness, as we find described in *The Cloud*. This is a transforming experience of God, an experience of origination, of new birth, of a new beginning,

Here psychoanalytic understanding, theological reflection, and spiritual practice work together. Psychoanalytic understanding serves self-

---

11. Jones, *The Mirror of God*, 56.

knowledge: helping us understand what within us is attracted to or re-pelled by these practices and experiences. Theological reflection serves their integration into our meaning system. Practice without reflection leads to experiences that cannot be integrated into the individual's life (at worst it leads to rote and meaningless activity). Reflection without grounding in practice leads to abstractions and reifications that produce no transformation. *The Book of Privy Counselling* and *The Cloud of Unknowing* contain a practical theology of spiritual transformation (that is, a set of practices and an experience-near description of the process and its goals) as well as a theology of God as "being." The medieval text of practice provides a pastoral account of a disciplined way of experiencing God as the source of our existence.[12] Such a theological articulation (perhaps augmented by a more contemporary expression in the theology of being in writers such as Paul Tillich or John Macquarrie can undergird the practice of spiritual direction and the deployment of disciplined spiritual practices in the lives of congregations and parishioners. Such concerns on the boundary of psychology, practical theology, and spiritual transformation are, clearly, at the heart of Professor Ulanov's life work.

12. A contemporary exposition of this practice can be found in Martin Laird, *Into the Silent Land: A Guide to the Practice of Christian Contemplation* (New York: Oxford University Press, 2006). See also Jones, *The Mirror of God.*

Healing Wisdom for Suffering and Evil

The Question of Evil:
An Answer *from*, Not *to*, Job

David W. Augsburger

> Is God willing to prevent evil, but not able? Then he is impotent. Is he able, but not willing? Then is he malevolent. Is he both able and willing? Whence then is evil?
>
> David Hume, *Dialogues concerning Natural Religion*, 1779

"Who hears the cries of the innocent?" "Why does evil happen to the good?" "Why do the evil prosper and the righteous suffer?" These are the questions of heartbreak. These questions are haunting social injustices and abuses, dismaying global dilemmas. As personal, social, communal, and global issues, they form the most troubling theological, philosophical, and, above all, pastoral problems. Answers range from the random nature of evil to the retributive punishment of an angry God.[1]

What "answer" does one offer the sufferers? — presence, silence, shared lament, and, in time, serious consideration of the questions of theodicy?[2] Theodicy, the branch of theology that seeks to reconcile the ex-

---

1. "As you sow, so shall you reap," was Saddam Hussein's comment on the September 11, 2001, attack on New York and Washington, DC. It was similar to the interpretation given by fundamentalist Jerry Falwell, who blamed the tragedy on pagans, abortionists, feminists, homosexuals, the ACLU, and People for the American Way. God allowed these attacks, Falwell claimed, because these groups were secularizing America. Loren Fisher, *Who Hears the Cry of the Innocent?* (Willets, CA: Fisher Publishing, 2002), 108.

2. The problems of good and evil are ancient, but "theodicy" is an early Enlightenment term from Gottfried Wilhelm Leibniz (1646-1716) and Christian Wolff (1679-1750). In *The*

istence of a benevolent God with the visible reality of evil, offers philosophical, biblical, and rational ways of thinking about suffering that are tormented by the inexplicable, tortured by their own agonized attempt to give answers. These are among the oldest of theological enigmas. They are the questions set to us by the biblical story of Job.

The subtitle of this chapter indicates that it draws from the writings of Carl Jung in his *Answer to Job*.[3] Jung concludes that it is necessary to offer his own answer to Job. But has he — or, we might well ask ourselves, have *we* — listened to the answer *from* Job? Unsatisfied with the answer that is finally given to Job, the sufferer who sat bereaved on an ash heap, rubbing his skin eruptions and confronting God, Jung offers his alternative response to Yahweh's reply. While we can learn from his answer, we may gain more by returning to the biblical text and reconsidering the answers from Job. Jung's purpose, much broader than individual suffering, was ultimately to address human responsibility for the nuclear threat. In the course of his long and multifaceted argument, there is a constant thread of human outcry against the perceived injustices of the Sovereign God. That protest offers an empathic voice to any counselor who sits with the bereaved, the abused, the sinned-against, the innocent victim in any pastoral situation.[4]

The story of Job, arguably the greatest epic drama of the Hebrew Bible, is a poetic debate, first between Job and his "comforting" friends, and second, between Job and God. The prose prologue and epilogue comprise what most scholars take to be an earlier narrative, indebted to Babylonian religious thought that pairs a good God and an evil God. Here the two are both part of Yahweh, and his "eyes" serve as the adversary who scans, sees, and reports on

---

Theodicy, Leibniz took the threefold task of demonstrating the goodness of God, the freedom of human will, and the origin of evil to define "the best of all possible worlds." Gottfried Wilhelm Leibniz, *Theodicy: Essays on the Goodness of God the Freedom of Man* (Charleston, SC: BiblioBazaar, 2007).

3. *Answer to Job* is a most difficult book. In one of his letters, Jung referred to it as philosophical idiocy, theological blasphemy, rational illogic, but psychological truth. Paul Bishop, *Jung's Answer to Job: A Commentary* (New York: Routledge and Kegan Paul, 2002), 70. Bishop's book sums up well the complementary, compensatory tenets of Jung's psychology and carries forward his psychology of religion.

4. Excellent critiques of Jung's commentary on Job exist in abundance. In this paper we will explore only one of several themes that have continuing pastoral significance, the view of the problem of good and evil and the direction he gives toward the psychological meaning of our human struggle to understand the justice of God.

the state of things on earth. We have turned the word "adversary" into a proper noun, "Satan." In this story, Job, a righteous Gentile, refuses to curse God and is ultimately rewarded for his unswerving fidelity. The poet splits this folktale in half, creating a prose envelope, and writes a radical reversal in the long debate that sets forth a God whose justice is not retributive. The elusive mystery of evil is not resolved, but as the drama unfolds, it is nuanced with profound theological reflection on the nature of divine justice.[5]

God-images and Facing the Mystery

In *The Wizard's Gate,* the wonderful narrative of an analyst and a dying analysand walking together along the escarpment of finitude, Ann Belford Ulanov offers an introductory word that sets the stage for this essay. Summarizing Jung's passionate investigation of our religious images, she writes:

> Among our instinctive faculties, he said, is a religious instinct, a consciousness of our relation to deity. This sense of relation expresses itself in God-images that we might understand as the religious instinct's perception of itself, or the self-portrait of the religious instinct. Here we find and create what acts as God within us, within our group, within our religious traditions. By entering these images of the center we climb our own Jacob's ladder toward the transcendent, only to discover that the ladder stops and breaks, and that we cannot reach to God on it. God reaches to us, crossing the gap between us and the Holy from the divine side. That is the never-ending miracle.[6]

The God-images we project and the self-images we create have a remarkable coincidence, unfolding and elaborating in parallel forms

---

5. Jung prefers the frame to the picture, the prose tale of God paired with Satan over the poetic drama of breakthrough to an actual God-encounter that silences and transforms Job's protest.

6. Ann Belford Ulanov, *The Wizard's Gate* (Einsiedeln: Daimon, 1994), 10. Ann Belford Ulanov has led the way in doing pastoral theology that draws creatively on depth psychology. She has extended our understanding of Jung's thought while not being contained or limited by his philosophical and theological assumptions, and in her constructive work has offered all of us who are indebted to her a model of dialogical conversation with a recognized master of psychology from a wider theological perspective.

through the first half of life, then undergoing transformation as we enter the second half. In "A Psychological Approach to the Dogma of the Trinity," Jung observes that there is an intriguing correspondence between the three stages of maturation of the self and the three persons of the Trinity.[7] Visualizing the Trinity as the ultimate archetype of the universal disposition toward wholeness, Jung postulates that there is a corresponding series of God-images — a Father-stage, a Son-stage, a Spirit-stage — that are types of human religious formation. In each of these, we will argue, answers that seem to satisfy the question of evil will be shaped by the dominant image and the perspective it offers.[8]

It is helpful to remind ourselves when reading Jung that as he speaks of God, he speaks as a psychologist. Rarely does he speak of God as God-self, but rather of God as the God-image, the God-representation in the soul, the God-concept that centers the self and has an empirical, clinical, observable referent. Even when he uses the word "God," he is referring to the God archetype within, to the image, the concept, the model arranged within the individual. In referring to the Trinity as an archetype, Jung is not debating whether God exists, or whether God exists as a Trinity; these are questions for theologians. Whether there is a threefold development of God-image in the psychological unfolding of the human religious experience, he argues, is a question for psychologists.[9] On this psychological question, he applies the trajectory familiar in Immanuel Kant, proceeding from the individual to the universal, but Jung alters it in his characteristic way by projecting an archetypical, Trinitarian-styled, three-stage model of self-development.

7. C. G. Jung, "A Psychological Approach to the Dogma of the Trinity," in *The Collected Works of C. G. Jung* (Princeton: Princeton University Press, 1942, 1954-71).

8. Michael Palmer, *Freud and Jung on Religion* (London: Routledge, 1997), 154-60. Jung views the archetypes of the Self and of God as virtually equivalent. Individual development will then follow the same course as the God-image development. What is true for ontogeny is true in phylogeny, and he suspects in theogeny. God is in movement from Yahweh to the God-man to the Holy Spirit as the dominant image expression. Is the Trinity, according to him, also maturing in this same sequence?

9. But can one really sidestep the problem that easily? What are the consequences for Jung's theodicy if the resolution of suffering, loss, pain, and the problem of evil is the assimilation of human anguish into a more mature God-image, but not a reconciliation with the transcendent? If there is a God, if that God does not support his own in their hour of need, what then? See Ann Belford Ulanov and Alvin Dueck, *The Living God and Our Living Psyche: What Christians Can Learn from Carl Jung* (Grand Rapids: Eerdmans, 2008).

On the theological question, Jung affirmed his knowledge of God without declaring that he was a theist. As he said in an interview near the end of his life, "All that I have learned has led me step by step to an unshakeable conviction of the existence of God. I only believe what I know. And that eliminates believing. Therefore I do not take his existence on belief — I *know* He exists."[10] He *knows* from empirical observation that the God-images within the psyche are undeniable, ineradicable, innate to human experience. As archetype, God is a psychic reality for Jung, an immediate, direct, uncontestable fact of psychic experience. The innumerable God-images in the individual psyche offer an imprint from which one may postulate an imprinter. Yet Jung's ambivalence in going beyond God as archetype to God as "actual Other" suggests that he is at least a Kantian agnostic. God's existence is postulated because it is necessary to our experience of moral obligation.[11]

Therefore, God exists, as a psychic reality. God-images exist as psychic knowledge of God, and various God-images form and unfold as the person matures from early life through midlife to mature human stature. The stages that tend to emerge in human maturation correspond, he argues, to those of the human developmental journey, and leave their imprint in relation to the Divine, no matter what religious tradition. (We shall bracket, for this discussion, the larger questions of universalizing a Western Christian worldview, assuming a common pattern for all cultures, and a critique of the limitations of all "thin description" rather than "thick description" that goes deeply into a particular case and social location.)

Three Stages, Three Theodicies

Jung argues that we humans conceive of God as parent — for him, as father — because it is an innate disposition to express the archetype of God as parent. The Father-stage correlates to the first stage of the process of individuation stretching from infancy through the first half of life. The Father-form of religious experience welcomes our dependency, offers the security of clearly defined law, inhibits question and reflection while rewarding

10. William McGuire and R. F. C. Hull, *Jung Speaking* (Princeton: Princeton University Press, 1977), 251.

11. John Macquarrie, *Twentieth Century Religious Thought* (London: SCM, 1971), 109.

obedience, and rewards our reverence with safety and success in life. This religious consciousness is that of a child who trusts the Father implicitly, honors his authority automatically, and identifies with the parental image. God, the world, and humanity form a unity that is accepted without criticism. The problem of evil is in our rebellious nature, not in the Father. The Oneness, the Omnipotence, the Omniscience, the Omnipresence of God are unquestioned, as are the goodness, benevolence, and freedom from any causation, authorization, or intention of evil. "Generally speaking, the Father denotes the earlier state of consciousness when one was still a child, still dependent on a definite, ready-made pattern of existence which is habitual and has the character of law."[12] This insight opens our understanding of immature religious experience, but Jung's perspective, made overly cautious by the language he uses to describe God, limited to the Enlightenment stereotype of a Deity who is a heteronomous being, does not allow for an active relationship between the subject and God.

The Son-stage emerges as the person individuates to the point of reflective, critical consciousness (emerging from the unreflecting and uncritical semi-consciousness of the childhood stance toward authority, reality, and the transcendent). The maturing ego in search of the true self seeks the truth about self and other and inevitably asks about the relationship to the Divine Other. Now the ego finds itself in conflict. The old images of God — gender, power, agency, responsibility — are up for debate. The world of the Father has now become the world of God-incarnate in a God-man. The Son who can question "why" becomes the image for the emerging self that can demand a reply. "The stage of the 'Son' is therefore a conflict situation par excellence: the choice of possible ways is menaced by just as many possibilities of error. 'Resisting the law of the Father' brings a sharpening of opposites, in particular of the moral opposites."[13] Theologically, Jung moves from a Kantian, heteronomous God to a Hegelian dialectic of paired opposites in tension and apposition — Father delegates and sacrifices Son; Son questions Father.

The Spirit-stage, in Jung's thought, is the achievement of authentic adulthood. As the ego discovers solidarity with all humanity and connects to the collective and wider web of relationships that provide a supra-

---

12. C. G. Jung, "A Psychological Approach to the Dogma of the Trinity" (1942), in *The Collected Works* (Princeton: Princeton University Press, 1954-71), 11:181.

13. Jung, "A Psychological Approach to the Dogma of the Trinity," 182.

individual identity, it internalizes images of union and wholeness, solidarity and human community. "Just as the transition from the first stage to the second demands the sacrifice of childish dependence, so, at the transition to the third stage, an exclusive independence has to be relinquished. . . . The Holy Ghost, the breath that heals and makes whole."[14] This stage opens the mind to the possibilities of Jung's idealism extended into mysticism. His theory of human advancement moves from the human scene to be projected onto the Trinity. We all create God in our own image, some of us in paltry ways, others in grand design. Does Jung's synthesis bring God down to us, rather than nudging us toward God? Is the human spirit actualized in a universal human consciousness rather than becoming a Spirit-transformed-humanity?

In examining these patterns, we might return in reductive analysis to the origin of the symbols in infancy and childhood, or we may turn to prospective analysis of the images and figures that anticipate the spiritual adventure. In Paul Ricoeur's language, this is a hermeneutic of original symbols and their causal effects, or a hermeneutic of symbols and images of future envisioning. In reductive analysis we focus particularly on the Father-stage images of God as parent, judge, benevolent Father Christmas, etc. In prospective analysis we move toward the vision of God as Spirit, the universal Presence, the call of the Divine to all humans in all relationships and cultures. In between lie the conflicts of the Son-stage, differentiating from the Father, protesting the justice and goodness issues of Divine inequity shown to us in the face of human suffering.

No series of stages is invariable, no chronological plotting of what is expected is without exception. They may overlap, occur out of order, appear simultaneously in response to differing tragedies, or one may remain in a single stage and venture no further.

However, these stages of progression in God-images are a true assessment of the human end of the bridge, the human abutment, as it were, of the suspension span reaching toward contact with God. They are worthy of thoughtful application to our problems of theodicy. What do they say to the confessional community and its struggles to make sense of natural and human evil and its horrific consequences?

14. Jung, "A Psychological Approach to the Dogma of the Trinity," 183, 185.

David W. Augsburger

The Parent-stage: Surrender in Theodicy

In the morning of life, the answers seem self-evident, the visible correspondence to our parental situation unmistakable. In a time of loss, the person whose inner religious experience is child-to-parent, what Jung calls the Father-stage, struggles under the weight of grief, cries out in anguish, but regresses to or remains in the subordinate position of childhood obedience. The questions are asked, but the "why" swings from the whining complaint of the victim to the querulous rage of an angry child; both pour out disillusionment that springs from abandonment. Either way, the sufferers show the sense of powerlessness that leaves them hesitant to wage a full-scale protest as a mature son or daughter. "There must be some reason, some plan, some purpose, some ultimate good hidden in this tragedy." Or, at the other pole, "No possible reason, no meaningful plan or purpose, nothing of lasting good can be worth this pain."

In stress, we all regress. It is most common in pastoral care of persons in shock to hear their unconscious return to the language of the Parent-stage. The God-talk will express fatalism — "It was his time." "God knows what he is doing." "God is in control, so what can we say?" "God took him quickly." "God answered our prayers and protected us when everyone around us suffered." "God needed our little flower to beautify his garden." "God takes care of his own." "I just think they had it coming." "I see God in the school shooting." "I just place it all in God's hands since he knows best." "If it is my time to go, what can I say? I've lived a good life." "The Lord will not put on you more than you can bear." "We will understand it better by and by." "God will get that drunk driver that killed my daughter." "You'll get *yours,* buddy." "God will get you for this."[15]

The fatalism easily shifts to a sense of entitlement that claims a special child relationship with "the Father in Heaven," or asserts the certainty of Divine sovereignty ordering life. This child-like trust relieves one of responsibility, reassures one in times of threat, protects one from the rage of abandonment and betrayal. In pastoral care of persons utilizing the language of the Parent-stage, listening and affirming the elements of healthy trust, supporting the gradual expression of questions and struggles with the absolutism of fate, assuring presence when the going gets hard in the

---

15. J. Timothy Allen, *A Theology of God Talk: The Language of the Heart* (New York: Haworth Press, 2002), 15.

future, offering a safe place to explore thoughts and feelings when they become admissible may open the future to a return to a more adult faith formation, or invite growth as the person gains a new perspective on personal and spiritual reality from the impact of the loss.

The Daughter/Son-stage: Protest and Theodicy

At the mid-day of life, the questions arise with new vigor. The security of sonship and the confidence of daughterhood emerge from the more individuated self that at midlife internalizes responsibility and authority for one's own destiny. Having assimilated this agency, this self can stand over against the God-image in courageous debate that calls Divine sovereignty and, indeed the Sovereign itself, into question. A striking correspondence appears between a clarified self-image as a person of depth and integrity and an emerging image of God as one whose justice can be weighed and challenged to be visible and demonstrable. Not only must justice be done, it must be *seen* to be done. Abraham is an archetypical symbol, in his debate with God over the potential justice of destroying two cities *in toto*. "Will not the judge of all the earth do what is just?" he argues (Gen. 18:25). And he prevails in the argument.

The anger of the Son toward the failure of the Father is an archetypical pattern of both human familial and human religious experience. In *Answer to Job*, when Jung "plays the roles at once of the emotionally involved psychotherapist and of the angry son who brutally confronts the Father with His shortcomings, these are precisely roles he played earlier . . . with his own father and with Sigmund Freud and psychoanalysis."[16] The God-talk of the daughter/son-stage is characterized by searching and questioning. "How could God have done this?" "Where is God in the midst of this pain?" "God does not do such cruel things to us, but does he allow it?" "Oh God, where are you in all this pain, where were you when it happened?" The language of anger, blaming, rage, and outrage may empower a passionate encounter with God, and with anyone seen as representing God. At the outset, pastoral caregivers need to listen, validating the right of the person to express the feelings of abandonment.

Most of the questions in this stage begin with "why?" In our psycho-

16. Murray Stein, *Jung's Treatment of Christianity* (Wilmette, IL: Chiron, 1985), 163.

logical age, caregivers are often trained to offer no answer at all, simply to be present with those who suffer, to "truly hear" the cry of pain and witness the authenticity of people crying out in fear, anger, loneliness, and confusion. But as weeks go by, they deserve support in seeking answers. They need a friend who thinks as well as a friend who feels, as they sort through the answers — fate, punishment, karma, needed growth, the journey of soul-making, the confidence that it is meaningful to God in some mysterious way, or the inexplicable mystery of suffering that will need the long perspective of eternity before it makes sense.

In the daughter/son-stage, the basic propositions of faith that have seemed consistent with logic in normal times now hit the wall. The encounter with evil, either human evil (war, abuse, torture, genocide) or natural evil (earthquake, tornado, tidal wave, untreatable illness), awakens profound contradictions, indeed deep inner conflicts in the primary symbols and central convictions of faith. These propositions are: (1) There is a God, one God; (2) who created the world, on whom we are dependent; (3) who is omnipotent, bringing about the state of affairs in which we live; (4) who is personal, relational, deeply concerned with and interested in all creatures; (5) who is perfectly good with intentions that are morally just and right; (6) *yet evil exists.* Suffering happens.

How can one combine propositions (3) Divine power, (5) Divine goodness, and (6) raw evil? What sort of logic could unite them? What sort of God could contain all three? Evil exists, of that we have no doubt. Does God? If God exists, then God is not good in our traditional human sense of the term. God's goodness and power must be different than ours. In this stage, the debate cannot be avoided; it is essential to spiritual integrity and corresponds to the internalizing of authority in the process of individuation of the self as it struggles with ego dominance in the search for depth. The daughter or son must stand over against the Father/Parent and demand some sort of an account of the dilemma of evil in every good. Out of the fire of thesis versus antithesis comes the synthesis of Spirit.

The Spirit-stage: Solidarity in Suffering and Theodicy

In the afternoon of life, the protest wanes and one accepts the common lot with all humanity. The Spirit-stage connects one to a wide world of suffering in the solidarity that marks authentic individuation. As the self matures, the public persona of face and the ego of self-will both soften and bend to own their darker sides. The maturing self assimilates the split-off and denied polarities of the shadow. Humility becomes possible, solidarity with fellow sufferers more evident in response to pain. Jung warns against the danger of this stage — the indwelling Spirit can be mistaken for the self, leading to self-inflation and even self-deification. The superman of Nietzsche, the narcissistic religious experience of self-above-all-else, endangers all true spirituality. The Spirit leads us to oneness with others, not superiority over all others.

The solidarity is experienced as inclusion in a wider humanity. "I do not want to be myself only; I want the other to be part of who I am and I want to be part of the other."[17] The Spirit-stage is the stage of solidarity with the suffering, joining with them in lament, struggling alongside them in working for change, recognizing that our hands are within God's hands as we work to alleviate pain, abuse, and injustice.

From the speechless moaning isolation of pain where suffering is turned in upon the self, we follow the Holy Spirit into a community of lament where we become fully aware of a greater justice that is needed in all existing structures. Finding our voice, we call for utopian aims through prayer, song, lament, and psalm to strive for transformative justice and structural change.[18]

So the problem of theodicy in the Spirit-stage is not pain on an isolated ash heap where one rubs the boils of suffering in solitude, rather it is shared with a community of fellow sufferers. There in community the problem of theodicy is likely to be stated with more certainty as well as with more ambiguity, since it must embrace a wider group of perspectives. In the Spirit-stage, one may affirm that God is, and God is known in the midst of God's gathered people. God is all-powerful, but with a different kind of power than that which we idolize. God is good, but with a different kind of goodness than we know. God creates a world that contains evil, but in a different dimension that does not contradict the existence and nature of God. Is this a word-game that empties the concepts of "good," "power," and "love" of linguistic meaning? Or can we recognize that it is essential to the mystery of the transcendent? We can still affirm that God loves creation and all creatures but in a way beyond our understanding (Job 38; Isa.

---

17. Miroslav Volf, *Exclusion and Embrace* (Nashville: Abingdon, 1996), 141.
18. Dorothée Sölle, *Suffering* (Minneapolis: Fortress, 1975), 73.

55). Is this the perspective of the final answer from Job? Does it not lead us beyond the arrogance of measuring God, goodness, and justice with the use of our personal criteria, or projecting our particular slant on the archetypes of ultimate values on the divine?

One might ask whether in the Spirit-stage the problems of theodicy are laid aside in the humility that comes from sharing the common lot of fellow sufferers — in the tracks of fellow strugglers and stragglers, the questions move from rebellion to relinquishment, from the courtroom where God is placed on trial to Gethsemane. The communitarian Anabaptist theologian John Howard Yoder suggests that any attempt at constructing a theodicy may well be as arrogant as it is awkward. Yoder offers three questions in critique of such formulations: (1) "Where do you get the criteria by which you evaluate God? Why are the criteria you use the right ones? (2) Why [do] you think you are qualified for the business of accrediting Gods? (3) If you think you are qualified for that business, how does the adjudication proceed? What are the lexical rules?"[19]

Ours is a world of massive suffering that no spiritually sensitive person can ignore. The outcry of astounded rage now becomes more muted by the conversation about human responsibility and the search for options to intervene or alleviate the pain of others. So, let us arrogantly suppose, you and I have arrived at the higher stage where the opposites within us, a God-the-Father in domination and a Son in dissidence, have come together in Spirit-formed-community of trust. What then? Have the problems of the horrifying dissonance between good and evil resolved themselves? Are there further answers we should wish to demand from Jung, or from Job, or from our community of suffering servants in inexplicable tragedy?

The Problem of Good and Evil

The problem of good and evil does not go away, no matter our form of protest. For Jung, the tension between God as "the greatest good" (the *summum bonum*) and the understanding of evil as the absence or "the priva-

---

19. John Howard Yoder, "Trinity Versus Theodicy: Hebraic Realism and the Temptation to Judge God," 1996. Available at: www.nd.edu/~theo/research/jhy_2?writings/home/ind-pstheo.htm.

tion of good" *(privatio boni)* could not be resolved in the classic division between the two as taught by Augustine (354-430) and Aquinas (1225-1274). According to them, God is the supreme good, who allows no evil to occur unless, in his power, he is able to draw good from every instance of evil. Thus evil is not evidence of God's ignorance or impotence, of his malevolence or unconcern, but must be seen as a part of his infinite wisdom and unfathomable goodness. Jung, in contrast, insisted on the necessity of what we perceive as good and as evil being present in "God" — the inner God-image and concept — and the possibility of a God beyond good and evil who in mystery includes both in God-self. The image of God he has created corresponds to the image of the self we are seeking to know and actualize in the process of individuation. The realization of this image is, for him, found in the Holy Spirit who is One, and who brings us into balanced unity in individuation, in relationships, in society. The trajectory of Jung's correspondence and complementarities of opposites moves toward the final integration of good and evil in the wholeness of the self, but it offers only the most general moral direction for one's witness to society. In *Answer to Job*, he focuses his final word toward confronting the nuclear threat posed by individuated man in possession of the bomb.

In the biblical text, Job protests the undeserved evil that has come upon him, and ultimately, God answers the suffering Job by bringing all assumptions of retributive justice to an end. In Jung's *Answer to Job*, speaking of and for God, Jung offers an alternate answer.[20] In search of a great synthesis, Jung places his final resolution of the opposites of human existence in an answer that unites conscious ego and the unconscious, and evil and good, by seeing the same contradictory divided and dissociated nature in the Divine as in the human. The internal conflicts evidenced in God are the same as those that are present in Jung, and perhaps, he reasons, in all humanity. In confronting the arbitrary, wanton, ruthless, autocratic and demonic side of God with which Job has collided, Jung reviews his own encounters with the Deity. In answering *for* God, he erases the distance between God and himself.[21] In answering *to* God, he is also answering to

20. Jung offers a threefold answer: (1) the incarnation of the Christ as the result of the encounter with Job; (2) the human experience of Jesus in his cry of abandonment on the cross; (3) and the Deity striving today to break out in the consciousness in every human soul.

21. Jung's argument in *Answer to Job* unites God and the Adversary into polarities of the One, and the struggle between the two sides of the Divine nature leads God to trifle with Job

Freud, and offering a counter view of the psychology of religious experience. Is he, may we also ask, revealing his greater consciousness of human depths, as compared to Freud? Is Freud bested by his one-time protégé as God is bested by his creature Job? And so our laments may be heard, heeded, and ultimately change the God-image within our souls. But do they change God?[22]

In Conclusion

In pastoral theology, caregivers tend toward the theodicies that arise from the cries of the soul rather than those devised by the brilliance of the mind. As Vento concludes: "Theodicy is the lived questions addressed to God about the suffering of the world, not a tidy answer to it."[23] One reads Job and listens to Jung differently, depending on one's social location. If one's social location is the troubled villages of Colombia, Nicaragua, or Guatemala, tidy answers are few. "For Latin Americans the Book of Job is a paradigm of protest by those who suffer unjustly. It is also a biblical source that provides a different way of speaking of the God of grace, 'from among the ashes' . . . the power of the Latin American reading has almost always been in its identification and solidarity with two voices expressing suffering

in a capricious way; when questioned by Job, God silences any demand for justice with an intimidating display of cosmic power, but in the process, shows a complete disregard for the moral law he has set forth for humankind. C. G. Jung, *Answer to Job* (London: Routledge and Kegan Paul, 1954), 25, 33. In Jung's eyes, Job is God's mid-life crisis; the sovereign God must finally admit that he has suffered a moral defeat before the integrity of his creature who consistently calls into question the brutality of divine injustice. Here Jung postulates that God's shadow side is the source of and thus responsible for the existence of evil. Jung, *Answer to Job*, 33, 35, 94, 108.

22. Job, according to Jung as analyst, reveals a greater degree of consciousness than Yahweh. Jung, *Answer to Job*, 68, 69. Out of finitude, frailty, and weakness, the human mind has been forced to develop "a somewhat keener consciousness based on self-reflection" than that of God who, protected by omnipotence in eternal safety, need not assimilate his unconscious and deal with his shadow side. Jung, *Answer to Job*, 20-21. But this scandalous encounter strips him of his denial and lack of self-awareness stimulating the desire to reunite with his creatures, regenerate himself through a rapprochement that is only possible in the incarnation as he takes on human existence in Jesus Christ. This act leads inevitably to the "Christification of many" as God enters humanity, and enables us to become God-men. Jung, *Answer to Job*, 180.

23. J. M. Vento, "Violence, Trauma and Resistance," *Horizons* 29, no. 1 (2002): 8.

through unjust poverty, disease and abandonment: Job's cries and those of the excluded of today."[24] Here the passages that speak for retributive justice, the speeches by Job's friends, repeat the empty promises of the prosperity gospel; the final protest is heard with acclamation.

One hears Job very differently in the midst of communities facing the HIV/AIDS threat and reality.

> When people worked diligently, it was generally accepted that they would reap the benefits of conforming to God's order. . . . The problem with this theology, of course, is that those who prospered by unjust means were presumed to have lived justly. Many houses and full barns, fine clothes and livestock, and extravagant imported goods were seen by society as signs of God's blessing for a good life. Remarkably, even though there was clear evidence to the contrary, this distorted theology of retribution endured. God, it was assumed, was in control, and so those who prospered must have pleased God by living according to God's order.
>
> This kind of theology has little understanding of structural injustice, and those who have advocated it tend to be those who benefit from systemic privilege, be it the racial privilege of apartheid, the middle-class privilege of capitalism, or the male privilege of patriarchy. What we now need to recognize is the devastating effects of this theology on people living with HIV/AIDS.[25]

Reading Job since the Holocaust opens our eyes to the final showdown between the protesting sufferer and the Almighty. The texts that have been translated as capitulation have been reexamined, and the depth of passion in Job, the nuances of his final words, suggest that instead of submissive repentance, he is still holding God to the question. Instead of "Therefore I despise myself, and repent in dust and ashes," he may still be saying, "Therefore I shudder with sorrow, I grieve for mortal clay that is but dust and ashes" (Job 42:6).[26] Since the Holocaust, virtually all theodicies have become increasingly difficult to sustain. Zachary Braiterman, in his book,

24. Elsa Tamez, "From Father to the Needy to Brother of Jackals and Companion of Ostriches: A Meditation on Job," in *Job's God*, ed. Ellen Van Wolde (London: SCM, 2004), 103.

25. Gerald West and Bongi Zengele, "Reading Job Positively in the Context of HIV-AIDS in South Africa," in Van Wolde, ed., *Job's God*, 115.

26. Jack Miles, *God: A Biography* (New York: Random, 1995), 325.

(God) After Auschwitz offers an anti-theodicy as a constructive response to the new reality since the "Final Solution." Perhaps, like Job's, our engagement with God and evil must end in protest. If we are to honor the ultimate justice of God, the question must go on, asking as Abraham asked, "Will not the judge of all the earth act justly?"[27]

Perhaps our final word needs to acknowledge the God who stands with us, like these words from Jacob Neusner.

> God's chosen ones suffer guiltlessly. It is what is called in Hebrew terminology, *gezeira,* an inscrutable divine decree. The decree is not that there be human suffering; the decree is that there be divine long-suffering with man in spite of man's criminal turpitude; indeed the decree that there be this world of man which could not stand without divine forbearance.[28]

Perhaps, at the mid-day of our lives, we can join Job, Jung, and sufferers around the world who read Job's ancient story. Will we, unlike Jung, gain answers from Job by hearing the Divine Answerer speak to him and to us?[29]

27. Zachary Braiterman, *(God) After Auschwitz: Tradition and Change in Post-Holocaust Jewish Thought* (Princeton: Princeton University Press, 1998).

28. Jacob Neusner, *Faith Renewed: The Judaic Affirmation beyond the Holocaust* (Macon, GA: Mercer University Press, 1994), 96.

29. I am indebted to many long conversations with Professor James Butler for his diligent attempts to help me understand the depth of wisdom in the Book of Job and its understanding of the non-retributive justice of God.

Scapegoating in Congregational and Group Life: Practical Theological Reflections on the Unbearable

K. Brynolf Lyon

Discussions of the modern psychological idea of scapegoating often refer to the ancient Hebrew Day of Atonement ritual described in Leviticus 16. In this purification rite, the high priest casts lots over two goats, with one offered as a sacrifice to the Lord and the other offered to a demon, Azazel. The priest is to lay hands on this latter goat and "confess over it all the iniquities of the people of Israel, and all their transgressions, all their sins, putting them on the head of the goat. . . . The goat shall bear on itself all their iniquities" (Lev. 16:21-22). The ritual transmits the sins of the people to the goat, who is then driven into the wilderness or "barren region," carrying away the sins and impurities of the people. Scapegoating as a collective-emotional concept describes one of the unconscious ways we attempt to deal with the unbearable in ourselves. We seek to drive it into the wilderness, as it were, by locating it in other people. There it resides in someone other than us, where we can treat it as if it were alien and separate, where we can act demonically, Azazel-like, toward it.

Scapegoating is one of the most common dynamics in group life. It is also one of the most virulent. Because of its virulence we might wish that congregations and other locations of ministry could (or should) do without it. While such a wish is certainly understandable, that wish is itself partly constitutive of the factors that generate scapegoating: the wish that what is painfully present in all of us would not be located in us but in someone else. It is an emotionally primitive effort to cleanse, to purge, to rid ourselves of what is encoded in our psyches and our social groups as dirty, shameful, wrong, or bad. In this sense it is, like the Day of Atonement ritual described above, an effort at moral and spiritual purification. When we scapegoat others we are unconsciously trying to locate and expel what is wrong or distasteful in ourselves and, thereby, appease the angry gods inhabiting our inner and intersubjective worlds.

The purpose of this chapter is several fold. First, I will discuss the systemic dynamics of scapegoating: why it arises in groups, the forms it takes, and its effects on group life. Second, I will address some of its sociocultural dimensions. I will pay special attention to the moral order of the group and the place of scapegoating within it. In addition, I will consider why we "choose" the particular persons or groups we do to fill the scapegoat role. Are those persons, like the goats in the Day of Atonement ritual, innocent bystanders, chosen by some sinister cast of the unconscious lots? Or are they somehow complicit in the process? How do we avoid "blaming the victim" in such situations? Third, such questions will lead me to consider the spiritual and theological dimensions of scapegoating as part of a reflection on the larger mysteries in which questions of holiness, justice, and compassion arise.

Systemic Dynamics of Scapegoating

Scapegoating can take shape in numerous ways in group life. Two such ways will occupy our attention in this chapter: scapegoating that is an ongoing part of the social and cultural structure of the group and scapegoating that emerges as a "here-and-now" event in the life of a group. In the first instance, scapegoating is built into or encoded in the very linguistic and structural fabric of social life, whereas in the second, scapegoating is triggered in the daily interactions of persons who live or work together. As we will see, these expressions of scapegoating are often deeply intertwined. Let me begin with the second form of scapegoating to discuss its development in group life, since it is the kind of scapegoating of which we most readily think.

The basic process of scapegoating is this: disturbing feelings in some group members are unconsciously projected onto another individual or subgroup.[1] In other words, as a way to protect against the pain

1. "Projection" refers to the unconscious emotional defense of attributing our own feelings and thoughts to others. This may involve attributing unacceptable wishes to others or

of recognizing and managing these disturbing feelings in themselves, these group members imagine that those feelings are not present in themselves but only in those identified others. The group acts, therefore, as if it is that other person or that subgroup of people who possess what is bad or distressing. It is important to emphasize that this is an unconscious process. The group doing the projecting does not know they are doing it, but rather simply notices the disturbing feelings or qualities in the others.

Think, for example, about this situation: a therapy group had spent several weeks doing some difficult emotional work. A member of the group spoke one evening about how she had ambivalent feelings about being in the group. While she was grateful for the changes she was noticing in herself, she found being in the group exhausting and painful. Immediately the other group members began questioning her commitment to the group, suggesting that she was not being a good group member by having those feelings. The other members, in other words, were acting as if they didn't have and couldn't understand ambivalent feelings about the hard work the group was doing. They acted as if those feelings existed only in the woman who admitted them, where they could be isolated or quarantined and "treated" or attacked as unworthy.

Here is another example: a minister had served a struggling congregation for some thirty years. While he was much beloved, there was also significant discontent with his leadership over the final few years of his ministry leading up to his retirement. The discontent was not shared with the minister, however, largely because the discontented members felt conflicted about upsetting their beloved pastor and his supporters. After his retirement, the newly hired minister was almost immediately attacked for his supposed shortcomings. The minister, it appeared, could do nothing right, though he had served very successfully at several previous congregations. The new minister was, in effect, being scapegoated by a certain subgroup in the congregation. He was a substitute for the feelings that could not be expressed toward the beloved prior pastor.

In most cases of scapegoating, as Marshall Edelson and David Berg have noted, a complex problem is simplified by splitting it into two sup-

---

dissociatively externalizing emotional residue of traumatic experiences. See Joseph Newirth, *Between Emotion and Cognition: The Generative Unconscious* (New York: Other Press, 2003), 75-77.

posedly mutually exclusive alternatives.[2] Both aspects actually coexist, but their coexistence is felt to be intolerable and, therefore, impossible. Thus, in the first example above, the group was having trouble holding together feelings of satisfaction and pride, on the one hand, and feelings of emotional pain and exhaustion, on the other hand. In the second case, the congregation could not find a way to manage their feelings of love and respect for the prior pastor at the same time that they acknowledged their feelings of disappointment and irritation. In each case both sets of feelings existed, but their existing together was not felt to be possible. The groups managed this impossibility through the defense mechanism called "splitting": the group that did the scapegoating projected one-half of the complex set of feelings onto someone else, seeing those feelings not in themselves but only in, or in relation to, that other (the scapegoated group member in the one case and the scapegoated new pastor in the other case).

What is split off and projected onto someone else in the scapegoating process are some disowned or unwanted qualities in us. In Jungian psychology, this is called "shadow projection."[3] While in projection proper, these qualities may be felt to be either good or bad, in scapegoating they are usually qualities that are experienced as "bad." Aspects of our shadow, qualities that we experience as bad or evil, are projected onto another. The other, the carrier of the "unwanted," as Edelson and Berg note, is then driven away or driven mad.[4] The scapegoat is isolated within the group and, if the scapegoating is successful, frequently made to feel "crazy" or is run off from the life of the group.

A group of persons within a conflicted congregation was at odds with the pastor and lay leaders. An elderly woman in the group received an angry, anonymous letter referring to her with several vicious epithets and complaining about her opposition to the pastor and lay leaders. When she expressed her pain over the letter to the lay leaders and pastor, she received little sympathy. Surely, she felt, they could agree that this kind of vituperative response was incompatible with the Christian witness. Nonetheless, she began to feel more and more isolated within the congregation and, in effect, "crazy." Whatever the leaders' evaluation of her behavior,

2. Marshall Edelson and David Berg, *Rediscovering Groups: A Psychoanalyst's Journey Beyond Individual Psychology* (London: Jessica Kingsley, 1999), 248.

3. Sylvia Brinton Perera, *The Scapegoat Complex: Toward a Mythology of Shadow and Guilt* (Toronto: Inner City Books, 1986), 30-33.

4. Edelson and Berg, *Rediscovering Groups,* 249.

their refusal to validate her perceptions left her feeling increasingly isolated.

Bertram Cohen and Victor Schermer have helpfully deepened our understanding of the scapegoated individual or subgroup by identifying two patterns.[5] These patterns are differentiated by the way in which the scapegoated individual or subgroup responds. In the first pattern, the antagonistic pattern, the scapegoat responds antagonistically to those doing the scapegoating while exalting or elevating himself or herself. In other words, the scapegoated person attacks, condemns, or withdraws from the group and inflates his or her own sense of self in relation to it. In the second pattern, the agonistic pattern, the scapegoat in effect joins with those doing the scapegoating. That is, the scapegoat, even though he or she may recognize they are being treated unfairly, feels that the qualities being attributed to them are indeed present in them and, therefore, condemns himself or herself and elevates or exalts the group. As Cohen and Schermer observe, the agonistic pattern of scapegoating is a prime example of projective identification, i.e., of identifying with the qualities that are being projected onto oneself.[6] In both patterns, the scapegoated individual ends up in a vicious cycle. The antagonistic response, by its very aggression or withdrawal, confirms the group's perceptions of them as dangerous or bad. The agonistic responder directly acquiesces to the perceptions of those doing the scapegoating and remains caught in this way in the projective cycle.

From the perspective of those doing the scapegoating, of course, the situation looks like one in which there is a troublesome individual or subgroup that needs to be dealt with in some way. If that individual could be "managed," the problem would be solved. In congregations and groups of all kinds, individuals often appear to be the source of the group's problems, the reason the group is not functioning as it should. This or that person is said to be emotionally unstable or a control freak or chronically antagonistic in a way that causes the problem within the organization. Individuals

---

5. Bertram D. Cohen and Victor L. Schermer, "On Scapegoating in Therapy Groups: A Social Constructivist and Intersubjective Outlook," *International Journal of Group Psychotherapy* 52, no. 1 (2002): 89-109.

6. For a very helpful discussion of projective identification in group life, see Ruthellen Josselson, *Playing Pygmalion: How People Create One Another* (Lanham: Jason Aronson, 2007). For an application of scapegoating as projective identification to the idea of the identified patient in family therapy, see Christian Gostecnik, "The Operative Mechanism in Family Scapegoating," *American Journal of Pastoral Counseling* 3, no. 2 (2000): 23-42.

can be troublesome, of course. Yet, the troublesome individual is frequently a means the group uses to avoid a social-systemic issue: the identified individual is often a "mouthpiece" speaking the unbearable aspects of
the situation for which the group as a whole is not taking responsibility.[7] In
this sense, the scapegoat carries important information that the congregation or group needs to understand itself more fully and to function better
in the future. So long as the scapegoating process continues, however,
there will be little hope of the group's learning from its experience.[8]

Groups tend to be fascinated by their scapegoats. They will complain
endlessly about them and want to know as much as they can about them.
Though groups complain about how disruptive or evil or malicious the
scapegoat is, they have a terrible time letting them go. They keep coming
back to the scapegoat, drawing attention to that person, inviting them to
remind the group how controlling or thoughtless or nasty they are. They
want to know the latest story, the most recent gossip that will confirm their
feelings toward them. And, of course, the group does this, it will say, because it has no choice. The scapegoat is felt to be so powerful that they simply must be the focus of attention. The group acts as if it is imprisoned in
the scapegoating process. If perchance they succeed in actually running
the scapegoat off, the group often recruits another person with the same
qualities to fill the scapegoat role.

A congregation, on the encouragement of a judicatory official, called
in a consultant to help them deal with a conflict between their current pastor and a group of persons within the church. As the consultant spoke with
members of the congregation, he learned that this church had fired its last
five pastors over the previous twenty years. When the consultant asked the
members of the congregation what might have led to this unusual outcome, he was told that the judicatory official with responsibility for their
congregation kept sending them bad ministers. Scapegoating can be a re-
silient process: for two decades this church had blamed its pastors and its

7. Anton Obholzer and Vega Zagier Roberts, "The Troublesome Individual and the
Troubled Institution," in *The Unconscious at Work: Individual and Organizational Stress in
the Human Services,* ed. Anton Obholzer and Vega Zagier Roberts (London: Routledge,
1999), 129-38.

8. See J. Kelly Moreno, "Scapegoating in Group Psychotherapy," *International Journal of
Group Psychotherapy* 5, no. 1 (2007): 93-104. See also K. Brynolf Lyon, "The Hatred of
Learning from Experience: Why Pastors and Congregations Fail One Another," *Encounter*
68, no. 1 (2000): 464-76.

denominational officials for its problems. The congregation simply could not learn and could not, as a consequence, deepen its life in faith. The congregation repeated over and again its unconscious scapegoating process, failing to learn from its experience the deeper conflicted realities of its life and the redemptive energies that might have led to more genuine transformation.

In all of this, scapegoats are treated as if they are objects rather than subjects. In other words, they are frequently treated as if they do not have a distinct inner world of feelings and thoughts that have worth and meaning apart from the interpretations of others. The persons doing the scapegoating, in other words, have lost the capacity for "mentalization": the ability to understand the scapegoat's behavior in terms of the scapegoat's own feelings, longings, and intentions.[9] The scapegoat appears as having cartoonish feelings and longings rather than complex and understandable ones. The loss of the capacity for meaningful mentalization is characteristic of persons or groups whose way of experiencing has collapsed into what is called a "paranoid schizoid" mode.[10]

The effect of scapegoating has been well stated by Cohen and Schermer: "To exile a scapegoat is to separate oneself from unacknowledged aspects of one's own self."[11] Scapegoating is a process of self-alienation. At the level of individual psychology, scapegoating derives from the failure to grieve: the failure to grieve our own shortcomings and losses, the ways we do not live up to (or fear we will not live up to) the expectations of our families, congregations, and work groups, the ways others do not live up to our hopes and expectations for them.[12] The scapegoating process derives, in other words, from unmetabolized (insufficiently grieved) losses of our lives. This failure to grieve has left shards of aggression, intimacy, and dependency/authority conflicts alive in us, ready

9. Peter Fonagy, Gyorgy Gergely, Elliot Jurist, and Mary Target, *Affect Regulation, Mentalization, and the Development of the Self* (New York: Other Press, 2002).

10. I have discussed this process in congregational conflict in K. Brynolf Lyon, "Paranoid Schizoid Phenomena in Congregational Conflict: Some Dilemmas of Reconciliation," *Pastoral Psychotherapy* 47, no. 4 (1999): 273-92.

11. Cohen and Schermer, "On Scapegoating," 107.

12. See Cynthia Burack, *Healing Identities: Black Feminist Thought and the Politics of Groups* (Ithaca: Cornell University Press, 2004). See also Vamik Volkan, *The Need to Have Enemies and Allies: From Clinical Practice to International Relationships* (Northvale, NJ: Aronson, 1988), and Martha Stark, *Working with Resistance* (Northvale, NJ: Aronson, 1994).

to be recruited by the anxiety of group life. Individual psychology in this sense permeates and is permeated by the dynamics of the social world.

Scapegoating and the Moral Ethos of the Group

Scapegoating is a socio-emotional process in the life of a group. As noted above, it emerges from the felt sense that two qualities or feelings that actually coexist are too unbearable to hold together. The ambiguity cannot be tolerated. A group therapy client once vehemently maintained that the difference between him and his wife was that she always felt that the glass was half empty whereas he felt that it was half full. The irony, of course, is that they were both correct: if a glass is half full it is also half empty. The couple had split apart the complex reality of their life together into two pieces, the wife carrying the pessimism and the husband carrying the optimism. Both were correct. What makes a complex emotional reality too unbearable to hold together? What shapes this dynamic that can lead to scapegoating?

Scapegoating is not simply a psychological process. It is also a process that functions at the level of the moral and spiritual ethos of the group. Scapegoating, in other words, protects not only the individual members of the group from their unwanted qualities, but even more fundamentally it protects the idealized "group self" that the members of the group share.[13] This idealized group self is composed largely of the norms, values, and beliefs that group members share in interaction with one another. Whether the glass is half full or half empty depends in part therefore on the larger values and meanings embedded within the idealized groups we carry within us. As Cohen and Schermer have put it, "A scapegoating process is most likely to gain momentum under conditions in which each member's group self, and hence the moral order of the group, is threatened."[14] Put another way, the scapegoated qualities appear within the group as a violation of the moral ethos and fiber of the group itself. Jungian analyst Sylvia Perera puts it this way: "Scapegoating . . . means finding the one or ones who can be identified with evil or wrong-doing, blamed for it, and cast out from the community in order to leave the remaining members with a feel-

13. Cohen and Schermer, "On Scapegoating," 91.
14. Cohen and Schermer, "On Scapegoating," 92.

ing of guiltlessness, atoned (at one) with the collective standards of behavior. . . . It gives the illusion that we can be perfect even as your father in heaven is perfect.'"[15] René Girard refers to this as the "scapegoat effect": the ability of the scapegoating process to unite and reconcile the remaining members of the group around the ideals that bind them together.[16] The group is reconciled with one another at the expense of the scapegoat. Scapegoating is rooted in the unbearable, therefore, because it emerges not simply from disappointing someone or being disappointed, but from the sense that we are threatened with being out of joint with the moral (and spiritual) order itself: the values and meanings that populate the very horizons of our experiencing. It is this unconscious threat that gives rise to scapegoating in the group-as-a-whole.[17]

The qualities that are most often projected in the scapegoating process are those connected with differences of power and status and the anxieties they evoke.[18] Thus, it should not be surprising that aggression, as well as intimacy, dependency, and authority issues, are ever-present in scapegoating processes.[19] The reason for this is relatively straightforward: these qualities are ones we frequently experience as dangerous to the emotional, moral, and spiritual balance of life in the groups we inhabit. Aggression, hostility, and anger are notoriously difficult to manage in congregations and most other groups. Because the Christian message is often interpreted as disallowing anger, these feelings are particularly difficult to bear in congregations. Without the possibility for the legitimate expression of anger, congregations become prime places for the projection of angry feelings or aggressive actions. Similarly, many people struggle to cope with intimate relationships. Sexuality and emotional vulnerability are often especially difficult to deal with in congregations and, therefore, become central arenas for scapegoating. Finally, our conflicted feelings about our own dependency and interdependency can be troubling for many groups, particularly in the relationship between leaders and followers. Discomfort with

15. Perera, *Scapegoat Complex*, 9.

16. James G. Williams, ed., *The Girard Reader* (New York: Crossroads Publishing, 1996), 12.

17. Alternatively, René Girard speaks of this as an effect of rivalrous mimetic desire. See Girard, *The Scapegoat* (Baltimore: Johns Hopkins University Press, 1986).

18. Edelson and Berg, *Rediscovering Groups*, 258-59.

19. See, for example, the discussion of Yvonne M. Agazarian, *Systems-Centered Therapy for Groups* (New York: Guilford Press, 1999).

or even hatred of dependency can lead to conflict, envy, and counter-dependency, dynamics which then can evoke scapegoating in congregations.

In relation to this larger realm of meaning we can see that scapegoats are not chosen at random, for no reason. They are not simply the "nearest available objects" for our projections, but rather problematic instances of the value-laden categorizations that make up group life, persons at the margins of the moral-spiritual order of group life, "others." As I implied above, they are often recruited because of their place within the status and power hierarchy. Race, class, gender, ethnicity, and sexual orientation are five of the most prominent categorizations within group life that frequently serve as markers for likely scapegoats. Other value-laden categorizations are also often used today: body characteristics (weight, height, etc.), liberal/conservative, and young/old categories. It is also frequently the case that persons with emotional vulnerabilities derived from chronic traumatization are chosen for the scapegoat role because of their more fragile place within the emotional economy of group life.

The psychoanalyst Vamik Volkan has argued that scapegoating has its precursors in the socio-emotional structuring of our earliest life. Our earliest groups (family, country, racial, ethnic, and religious communities) offer up what Volkan calls "suitable targets for externalization."[20] In other words, we learn from our earliest life which "others" our idealized groups identify as appropriate objects onto which we may project unwanted qualities. We grow up with particular subgroups of people already identified (even if unconsciously) as legitimate targets for scapegoating. The world is divided into "us" and "them." This categorization of the social world becomes encoded in the unconscious. Our psyches are racialized and gendered and sexed as we internalize the socially categorized world.[21] Thus, when we are caught up in scapegoating processes in adult life, we are unconsciously drawn to the categories of "others" encoded within us.

In a small training group, organizational consultants were to study their behavior as a group while various members took turns consulting. The anxiety was high as members sought to impress the supervisor in the

20. Volkan, *The Need to Have Enemies*, 31.

21. See Farhad Dalal, *Race, Colour, and the Processes of Racialization: New Perspectives from Group Analysis, Psychoanalysis, and Sociology* (Hove, England: Brunner-Routledge, 2002), and K. Brynolf Lyon, "Uses of Otherness in Group Life: Racism, White Privilege and Christian Vocation," *Encounter* 68, no. 1 (2007): 19-32.

room. During one such session a gay Hispanic member began to be questioned by other members for what they perceived as his lack of participation. The questioning became arguing. Why was he being so quiet? Did he think he was better than the rest of the group? What was he withholding? While other members of the group had been even quieter than he, the otherwise white, heterosexual group "chose" the gay, Hispanic member onto whom to project their own anxiety and distress.

Does all this mean that scapegoats are innocent victims of their persecutors' projected feelings? In some cases, the answer is resoundingly "yes." However in many situations the answer is more complex. Scapegoats are often recruited by the group because such persons have vulnerabilities to being used by the group to exhibit the problematic behavior or feelings that are being attributed to them. In other words, if the group is struggling with anger, it might unconsciously seek to recruit a member who is especially struggling with anger issues into whom they can deposit the group's unresolved anger. The group exploits the vulnerability of the scapegoated member or subgroup and uses that vulnerability to evacuate its own unwanted qualities. The scapegoat, in other words, often does in fact exhibit the behavior or feelings the scapegoaters are complaining about. The scapegoat is not "innocent" in that sense. The bottom line is this: scapegoats are made to carry the faults of others, in addition to their own shortcomings. The injustice is not inherently that a person without sin or blame was falsely accused. The injustice is that the burden they are made to carry alone belongs to the whole group. Scapegoats and scapegoaters alike are caught up in a process in which aspects of being human are extruded or expelled to the boundary or beyond of the group's moral-spiritual order. The scapegoats are pushed (and sometimes push themselves as well) to the margins, the wilderness, the barren-regions of group life, there to bear away what is unbearable for those who remain behind.

Spiritual and Theological Reflections

The problem of scapegoating in congregational and group life, I have suggested, is not only a socio-emotional problem but also a problem that appears against the backdrop of the moral order of the group. It is, as well, a problem that appears within the spiritual register of our lives: a problem at the edges of desire that reaches into that final mystery that surrounds our existence. The conflicts that emerge from the desire to be both vigorously alive to ourselves and others and at one with the deepest dimensions of existence tend to distort and skew our lives. We suffer in all this the incompletions of our grieving: the ways we could not feel our losses fully, the mourning interrupted or disallowed by the pain and confusion of others, the depths of life itself seemingly inhospitable to our suffering and our longing. The unbearable emerges, ready to be evoked by the anxieties of group life. An enemy must be found. Violence against another is a misguided solution to redeem the violence against ourselves — to carry the unbearable away from ourselves into the wilderness of the other, reconciling us with one another at the other's expense, through the ideals that otherwise threaten to overburden us. Scapegoating is, because of this, sin: an expression of the violence we do to one another that draws on the socially sanctioned violence encoded in the "others" and "otherness" that our groups offer to us as suitable victims. Scapegoating in this perspective is both present sin and expressive of, as Marjorie Suchocki would have it, "original sin" since it draws on social and institutional forms of violence into which we are born and live.[22]

Religion is no stranger to violence. Collective religious violence against "others" is a well-known feature of our history and our contemporary lives. Religious violence against gays and lesbians, against persons of other faiths, against persons of color, against women, against children, against the different and marginalized is frighteningly common. Few things rally support, money, and motivating anger more quickly in religious groups than identifying an enemy that threatens what it is believed God demands of us. With the evil located over there in someone else, it can be attacked, the moral order of the community reinforced and restored. Since we believe we are acting on God's behalf, purging the community of what God despises, there is often little leverage for us to see it is our will, not God's, that we are serving.

From a theological perspective, scapegoating is a kind of works righteousness. It rests in the belief that we both can and should expel the disturbing, frightening, and unwanted from ourselves. It is an unconscious effort to make *ourselves* holy and acceptable "unto the Lord" or, at least, unto the gods who occupy our own inner worlds and the intersubjective

---

22. Marjorie Hewitt Suchocki, *The Fall to Violence: Original Sin in Relational Theology* (New York: Continuum, 1994).

worlds of our idealized group selves. Through the actions of scapegoating, we unconsciously believe that we can reconcile ourselves to God and the gods we serve. Yet, in Christian faith, we claim that God alone is the author of our redemption. God alone reconciles us to Godself and this as unmerited gift. In effect God frees us to be precisely who we are (in all our good and evil, worthy and unworthy dimensions) and, in so doing, makes it possible for us to seek the transforming of our selves and the world. Such transforming does not mean, however, that we overcome the qualities most disturbing to us. God does not erase those qualities in us. Thus, scapegoating remains within and between us. The end of suffering, as Johann Baptist Metz used to say, awaits the end of history. Yet, it is in recognizing this that we may gain the leverage available to us *within* history, to take the kind of limited but nonetheless real responsibility we can for ourselves and our communities.[23] Perhaps in this way, in Catherine Keller's words, "the patterns of enmity can be softened, tilted toward some common humanity."[24]

Within many historically central Christian atonement traditions, of course, Jesus *is* the scapegoat who reconciles us to God. In some versions of this tradition, suffering itself is valorized. In Mark Heim's recent reinterpretation, strongly influenced by René Girard, Jesus is the sacrifice to end sacrifice. The cross is not meant to endorse sacred violence but rather to end it. As Heim puts it, "But the God of Israel becomes a God who sides with Job and with the persecuted victims of the Psalms, the God of the Prophets. And in the New Testament, God becomes the scapegoat. . . . It is God who undergoes the sacrificial process in order to turn it inside out. Sacrifice is turned against sacrifice."[25] In Heim's interpretation, Jesus is the incarnate one who takes the role of innocent scapegoat once for all to break through the powers of the world.

In my own perspective, Jesus reveals the ongoing divine action of God: less once for all in the traditional sense than revealing God's perpetual suffering and redeeming presence in the scapegoating processes of our

23. Pamela Cooper-White, *Many Voices: Pastoral Psychotherapy in Relational and Theological Perspective* (Minneapolis: Fortress, 2007), 131-32.

24. Catherine Keller, *On the Mystery: Discerning God in Process* (Minneapolis: Fortress, 2008), 122.

25. S. Mark Heim, "No More Scapegoats," *Christian Century* (September 5, 2006): 29. See also S. Mark Heim, *Saved from Sacrifice: A Theology of the Cross* (Grand Rapids: Eerdmans, 2006).

lives. That we too may be called to suffer with persons does not mean that we are called to suffer (as is the scapegoat) so that some do not have to face the realities of their own lives. As Christians we are not called to become scapegoats but rather to participate in others' suffering — and, subsequently, in the suffering of God — in a way that discloses and makes manifest the redemptive presence of God.[26] Or perhaps to put it in a more provocative way, it is only in the encounter with the "other" as one who leads us into (rather than away from) the very midst of our lives that God, the Other, is known.[27] Seen in this way, what appears as the scapegoat's "transgression" may in fact allow us to glimpse the otherwise hidden holy, or, in the words of Georges Bataille's atheology, may allow us to glimpse the edges of the unspeakable where even the polarity of ecstasy and anguish is overcome.[28]

Ann Ulanov writes that the peculiarly Christian fear of the psyche is rooted in part in the supposed opposition between the personal and the social. Christians, she observes, often believe that "our personal and social dimensions are mutually exclusive — or worse, hostile to each other. . . . The personal and the social are not separable categories. . . . What is needed . . . is a living inward connection to the living psyche — conscious and unconscious — and recognition in other persons of a similar fullness of psyche, whether actual or potential."[29] The problem of scapegoating in congregational and group life clearly illuminates her point. Scapegoating is a social "solution" to an intrapsychic, intersubjective, and ultimately spiritual problem. Scapegoating shows us that the social and the personal are not mutually exclusive. Rather, they are deeply intertwined. For social justice and compassion to be more fully realized, we must be aware of the interrelatedness of personal and social dynamics, and the effects of unconscious processes in both.

26. Paul Fiddes, *The Creative Suffering of God* (New York: Oxford University Press, 1992).

27. Eric L. Santner, *The Psychotheology of Everyday Life: Reflections on Freud and Rosenzweig* (Chicago: University of Chicago Press, 2001).

28. Georges Bataille, *InnerExperience* (Albany, NY: SUNY Press, 1988).

29. Ann Belford Ulanov, "The Christian Fear of the Psyche," *Union Seminary Quarterly Review* 30, nos. 2-4 (Winter 1975): 147-48.

Ministry amid Scapegoating

What general orientation should guide ministry in the face of the scapegoating dynamic? Let me briefly mention four features. First, reconciliation begins in our own confession, while trusting in the assurance of God's grace and compassion. We must work toward accepting the complexity of our own lives: the good and ill, the despised and the loved, the shameful and the honorable. We must do the hard work of recognizing the coexistence of these apparent polarities within us. However, we so frequently point to others, believing that reconciliation must begin in *their* confession since it is their sin rather than ours that is creating the problem. Yet, it is with us first that confession must start, assured that we will not be cast off from God in facing honestly the truth about us. The scapegoat is only relieved from the burden the group is unfairly asking them to carry if we take responsibility for the reality in us of what we have seen only in them, making conscious our unconscious projections. This might involve acknowledging that we share the disturbing qualities that we have isolated in the scapegoat. Or it might involve acknowledging that the "otherness" of the scapegoat is less a threat we must defend ourselves against than disclosive of a limitation of our group's moral and spiritual orders.[30]

Second, we must make sure the role and authority structures of the group are in place, just, and functioning well. In other words, we must tend to whether leaders are performing their role responsibilities well and whether committee structures are functioning appropriately. Are role responsibilities clear? Are people performing their roles fully, vigorously, and within the boundaries in which they are authorized to act? Anxiety within the group tends to amplify problems that may exist in these areas of the role and authority structure of organizations. When anxiety, fear, or distress increases in the group, the potential for scapegoating behavior increases as well. While we may not always think of it this way, role and authority structures can be means of grace and blessing.[31] They can also, of course, be means of oppressing the marginalized within the group. Careful

30. Not all otherness, of course, is benign or an aspect of goodness suppressed. Some otherness is inimical to the good. To thoughtfully distinguish these amidst the ambiguities of scapegoating is a difficult but necessary calling of the church. See Richard Kearney, *Strangers, Gods and Monsters: Ideas of Otherness* (London: Routledge, 2002).

31. For a fuller discussion, see Lionel Stapley, *Individuals, Groups, and Organizations* (London: Karnac, 2006).

attention to role and authority structures can help mitigate scapegoating dynamics by providing group processes which contain (compassionately and justly respond to) emotional distress within the group.

Third, as individuals and as groups we must grieve the losses that confront us. In rapidly changing times in our social and personal lives, losses confront us at nearly every turn. While loss is necessary to growth and change, it is also painful and therefore avoided. Losses are often ungrieved and unconscious and, subsequently, operate to shape and channel our reactions to others at levels well below those of our awareness. The failure to grieve, as I mentioned above, can precipitate scapegoating within a group. Thus, in order to help mitigate the impulse for scapegoating there are important ministerial tasks awaiting us: offering emotional room and support to grieve individually and together the losses and changes we face, giving people the opportunity to have the complex and uncomfortable feelings they feel in the midst of that grieving, and not asking them to manage our discomfort for us by the way they grieve. In religious education, worship, and pastoral care we can help individuals and communities recognize loss, bring its conscious and unconscious dimensions to fuller expression, work through its meanings in our lives, and resist the tendency to enact the pain through scapegoating rather than doing the hard work of mourning.

Finally, in a larger sense congregations can practice being places where the full scope of being alive (acknowledging one's deepest longings and fears, seeing the interweaving of the intentional and the unconscious) can be acknowledged and brought into the worship of God. Can the church become a place where the unbearable is less acted out in sociopathogenic ways than compassionately held with one another? Can we jointly acknowledge and work through the depths of suffering, longing, and fear that might otherwise be directed toward scapegoating? In particular, can we provide potentially transformative experiences where "others" and "otherness" might be felt and known as enriching of the moral and spiritual orders of our communities rather than simply a threat to them? In congregations can we finally companion one another on a journey of faith that enables us to take responsibility for our lives in all their complexity, their joy, and their terror, and that holds "others" as equally complex and beloved? Can we amid all the inevitable losses and failures of our lives practice the age-old arts of forgiving and being forgiven?

Resistance Is Not Futile:
Finding Therapeutic Space between
Colonialism and Globalization

Cedric C. Johnson

Introduction

Anyone familiar with the science fiction series *Star Trek* may recognize the title of this essay. One of the abiding hallmarks of the series is its portrayal of futuristic characters in plots that address the cultural issues of the present day. The original *Star Trek* series has now gained "cult" status and spawned numerous television and movie spin-offs. The title of this essay, however, reverses a phrase uttered by one of the most feared species in the entire *Star Trek* franchise — the Borg. The Borg is a ruthless and relentless species that uses superior technologies to conquer and dominate other species. They travel throughout the universe attacking every planet they encounter, assimilating its inhabitants into the Borg collective known as the "hive." Once assimilated into the "hive," that species is subjugated. The particularities of their culture are erased. Their identity is now derived from their connection to the collective mind of the "hive." As the Borg descends upon each unsuspecting species, if that species struggles in any way to maintain the distinctiveness of its own cultural identity, the Borg responds, "Resistance is futile!"

While the tyranny depicted in these futuristic portrayals is fictional, the tragic reality is that countless communities around the world are in fact gravely endangered by various forms of domination. Capitalism's global interests have historically been embedded in Western European and North American colonial projects. These colonial projects have typically entailed attempts by the colonizer to dominate indigenous communities, in so doing effectively dismantling their cultural, religious, and economic systems and imposing "alien" versions of these structures on their colonial subjects. People who live in colonized communities are therefore constantly faced with the threat of assimilation or annihilation. Now, in light of the emergence of globalization, societies throughout the world are increasingly becoming subject to forces that similarly threaten to erode and undermine their cultural identities and traditions.

This essay seeks to inform pastoral care with communities that have been subjugated by colonial rule or are threatened by the global expansion of capitalism. The challenges facing these communities are daunting. How can populations confronted by such profound forces discover the capability to resist structures of domination? This chapter will put forth a conceptual framework that aids in the identification of "therapeutic spaces" that function as communal sites of resilience and resistance. I will argue that indigenous religious practices found on the fringes of a dominated society can serve in this capacity. Three major theoretical strands will be woven together to construct this framework. The three strands include: D. W. Winnicott's understanding of play and cultural space, Michel Foucault's concept of heterotopias as "spaces of liberty," and Ann Ulanov's understanding of religious experience. I will suggest that a *heterotopic praxis* — that facilitates the identification and creation of communal spaces of alternate ordering — is central to any pastoral theology concerned with caring for these societies. For in the context between colonialism and globalization, one of the primary tasks of pastoral theologians will be to empower, equip, and enable communities to declare, "resistance is *not* futile."

Between Colonialism and Globalization:
A Context for Pastoral Care

Frantz Fanon states, "Colonialism is not simply content to impose its rule upon the present and the future of a dominated country. Colonialism is not satisfied merely with holding a people in its grip and emptying the native's brain of all form and content. By a kind of perverted logic, it turns to the past of the oppressed people, and distorts, disfigures and destroys it."[1] The history of colonialism is largely a history of oppression, negation, and exploitation. It is a history of the encounters of indigenous communities

---

1. Frantz Fanon, *Wretched of the Earth* (New York: Grove Press, 1963), 169.

and cultures with foreigners and the terrorism and abuse that resulted from that contact. It is largely a violent history in which the colonized have been dehumanized, their identities distorted and their true histories and traditions denied. At the heart of the colonial relationship is a process that results in the "enforced invisibility" of the colonized. It is a process prompted by imperialism that ultimately seeks to extract a community's resources and undermine its capacity for resistance and rebellion. The imposition of colonial rule may therefore be seen as a means of subjugating and silencing indigenous societies.

In *Cocoa and Chaos in Ghana* (1992),[2] for example, Gwendolyn Mikell outlines how the colonial imposition of capitalist ideologies and European cultural values destabilized the local economy and undermined the traditions of the Ashanti people. Mikell notes that before European colonialism the Ashanti were a matrilineal society. Historically, family lineage descended through women and women participated in the society's decision-making processes. Economic systems were clan-based and agricultural efforts were directed primarily toward subsistence farming. There was no private ownership of land. Under British rule, colonial authorities imposed practices such as private property, export-oriented agriculture, and a patriarchal social structure. These practices shattered the Ashanti's social organization by placing women at the bottom of the societal hierarchy. Communal clan-based structures were dislocated and replaced with state bureaucracy. The Ghanaian agricultural system shifted from subsistence farming to an emphasis on exports. Subsequently, greed for land increased. People were displaced and unable to feed themselves. Slave labor spread. This self-sustaining indigenous society was despoiled, its social organization dismantled and its cultural identity disrupted by colonial rule. The traditional ways of life and collective identity of the Ashanti were devastated by colonial "weapons of mass destruction."

In light of the internationalization of capitalism, the cultural identities of societies around the world may now be increasingly threatened by forces that tend to recast all relationships in terms of models of the marketplace. The increasingly flexible flow of capital has undermined older divisions that were considered static. In the wake of the collapse of communism in the Soviet Union and Eastern Europe, massive and fluid

2. Cited by Rebecca Todd Peters in *In Search of the Good Life: The Ethics of Globalization* (New York: Continuum International Publishing Group, 2004), 142.

movements of capital and migrants have turned some areas into "emerging markets" while others have been marginalized into socioeconomic "basket cases," producing "Third World" enclaves in the United States and generating "First World" capitalist miracles in India. The diminishing significance of the nation-state as the center of cultural, political, and economic activity and the emergence of powerful transnational corporations have facilitated the global expansion of a capitalist economic order.

The term "globalization" has been employed to characterize this emerging transregional interconnectedness involving networks and cultural flows across local and national boundaries. While globalization is often reduced to an economic process characterized by increased trade and the creation of a single global economy, this represents only one conception of globalization.[3] Globalization represents different realities to different people. Those connected to the World Trade Organization understand globalization to be a means to increased trade and international commerce. For transnational corporations globalization represents access to new markets and cheap labor pools. Countless indigenous and marginalized communities throughout the world, however, experience globalization as a new form of colonial domination. For what is not emphasized often enough is the fact that these transregional networks and cultural flows are to a large extent asymmetrical. From this perspective globalization might actually be understood as a code used for the exportation of "empire" — North American and Western European capitalist interests and cultural values — into every corner of the inhabited world.

---

3. There is much debate regarding the nature of globalization. The idea of globalization is a concept that is still being defined. Different disciplines that employ the term often have specific ideas about what they mean by it. These definitions are not always shared by other groups. Even within traditions and disciplines, no singular account of globalization has achieved the status of orthodoxy. There is, however, an identifiable cluster of perspectives that have emerged which frame the globalization debate. In this essay globalization is understood as a form of neocolonialism. For an examination of the range of themes central to the globalization debate, see David Held and Anthony McGrew, eds., *The Global Transformations Reader: An Introduction to the Globalization Debate*, 2nd ed. (Cambridge and Oxford: Polity Press, 2003). For a discussion of the primary perspectives on globalization, including globalization as neocolonialism, see Rebecca Todd Peters, *In Search of the Good Life*. Also, see Michael Hardt and Antonio Negri, *Empire* (Cambridge, MA: Harvard University Press, 2000), and James Petras and Henry Veltmeyer, *Globalization Unmasked: Imperialism in the 21st Century* (Halifax: Fernwood/London: Zed Books, 2001), for discussions of globalization as a form of imperialist empire.

These movements involve the imposition, in whole or in part, of Euro-American worldviews on every culture they encounter. This includes the proliferation of Euro-American media images, attitudes, and capitalist values that are inundating the rest of the world. Globalization thus threatens the identities and cultural traditions of indigenous populations. It can be understood as re-presenting the threat of colonialism in a sophisticated and seductive package that promises possessions, prosperity, and attainment of the myth of the "American dream." Rebecca Todd Peters notes that these dynamics produce "a form of globalization that seeks uniformity and threatens to destroy the difference and distinctiveness it encounters in other cultures."[4] Globalization therefore erodes and undermines indigenous identities and traditions to the extent that it is able to commodify, trivialize, or supplant local cultures.[5]

Transnational corporations have therefore re-created many of the problems associated with colonialism. Peters states, "Through their trading practices, corporations can force small farmers and producers out of business, causing them to sell or abandon their land and become dependent on wage labor, thereby radically changing the traditional way of life in rural communities."[6] She notes that, increasingly, powerful transnational corporations are forcing nation-states to comply with business and trade policies that benefit big business at the expense of local cultures and communities. An example of the growing influence of transnational corporations on indigenous societies, Peters indicates, is found in Nigeria. Described as a country designed by corporations for corporations, which "disregards the people who live there," Nigeria's cultural affairs have been shaped to a large extent by corporate interest in their rich oil deposits.[7] Though corporate interest in Nigeria's natural resources has brought jobs to the region, it has also contributed to the social and economic chaos that grips the nation's communities. Nigeria's civil war has been linked to the corporate struggle for control of the country's oil reserves.[8] The interna-

4. Peters, *In Search of the Good Life,* 150.

5. Peters, *In Search of the Good Life,* 152.

6. Peters, *In Search of the Good Life,* 150.

7. Oronto Douglas, "The Case of Nigeria: Corporate Oil and Tribal Blood," in *Views from the South: The Effects of Globalization and the WTO on Third World Countries,* ed. Sarah Anderson (Chicago: Food First Books, 2000). Cited by Peters, *In Search of the Good Life,* 149.

8. Douglas, "The Case of Nigeria." Cited by Peters, *In Search of the Good Life,* 149.

tionalization of capitalism continues then to "reterritorialize" the world, producing new forms of domination.

To be taken seriously by populations that are subjugated pastoral theology will need to have the capacity to engage systems of power. Christie C. Neuger concurs, noting that any situation involving pastoral care requires a thorough analysis of how the dynamics of power and difference are functioning in the lives of those who have come for care.[9] Pastoral theology needs theoretical resources that not only provide psychological insights, but can also interpret the wider cultural, social, economic, and political contexts. Pastoral care in the context between colonialism and globalization will thus need frameworks that can attend to both the human relationships *and* larger power structures within which subjectivity is formed.

The Spaces Where We Live

In *Playing and Reality*, D. W. Winnicott contends that any conception of human living that focuses solely on the inner life of the individual or the external environment is inadequate. He claims, "It is useful . . . to think of a third area of human living, one neither inside the individual nor outside in the world of shared reality."[10] This third zone of living is comprised of "an intermediary area of experiencing to which inner reality and external reality both contribute."[11] This intermediary area might be thought of as occupying a potential *space*. This third space is defined by neither the objective environment nor the isolated individual, but rather by the interaction between them. For it is a "product of the experiences of the individual . . . in the environment."[12] Winnicott employs the terms "holding environment," "transitional object," "space," and "play" to describe the dynamics inherent in this intermediate area between the subjective and that which is objectively perceived.

Winnicott's understanding of this third intermediary area of living is

9. See Christie Cozad Neuger, "Power and Difference in Pastoral Theology," in *Pastoral Care and Counseling: Redefining the Paradigms*, ed. Nancy J. Ramsey (Nashville: Abingdon Press, 2004), 65-85.

10. D. W. Winnicott, *Playing and Reality* (London: Brunner-Routledge, 1971), 110.

11. Winnicott, *Playing and Reality*, 2.

12. Winnicott, *Playing and Reality*, 107.

informed by his observations of the interactions between infants and their mothers. He argues that healthy human development requires the provision of a *holding environment*. The quality of the holding environment has to do with the mother's capacity to help the infant work through the process of differentiation — the child's transition from a state of fusion with the mother to a state of being in relation to the mother as someone outside and separate. For Winnicott a quality holding environment provides an infant with sufficient trust in life's dependability, allowing the infant to venture beyond the boundaries of his or her private world. Memories of good "holding" experiences lay the psychological groundwork for the emergence of a *transitional object*. Central to the infant's ability to move into the outside world is the use of a transitional object that embodies the security of the mother-child relationship. It represents the infant's connection to the mother and is used to ease the movement from that first interpersonal relationship into the larger world. Linus's blanket, popularized in the Charlie Brown cartoon series, is a familiar transitional object.

Winnicott notes that children "play" with their transitional objects. *Play* is therefore a crucial component of the transitional process. Play occurs in the potential *space* between inner and external reality. Occurring in this intermediary space, it evokes the security of the relationship between the mother and child. Winnicott encourages us to consider the preoccupation that characterizes the playing of children. He writes, "Into the play area the individual gathers objects or phenomena from external reality and uses these in the service of some sample derived from inner or personal reality. . . . In playing, the child manipulates external phenomena in the service of the dream and invests chosen external phenomena with dream meaning and feeling."[13] The "play area" then transcends the dichotomy between the subjective and objective or between the outer and the inner, and creates an interpersonal psychological space between both worlds. For Winnicott, "It is an area that is not challenged, because no claim is made on its behalf except that it shall exist as a *resting place for the individual engaged in the perpetual human task of keeping inner and outer reality separate yet interrelated*."[14] While no human being is ever free from the strain of relating inner and outer reality, relief is provided by entering the potential *space* created in this intermediate area of experience. Playing then be-

13. Winnicott, *Playing and Reality*, 51.
14. Winnicott, *Playing and Reality*, 2; italics added.

comes a *therapeutic activity*, for it facilitates emotional growth and psychological health.

Play in transitional space is not limited to infancy. The transitional phenomena and play that began in relation to the mother later spreads out to "the whole intermediate territory between 'inner psychic reality' and 'the external world as perceived by two persons in common,' that is to say over the whole cultural field."[15] Winnicott makes it clear that he is not just talking about "child's play." He is, in fact, postulating a psychological framework for an understanding of cultural space. Winnicott is proposing the creation of intermediary areas or "spaces" within which not only individuals but also groups and communities can find relief from the "strain" of relating inner and outer reality. Winnicott's understanding of the relationship between play and culture therefore has important implications for those interested in caring for communities. Ann Belford Ulanov notes that Winnicott's research "opens up for us spaces we reconnoiter throughout our whole life."[16] She notes that it is in these spaces that we find "the origin of psychic reality" and "the basis for creativity." Winnicott's theories thus posit the possibility of finding or creating communal spaces — intermediary areas of experience that serve as therapeutic "resting places" for entire communities. Undoubtedly, the identification of therapeutic communal spaces is a critical component of care for groups whose identities and traditions have been subjugated by colonial domination or threatened by globalization. However, while Winnicott's understanding of play and culture allows for the creation of communal spaces, he does not attend fully to conditioning structures of power and the way communities respond to living within hegemonic structures that don't reflect their experiences and needs. For assistance in these areas we turn to the theoretical work of Michel Foucault.

Power and "Playful" Resistance

Shortly before his death in 1984, Foucault noted that his objective for over twenty-five years had been to "sketch out a history of the different ways in

15. Winnicott, *Playing and Reality*, 5.
16. Ann Belford Ulanov, *Finding Space: Winnicott, God, and Psychic Reality* (Louisville: Westminster John Knox Press, 2001), 6.

our culture that humans develop knowledge about themselves."[17] Central to the work of Foucault is the notion of *discourse*. Discourse is the term he employs to examine the complex web of interrelatedness among language, institutions, power, subjects, objects, and practices. He contends that language is not benign. Foucault asserts that language has the capacity to create. The simplest level of linguistic organization is what Foucault calls *signs*. Signs are organized according to a schema, such as words organized into a sentence. Signs become a *statement* when they are situated in a web of other statements. Statements can be connected in a series, forming an argument, narrative, or conversation. These larger linguistic entities comprised of connected statements are what Foucault calls *discourse*. He argues that what is put forth as "truth" in any society involves privileging certain types of discourse, sanctioning certain ways of distinguishing true from false statements, underwriting certain techniques for arriving at the truth, and according a certain status to those who competently employ those techniques. Within any given society certain discourses are therefore privileged while other discourses are concurrently repressed and excluded. "Truth" therefore is not an objective reality to be discovered. Rather, the dynamics of power are inextricably connected with discourse. Truth emerges, for Foucault, as a result of multiple practices of power. In other words, power produces "reality," it produces what a society comes to understand as truth. An analysis of the discourses of any society therefore presses one to ask: Who among the totality of speaking individuals has been socially authorized or accorded the privilege to speak and who has not?

One of the ideas that then came to guide Foucault's investigation was the constitution of subjectivity through power relations. He states that "the individual impact of power relations does not limit itself to pure repression but also comprises the intention to teach, to mold, to conduct, [and] to instill forms of self-awareness and identities."[18] The conception of power as a network of relations in which we are always enmeshed did not seem, however, to allow for the opening up of "space" that would enable the kind of reflective capacities needed for the construction of subversive

17. Michel Foucault, "Technologies of the Self," in *Technologies of the Self,* ed. Luther H. Martin, Huck Gutman, and Patrick H. Hutton (Amherst: University of Massachusetts Press, 1988), 18.

18. Michel Foucault, *Power,* ed. James D. Faubion (New York: New Press, 1994), xix.

discourses. For if the self-reflecting subject is nothing but the effect of power relations, how are we to understand the emergence of modes of resistance to structures of power and domination?

In response to these critiques, Foucault posits a multidimensional framework. This framework includes four interrelated and interdependent spheres. They include: (1) technologies of production; (2) technologies of sign systems; (3) technologies of power; and (4) technologies of the self.[19] Power is now construed in the way these four spheres act on and modify each other. *Technologies of production* enable us to produce, transform, or manipulate things. They include capitalist modes of production, such as transnational media conglomerates. *Technologies of sign systems* enable us to use signs, meanings, symbols, or signification. They include the narratives, metaphors, and myths that govern our lives and shape our realities, such as psychoanalytic psychologies, imperial ideologies, and racist or sexist discourses. *Technologies of power* determine the conduct of individuals and submit them to certain ends of domination. This includes South African apartheid, chattel slavery, colonialism and empire. *Technologies of the self* enable individuals and groups to transform themselves and effect liberative changes in their bodies, psyches, thoughts, behaviors and environments.[20] Technologies of the self represent the techniques whereby communities resist structures of power. Foucault's multidimensional typology thus serves as a framework for understanding how therapeutic spaces can emerge in the context between colonial domination and globalization.

In "Of Other Spaces," Foucault notes, "we do not live in a kind of void . . . we live inside a set of relations that delineates sites which are irreducible to one another and absolutely not superimposable on one another."[21] He contends that the space in which we live then is a heterogeneous space. Foucault calls these spaces *heterotopias.* He describes heterotopias "as a sort of simultaneously mythic and real contestation of the space in which we live."[22] Heterotopias might be understood then as communal spaces created in the intermediary areas between the subjective and that which is objectively perceived. Foucault notes, "They are privileged or sacred or

19. Foucault, "Technologies of the Self," 18.
20. Foucault, "Technologies of the Self," 18.
21. Michel Foucault, "Of Other Spaces," *Diacritics* 16, no. 1 (Spring 1986): 23.
22. Foucault, "Of Other Spaces," 24.

forbidden places reserved for individuals who are, in relation to society and to the human environment in which they live, in a state of crisis."[23] He posits that some heterotopias also have a compensatory function within a society. Their role is to create a space inside of which human life is partitioned and organized when all other societal spaces are "ill constructed and jumbled." Foucault defines them as spaces of "liberty" outside of social control or places of alternate ordering. They are, therefore, spaces of freedom and change. This is consistent with his notion of "margins of liberty" or "sites of resistance" that mediate relationships of power. In essence they provide opportunities where subjects can deflect or detach themselves from hegemonic structures of power and make creative use of "space" for formation of the self. The emergence of the reflective capacities needed for the construction of "technologies of the self" — modes of resistance to structures of power and domination — might now be understood as being constituted in heterotopic space. I would contend therefore that a *heterotopic praxis* — that facilitates the identification and creation of communal spaces of alternate ordering outside of social control — is central to any pastoral theology that seeks to care for communities in the context between colonialism and globalization. Foucault's understanding of the conditioning structures of power and the way heterotopias can emerge within those structures is vital for those interested in caring for these communities.

The creative use of heterotopic space as a site of resistance, however, requires "playfulness." The articulation of expressions of resistance is contingent upon a community's capacity to transcend the dichotomy between external structures of domination and the inner impulse for self-determination to create "therapeutic spaces" in the third area of living between both worlds. This requires playfulness, for it entails a community's ability to manipulate "transitional objects" in order to deflect or detach itself from hegemonic structures of power in the service of that community's dream of freedom. The capacity to "play" in heterotopic space is thus the very ground for cultural resistance. If play is in fact the ground for cultural resistance and if play is therapeutic — promoting emotional growth and psychological health as Winnicott has argued — we can now construct a framework in which *cultural resistance can be understood as therapeutic.*

The implications for a heterotopic praxis are intriguing. For an under-

23. Foucault, "Of Other Spaces," 24.

standing of cultural resistance as therapeutic points to the importance of pastoral care practitioners being involved in initiatives not traditionally associated with the discipline. It entails an understanding of communal care that connects psychological health to participation in global resistance movements and the putting forth of a political pastoral theology in public spaces. It calls for pastoral theologians, pastors, and faith communities to be involved in movements that resist the imposition of "alienating western ways of thinking on tricontinental societies."[24] It calls for practitioners of pastoral care to identify and support efforts that resist "all forms of exploitation (environmental as well as human) and all oppressive conditions that have been developed solely for the interests of corporate capitalism."[25] This includes detecting "indigenous" responses to domination that occupy subliminal spaces in local communities.

Religious Experience as Heterotopic Space

In *Finding Space,* Ann Belford Ulanov draws upon insights from depth psychology to illumine our understanding of religious experience. She appropriates Winnicott's theories in an attempt to uncover fresh ways of "looking at what opens in the space between our experiences of our self and our experiences of God."[26] Ulanov notes that while psychology has traditionally studied religion as a subjective experience, theological studies have been more interested in examining the objective existence of God. She states that if we stand in transitional space and examine religious experience from that perspective, we discover that religion is neither solely about our human experience nor solely some objective truth about God. It is in fact neither and both. According to Ulanov, religious experience is located in the "space in-between subjectivity and objectivity, between our unconscious and conscious, between faith and fact" (18). She states,

> Located in this transitional space, we see that our religious experience
> arrives neither totally from outside ourselves, like a lightning bolt, nor

24. Robert J. C. Young, *Postcolonialism: A Very Short Introduction* (New York: Oxford University Press, 2003), 113.

25. Young, *Postcolonialism,* 113.

26. Ulanov, *Finding Space,* 6. Hereafter, page references to this book will be given parenthetically in the text.

totally from inside ourselves, as from a dream, but in the space in between. In theological discourse this means God is disclosed neither as
totally transcendent to human life — apart from us, unaffected by us,
untouched by human suffering, a self-enclosed, self-propelling being —
nor as totally immanent within human experience — as found in some
part of ourselves, as part of nature, the created order, [or] a product . . .
of human psychology. (20)

Religious experience cannot be reduced to our projections. It takes
place in the spaces in-between subjective-object God-images (pictures of
God covered in our projections), objective-object God-images ("traditional" images of God we find "laying around" in culture), and the transcendent reality many religions call God.

If we analyze Ulanov's argument from a perspective informed by
Foucault, she seems to indicate that religious experience can function as
heterotopic space. Ulanov states that totalitarian structures tend to destroy
hope and render individual and communal creativity ("playfulness") useless by attempting to annihilate the space between subjectivity and objectivity (47). In order to live our "creative self," she notes, we need an "other"
to reflect back to us our spontaneous gestures and discoveries. If we lack
such an "other" or find instead others who refuse to see that self or who try
to annul the self by asserting that nothing exists there to find and create,
we can be left resourceless with an unmet dependency (135). If we are not
reliably "held" when we are dependent — if we are dropped from our parent's attention — we may experience "the threat of annihilation through
disintegration" (44). Ulanov intimates that religious experience can facilitate the (re)constitution of individual and collective identities. She asserts,
"God as subjective-object functions to keep our ego in being. Like a mirror
— or a mother — the subjective-object God reflects our ego back to us in
the fullness of its identity, whether personal or social. Such a God-image
may function positively as a resource in time of trouble, as refuge in time
of sorrow" (23). According to Ulanov, subjective-object God-images function to hold us in being both individually and as a group, conferring a
sense of self on us that we ourselves help to create. She indicates that for
adherents of the Christian faith, "The body of Christ offers a community
whose members imaginatively hold one another in being" (47).

Ulanov's assertion that we can be left resourceless if an "other" refuses
to see our "creative self" or tries to annul that self by asserting that nothing

exists there to find and create, I believe, illumines our understanding of the psychic damage perpetuated against populations that are rendered "invisible" in the context between colonial domination and globalization. As stated, the imposition of colonial rule entails processes that demean, disrupt, and distort indigenous identities and traditions. Globalization undermines indigenous identities and traditions by commodifying, trivializing, or supplanting local cultures. When structures of power undermine the cultural and psychic structures that serve as facilitating environments for communities — when a *people* are not reliably "held" — they can collectively experience the threat of annihilation and disintegration. A unique contribution that religious experience makes available is its capacity to provide a holding environment that allows us to go back and look into "gaps of disassociation" and begin slowly and carefully to knit together what was broken apart (49). Religious experience, I would argue, therefore has the capacity to lay the psychological groundwork for the (re)emergence of "playfulness" in the context between colonialism and globalization. It has the capability to function as heterotopic space and enable a community to knit back together the psychic damage inflicted on its collective identity by oppressive structures. It appears then that one thing which can open in the space between our experiences of our self and our experiences of God is the capacity for psychological resilience and cultural resistance.

The Excluded Possibility

From Manifest Destiny's justification of the enslavement of Africans to Islamic extremism's involvement in the vicious attack on the World Trade Center, history reveals that religious beliefs have also encouraged some of humankind's greatest atrocities. Religious practices have undeniably been experienced not only as spaces of resistance, but also as sites of oppression. Ulanov notes that the "archetypal undertow" of a powerful image of God that one group thinks validates them as carriers of truth can cause that group to commit acts of insanity. She considers it a form of "theological sadism" when one group attempts to impose its image of God onto another group, insisting that their "image" is the only true depiction of the Sacred (38). Those who hold different pictures of the Sacred are then characterized as primitive or heretics and are oftentimes persecuted. Religious pathology arises, according to Ulanov, when the "space" between the subjective and objective collapses. When space disintegrates from the objective side, "official" interpretations of God (objective object God-images) are put forth that *exclude* our personal participation. These "official" interpretations of God "crowd out our spontaneous gestures toward the divine" and dictate how we should believe — religiously, politically, sexually, culturally, and economically (38). Ulanov states, we subsequently feel *invaded* and *imposed upon* by these "official" religious interpretations. However, if totalitarian structures tend to destroy hope and render communal creativity useless by attempting to "crowd out" personal gestures toward the divine, where can we detect subjective-object God-images that are capable of facilitating heterotopic spaces? Where in the context of totalitarian structures can we find religious practices that can function as sites of resistance?

According to Richard Fenn, "many societies claim that they represent some sort of an improvement on other societies or on nature itself precisely because they exclude certain possibilities on the basis that what is excluded is underdeveloped, unworthy or even barbaric."[27] Like Foucault, Fenn asserts that the line between what a society includes and excludes usually reinforces its normative boundaries and separates the conceivable from the inconceivable, the possible from the impossible, and the sacred from the profane. Fenn notes, however, that outside the boundaries of a society lie other ways of being human, but these must be excluded successfully or otherwise discredited as being uncivilized and primitive. Interestingly, Fenn contends that "religious language is pre-eminently the place where one looks for these excluded possibilities."[28] For Fenn, religious forms relegated to the fringes of a society typically function as depositories for excluded possibilities — excluded possibilities about other ways of being human; excluded possibilities discredited by structures of domination; excluded possibilities crowded out by the imposition of alien images of God; excluded possibilities that undermine the cultural imperialism inherent in colonialism and globalization. Fenn's conception of religious language appears to support the thesis that, even in the context of structures of power, religious practices can emerge that facilitate the construction of communal sites of resistance and liberation.

As Diana Fuss similarly notes, colonial domination "works in part by

27. Richard K. Fenn, *The Return of the Primitive* (Burlington: Ashgate, 2001), 1.
28. Fenn, *The Return of the Primitive*, 24.

policing the boundaries of cultural intelligibility, legislating and regulating which identities attain full cultural signification and which do not."[29] Like Foucault and Fenn, Fuss recognizes that "truth" emerges as a result of who in a society has been privileged to speak and who has been excluded. A critical question for pastoral care practitioners is to ask to what extent do the *dominant* pastoral theological discourses also "police the boundaries" of cultural intelligibility, legislating and regulating which forms of communal resilience and resistance attain full cultural signification and which do not? Pastoral care practitioners working with subjugated populations will therefore need to be careful not to unwittingly employ "hegemonic" frameworks that *exclude* heterotopic spaces encoded in hybridized religious forms operating on the fringes of societies. We will need to be careful not to put forth pastoral care frameworks that are "theologically true" for centers of power, but "psychologically false" for the communities we serve. Indigenous religious practices found on the margins of a society are therefore places where we can detect heterotopic spaces.

African American Spirituals: Songs of Resistance in a Strange Land

Black religious practices have historically been relegated to the fringes of American society. They have represented the "excluded possibility" and in many ways functioned as heterotopic spaces. Cornel West indicates that the use of communal space has been central to the survival of Africans in America. He states, "The genius of our black foremothers and forefathers was to create powerful buffers to ward off the nihilistic threat, to equip black folk with cultural armor to beat back the demons of hopelessness, meaninglessness, and lovelessness. These buffers consisted of cultural structures of meaning and feeling that created and sustained communities."[30] African American spirituals represent one mode of religious expression that has functioned as a "buffer" for black people. Through the use of the spirituals enslaved Africans built new structures that enabled them to exist and resist in a "strange land." W. E. B. DuBois states in his monumental work, *The Souls of Black Folk,*

---

29. Diana Fuss, "Interior Colonies: Frantz Fanon and the Politics of Identification," *Diacritics* 24, no. 2/3 (Summer-Autumn 1994): 21.

30. Cornel West, *Race Matters* (New York: Vintage Books, 1993), 24.

The Music of Negro religion is that plaintive rhythmic melody, with its touching minor cadences, which, despite caricature and defilement, still remains the most original and beautiful expression of human life and longing yet born on American soil. Sprung from the African forest, where its counterpart can still be heard, it was adapted, changed, and intensified by the tragic soul-life of the slave, until, under the stress of law and whip, it became the one true expression of a people's sorrow, despair, and hope.[31]

The central concept in African American spirituals is the divine liberation of the oppressed from slavery. James Cone states, "The theological assumption of black slave religion as expressed in the spirituals was that *slavery contradicts God,* and *God will therefore liberate black people.*"[32] The Bible, which was employed by whites to justify the enslavement of blacks, now provided a rationale for resistance. The story of the liberation of the children of Israel from Egyptian bondage was appropriated by African Americans and infused with new meaning in the spirituals. The Exodus narrative assured blacks that God would also deliver them:

When Israel was in Egypt's land,
Let my people go;
Oppressed so hard they could not stand,
Let my people go;
Go down, Moses, 'way down in Egypt's land;
Tell ole Pharaoh
Let my people go.

Cone indicates that the spirituals enabled African Americans to define their present history in light of their promised future. The spirituals, however, did not simply point to an eschatological hope beyond space and time. Blacks were able, through the spirituals, to "transcend the enslavement of the present and to live as if the future had already come."[33] The spirituals represent a mode of resistance that functioned to lift African Americans from the degrading images of a white supremacist capitalist society and enable them to draw their own conclusions about their personhood and their possibilities. They provided "material for worship

31. W. E. B. DuBois, *The Souls of Black Folk* (New York: Signet Classics, 1995), 212.
32. James H. Cone, *The Spirituals and the Blues* (Maryknoll: Orbis Books, 1972), 65.
33. Cone, *The Spirituals and the Blues,* 86.

and praise to the One who had continued to be present with black humanity despite European insanity."[34] The spirituals supplied African Americans with the "courage to be" in a society that sought to subjugate and silence them. They are a vibrant expression of black people's determination
to resist domination and their desire to be free.

> O freedom! O freedom!
> O freedom over me!
> And before I'll be a slave,
> I'll be buried in my grave,
> And go home to my Lord and be free.

The image of "heaven" in the spirituals was central to the impulse for
freedom. For some blacks heaven meant attempting the treacherous journey to freedom in the North and Canada, for others heaven meant having
the courage to actively engage in slave rebellions, and for others heaven
was a perspective that sustained them and enabled them to survive the
horrors of chattel slavery. In the midst of one of the greatest atrocities committed against humanity, the spirituals helped African Americans to have a
sense of worth when the larger society deemed them worthless. They
served as a resource in a time of trouble and a refuge in a time of sorrow.
They helped blacks to have a sense of hope when their external reality
seemed utterly hopeless. They were songs of resistance in a strange land.

From a perspective informed by Winnicott, black spirituals might be
understood as facilitating "play" in the third area of human living. The African American appropriation of the Exodus narrative in the spirituals
served to open up "therapeutic spaces" that empowered blacks to overcome the dichotomy between their external experiences of oppression and
their inner understanding that they were in the care of a Transcendent Reality. The spirituals provided a psychological space that functioned as a
therapeutic "resting place" for a community seeking relief from the strain
of relating their inner reality and the external world. Drawing upon the insights of Foucault, the African American spiritual might be understood as
a "technology of the self." They enabled blacks to deflect the conditioning
structures of domination and change their attitudes and behaviors. Ulanov
allows us to see that the spirituals gave expression to subjective-object God

34. Cone, *The Spirituals and the Blues*, 66.

images that conferred a sense of self on African Americans. They functioned to (re)constitute collective identities and rectify the falsification and harm done by colonial misrepresentations. African American spirituals therefore acted as heterotopic spaces, for they supplied blacks with communal sites of alternate ordering. They provided spaces of freedom.

Conclusion

This essay has sought to introduce the components of a model for communal care that attends to the identification of therapeutic spaces in the context between colonialism and globalization. Drawing primarily upon the work of Winnicott, Foucault, and Ulanov, this study suggests that a praxis which is attentive to the relational matrices, dominant discourses, and dynamics of power wherein subjectivity is formed is central to the care of subjugated societies. A therapeutic rationale for cultural resistance was introduced which provides a basis for the active participation of pastoral theologians, pastors, and faith communities in global and grassroots resistance movements. To this end, indigenous religious practices located on the fringes of dominated societies were identified as being capable of functioning as heterotopic spaces or "communal sites of alternate ordering." African American spirituals were examined as an example of a marginalized religious practice that has served in this capacity. The ability of indigenous religious practices to function as sites of resistance also calls, however, for practitioners of pastoral care to be sensitive to the ways in which our pastoral theological frameworks may "exclude" responses to domination that occupy these "subliminal" cultural spaces.

I began this essay reflecting on the tyranny of the Borg, a fictional species that travels throughout the universe subjugating and assimilating other species. Interestingly, one of the last installments of the Star Trek franchise, entitled *Voyager*, features a character called Seven of Nine who has been severed from the hegemonic grip of the Borg. Formerly human, Seven was assimilated into the Borg collective as a child. One of the ongoing subplots of the series involves Seven's struggle to "decolonize" her mind and (re)gain the distinctiveness of her human identity. Today countless societies throughout the world are engaged in this very struggle. It is my hope that this essay in some way furthers the causes of colonized and commodified communities in their fights for freedom. Resistance is not futile.

Ann Belford Ulanov: A Brief Biography

Christiane Brooks Johnson Memorial Professor of Psychiatry and Religion
Union Theological Seminary, New York City

Ann Belford Ulanov graduated with a B.A. from Radcliffe College in 1959 and received the M.Div. and Ph.D. from Union Theological Seminary, in 1962 and 1967, respectively. She has received honorary doctoral degrees from Virginia Theological Seminary, Loyola University in Maryland, and Christian Theological Seminary, Indianapolis.

Professor Ulanov is an Episcopalian, and her teaching and research are in psychiatry and religion, with a special interest in issues of prayer and the spiritual life, aggression, anxiety, fantasy and dream, identity, and the feminine.

She is the author of *The Feminine in Christian Theology and in Jungian Psychology; Receiving Woman: Studies in the Psychology and Theology of the Feminine; Picturing God; The Wisdom of the Psyche; The Female Ancestors of Christ; The Wizards' Gate; The Functioning Transcendent; Spirit in Jung; Finding Space: Winnicott, God, and Psychic Reality; Attacked by Poison Ivy: A Psychological Study; Spiritual Aspects of Clinical Work; The Unshuttered Heart: Opening to Aliveness/Deadness in the Self;* and, with Alvin Dueck, *The Living God and Our Living Psyche.*

With her late husband, Barry Ulanov, she is the author of *Religion and the Unconscious; Primary Speech: A Psychology of Prayer; Cinderella and Her Sisters: The Envied and the Envying: The Witch and the Clown: Two Archetypes of Human Sexuality; The Healing Imagination;* and *Transforming Sexuality: The Archetypal World of Anima and Animus.*

Adapted from the Union Theological Seminary website at: https://www.utsnyc.edu/ Page.aspx?pid=339

Professor Ulanov is the recipient of the Distinguished Alumna Award from the Blanton/Peale Graduate Institute; the Vision Award from the National Association for the Advancement of Psychoanalysis; the Oskar Pfister Award from the American Psychiatric Association for Distinguished Work in Depth Psychology and Religion; and the Gradiva Award in Psychiatry and Religion 2002 from the National Association for the Advancement of Psychoanalysis for *Finding Space: Winnicott, God, and Psychic Reality.*

Prof. Ulanov is a psychoanalyst in private practice in New York City. She is also an active member of the International Association of Analytical Psychiatry, the Jungian Psychoanalytic Association, and the American Association of Pastoral Counselors. She serves on the Editorial Board of the *Journal of Pastoral Care* and on the Advisory Boards of both the *Journal of Analytical Psychology* and the Center for Spirituality and Psychotherapy of the National Institute for Psychotherapies.

Constantly sought after as a speaker, Professor Ulanov was particularly in demand in the aftermath of the World Trade Center Disaster for her message about the relationship between religion and aggression, understanding unconscious processes, and the need for healing the psyche, which she sees as the most crucial deterrent to violence in the world.

Ann Belford Ulanov: Selected Bibliography

Books

The Feminine in Jungian Psychology and in Christian Theology. Evanston: Northwestern University Press, 1971.

Religion and the Unconscious. With Barry Ulanov. Philadelphia: Westminster, 1985. First published 1975. Korean translation 1996.

Cinderella and Her Sisters: The Envied and the Envying. With Barry Ulanov. Einsiedeln, Switzerland: Daimon, 1998. First published in 1981. Italian translation 2003.

Receiving Woman: Studies in the Psychology and Theology of the Feminine. Einsiedeln, Switzerland: Daimon, 2002. First published in 1981.

Guest editor, Psychiatry and Religion issue of the *Union Seminary Quarterly Review* 36, nos. 2 and 3 (Winter/Spring 1981).

Primary Speech: A Psychology of Prayer. With Barry Ulanov. Louisville: Westminster John Knox Press, 2000. First published in 1982. British edition, London: SCM Press, 1982.

Picturing God. Cambridge, MA: Cowley, 1986.

The Witch and the Clown: Two Archetypes of Human Sexuality. With Barry Ulanov. Wilmette, IL: Chiron, 1987.

The Wisdom of the Psyche. Einsiedeln, Switzerland: Daimon, 2000. First published in 1988.

The Healing Imagination: The Meeting of Psyche and Soul. With Barry Ulanov. Einsiedeln, Switzerland: Daimon, 1999. First published in 1991.

The Female Ancestors of Christ. Einsiedeln, Switzerland: Daimon, 1998. First published in 1993. Czech translation 2004.

The Wizard's Gate: Picturing Consciousness. Einsiedeln, Switzerland: Daimon, 1994.

Transforming Sexuality: The Archetypal World of Anima and Animus. With Barry Ulanov. Boston: Shambala, 1994.

The Functioning Transcendent: Studies in Analytical Psychology. Wilmette, IL: Chiron, 1996.

Religion and the Spiritual in Carl Jung, Mahwah, NJ: Paulist, 1999. Also published as *The Spirit in Jung.* Einsiedeln, Switzerland: Daimon, 2005.

Finding Space: Winnicott, God, and Psychic Reality. Louisville: Westminster John Knox Press, 2001.

Attacked by Poison Ivy: A Psychological Understanding. York Beach, ME: Nicolas-Hays, 2001.

Spiritual Aspects of Clinical Work. Einsiedeln, Switzerland: Daimon, 2004.

The Unshuttered Heart: Opening to Aliveness and Deadness in the Self. Nashville: Abingdon Press, 2007.

The Living God and Our Living Psyche: What Christians Can Learn from Carl Jung. With Alvin Dueck. Grand Rapids: Eerdmans, 2008.

Publications in Books

"The Psychological Reality of the Demonic." In *The Disguises of the Demonic: Perspectives on the Power of Evil,* edited by A. Olson, pp. 134-49. New York: Association Press, 1975.

"God and Depth Psychology." In *God in Contemporary Thought,* edited by S. A. Matczak, pp. 939-56. New York: Learned Pub., 1977.

"The Search for Paternal Roots: Jungian Perspectives on Fathering." In *Fathering: Fact or Fable?* edited by E. V. Stein, pp. 47-67. Nashville: Abingdon Press, 1977.

"C. G. Jung on Male and Female." In *Male and Female: Christian Approaches to Sexuality,* edited by R. Barnhouse and U. Holmes, pp. 197-210. New York: Seabury, 1978.

"Aging: On the Way to One's End." In *Ministry with the Aging: Designs, Challenges, Foundations,* edited by W. M. Clements, pp. 109-23. San Francisco: Harper & Row, 1981.

"Spiritual Aspects of Clinical Work." In *Jungian Analysis,* vol. 1, edited by M. Stein, pp. 50-78. La Salle: Open Court, 1982.

"Transference/Countertransference: A Jungian Perspective." In *Jungian Analysis,* edited by M. Stein, pp. 68-85. LaSalle, IL: Open Court, 1982.

"The Anxiety of Being: Paul Tillich and Depth Psychology." In *The Thought of Paul Tillich,* edited by J. L. Adams, W. Pauck, and R. L. Shinn, pp. 119-36. New York: Harper & Row, 1985.

"Image and Imago: Jung and the Study of Religion." In *Essays on Jung and the Study of Religion,* edited by L. H. Martin and J. Goss, pp. 2-25. Lanham, MD: University Press of America, 1985.

"The God You Touch." In *Christ and the Bodhisattva,* edited by D. Lopez and S. Rockefeller, pp. 117-39. Albany: State University of New York Press, 1986.

"Prayer and Personality: Prayer as Primary Speech." With Barry Ulanov. In *The Study of Spirituality*, edited by C. Jones, G. Wainwright, and E. Yarnold, pp. 24-33. New York: Oxford University Press, 1986.

"Foreword." In *Imprints of the Future*. By George Czuczka, pp. v-vii. Einsiedeln, Switzerland: Daimon, 1987.

"The Self as Other." In *Carl Jung and Christian Spirituality*, edited by R. L. Moore, pp. 38-65. New York: Paulist, 1988.

"Between Anxiety and Faith: The Role of the Feminine in Paul Tillich's Thought." In *Paul Tillich on Creativity*, edited by J. Kegley and J. L. Adams, pp. 131-55. Lanham, MD: University Press of America, 1989.

"Two Sexes." In *Men and Women: Sexual Ethics in Turbulent Times*, edited by P. Turner, pp. 19-48. Cambridge: Cowley, 1989.

"Disguises of the Anima." In *Gender and Soul in Psychotherapy*, edited by N. Schwartz-Salant and M. Stein, pp. 25-54. Wilmette, IL: Chiron, 1990.

"The Objectivity of Subjectivity: The Feminist and Spiritual Strengths of Psychoanalysis." In *Jung and Christianity in Dialogue*, edited by R. L. Moore and D. Mickel, pp. 140-69. New York: Paulist, 1990.

"Religious Devotion or Masochism: A Psychoanalyst Looks at Thérèse." In *Experiencing Saint Thérèse Today*. Carmelite Studies V, edited by John Sullivan, pp. 140-56. Washington, DC: ICS Publications, 1990.

"Scapegoating: The Double Cross." In *Lingering Shadows: Jungians, Freudians, and Anti-Semitism*, edited by A. Maidenbaum and S. Martin, pp. 223-40. Boston: Shambala, 1990.

"The Holding Self: Jung and the Desire for Being." In *The Fire of Desire: Erotic Energies and the Spiritual Quest*, edited by F. Halligan and J. Shea, pp. 146-64. New York: Crossroads, 1992.

"The Perverse and the Transcendent." In *Chicago 92: The Transcendent Function: Individual and Collective Aspects — Proceedings of the Twelfth International Congress of Analytical Psychology 1992*, edited by M. Mattoon, pp. 212-32. Einsiedeln, Switzerland: Daimon, 1993.

"Reaching for the Unknown: Religious Dimensions of Clinical Work." With Barry Ulanov. In *Clinical Handbook of Pastoral Care*, vol. 2, edited by R. J. Wicks, R. D. Parsons, and D. E. Capps, pp. 7-26. New York: Paulist, 1993.

"Including Even Our Mad Parts." In *Parabola Book of Healing*, edited by L. Sullivan, pp. 122-24. New York: Continuum, 1994.

"Jung and Prayer." In *Jung and the Monotheisms: Judaism, Christianity, and Islam*, edited by J. Ryce-Menuhin, pp. 91-110. London: Routledge, 1994.

"Mending the Mind and Minding the Soul: Explorations Towards the Care of the Whole Person." In *Pastoral Care of the Mentally Disabled: Advancing Care of the Whole Person*, edited by S. Severino and R. Liew, pp. 85-101. Ithaca: Haworth, 1994.

"Jung and Religion: The Opposing Self." In *Cambridge Companion to Jung*, edited by P. Young-Eisendrath and T. Dawson, pp. 296-313. Cambridge: Cambridge University Press, 1997. Also included in *Cambridge Companion to Jung,* 2nd ed., pp. 315-332.

"Looking: Subjectivity and the True Self," With Barry Ulanov. In *Powers of Being: David Holbrook and His Work,* edited by E. Webb, pp. 173-90. Cranbury, NJ: Associated University Presses, 1995.

"Self Service." In *Cast the First Stone: Ethics in Analytic Practice,* edited by L. Ross and M. Roy, pp. 126-38. Wilmette, IL.: Chiron, 1995.

"*Coniunctio* and Marriage." In *Psyche and Family: Jungian Applications and Family Therapy,* edited by T. Gibson and L. Dodson, pp. 113-29. Wilmette, IL: Chiron, 1997.

"The Dread of the Good: On Good and Evil." In *The Book of Women's Sermons: Hearing God in Each Other's Voices,* edited by L. Hancock, pp. 228-35. New York: Penguin Putnam, 1999.

"Epilogue." In *The Guide to Pastoral Counseling and Care,* edited by Gary Ahlskog and Harry Sands, pp. 379-82. Madison, CT: Psychosocial Press, 2000.

"Foreword." In S. Sorajjakool, *Wu Wei, Negativity, and Depression: The Principle of Non-Trying in the Practice of Pastoral Care,* pp. xi-xii. Binghamton, NY: Haworth, 2001.

Articles

"The Relation of Religion to Pastoral Counseling." *Journal of Religion and Health* 7, no. 1 (January 1968): 26-42. Published under the name Ann Belford.

"Where Depth Psychology and Theology Meet." *Union Seminary Quarterly Review* (January 1968): 150-67.

"The Person Each of Us Is." *Concern* (July-August 1968): 9-11. Published under the name Ann Belford.

"Aggression." *Concern* (October 1968): 14.

"Selflessness." *Concern* (November 1968): 25.

"All Can Be Lost, All Can Be Given Again." *Concern* (December 1968): 28.

"Does Pastoral Counseling Bring a New Consciousness to the Mental Health Field?" *Journal of Pastoral Care* 26, no. 4 (December 1972): 253-55.

"The Self as Other." *Journal of Religion and Mental Health* 12, no. 2 (April 1973): 140-68.

"Birth and Rebirth: The Effect of an Analyst's Pregnancy on the Transference of Three Patients." *Journal of Analytical Psychology* 18, no. 2 (July 1973): 146-64.

"The Two Strangers." *Union Seminary Quarterly Review* 28, no. 4 (Summer 1973): 273-83.

"Response," to Richard F. French, Paul L. Lehmann, J. Louis Martyn, and Jeffrey Rowthorn, "Collegiality: An Initial Exploration. Theological Perspectives for the Practice of Collegiality in Union Theological Seminary." *Union Seminary Quarterly Review* 28, no. 4 (Summer 1973): 297-98.

"On the Feminine in Theology." *Mid-Stream: An Ecumenical Journal* 13, no. 1-2 (Fall-Winter 1973-74): 10-17.

"The Birth of Otherness." *Religion in Life* 42, no. 3 (Autumn 1973): 301-21.

"Dreams and the Paradoxes of the Christian Spirit." *The Christian Ministry* 5, no. 6 (November 1974): 15-18.

"The Feminine and the World of C.P.E." *Journal of Pastoral Care* 29, no. 1 (March 1975): 11-22.

"The Christian Fear of the Psyche." *Union Seminary Quarterly Review* 30, nos. 2-4 (Winter-Summer 1975): 140-52.

"The Disguises of the Good." *Union Seminary Quarterly Review* 31, no. 2 (Winter 1975): 113-25.

"The Place of Religion in Training Pastoral Counselors." *Journal of Religion and Health* 15, no. 2 (April 1976): 88-93.

"The Witch Archetype." *Quadrant* 10, no. 1 (Fall 1977): 33-61.

"Bewitchment." With Barry Ulanov. *Quadrant* 11, no. 2 (Winter 1978): 33-61.

"Being and Space." *Union Seminary Quarterly Review* 33, no. 1 (Winter 1978): 11-22.

"What Do We Think People Do When They Pray?" *Anglican Theological Review* 60, no. 4 (October 1978): 387-98.

"Follow-Up Treatment in Cases of Patient/Therapist Sex." *Journal of the American Academy of Psychoanalysis and Dynamic Psychiatry* 7, no. 1 (January 1979): 101-10.

"Heaven and Hell: An Anti-Reductionist View." *Union Seminary Quarterly Review* 34, no. 2 (Summer 1979): 239-48. Korean translation by Ee Kon Kim: "Heaven and Hell: An Anti-Reductionist View [1]." *Presence* (현존), no. 109 (March 1980): 31-38; "Heaven and Hell: An Anti-Reductionist View [2]." *Presence* (현존), no. 110 (April 1980): 43-47; "Heaven and Hell: An Anti-Reductionist View [3]." *Presence* (현존), no. 112 (June 1980): 23-31.

"Fatness and the Female." *Psychological Perspectives* 10, no. 1 (Spring 1979): 18-36.

"The Clown Archetype." *Quadrant* 13, no. 1 (1980): 4-27.

"A Symposium: How Do I Assess Progress in Supervision?" With Alfred Plaut, Gustav Dreifuss, Michael Fordham, Joseph L. Henderson, Elie Humbert, Mario Jacoby, and Hans-Joachim Wilke. *Journal of Analytical Psychology* 27 (1982): 105-30. Reprinted in *Jungian Perspectives on Clinical Supervision,* edited by Paul Kugler, pp. 145-81. Einsiedeln, Switzerland: Daimon, 1995.

"Picturing God." Excerpts in *Phos* [a newsletter of Trinity Institute, New York City] (1983).

"A Shared Space: Jung and Others." *Quadrant* 18, no. 1 (Spring 1985): 65-80.

"Picturing God." *Journal of Religion and Intellectual Life* 2, no. 4 (Summer 1985): 83-101.

"Spirituality and Women." *Vogue* (June 1985).

"Religion: A New Force." *Vogue* (December 1985).

"For Better and for Worse." *Psychoanalytic Review* 73, no. 4 (Winter 1986): 618-20.

"Interview." With Barry Ulanov. *Soundings [Minnesota Episcopal News]* (1986).

"The God You Touch." *Parabola* 12, no. 3 (Fall 1987): 18-33.

"Important Books in Psychiatry and Religion." *Commonweal* (February 1988): 149-50.

"Vocation: The Denying of Denial." *Anglican Theological Review* 71, no. 2 (Spring 1989): 176-80.

"The Foxes Have Holes . . ." *Issues and Trends* [a newsletter of The Consortium for Endowed Episcopal Parishes] (1990).

"Le Pervers et le Transcendant." *Cahiers Jungiens de Psychanalyse* 77 (May-June 1993): 71-87.

"Inside Talk: The Prayer of Conversation." With Barry Ulanov. *Living Pulpit* 2, no. 3 (July-September 1993): 20-21.

"Mapping the Territory." With Barry Ulanov. *Journal of Religion and Health* 33, no. 1 (Spring 1994): 3-5.

"Seeing Straight with Crooked Lines." With Barry Ulanov. *Journal of Religion and Health* 33, no. 2 (Summer 1994): 105-6.

"Nursing as Nourishment." With Barry Ulanov. *Journal of Religion and Health* 34, no. 2 (Summer 1995): 97-98.

"Envy: Further Thoughts." *Journal of Religion and Health* 34, no. 4 (Winter 1995): 313-16.

"A Matter of Faith." With Barry Ulanov. *Journal of Religion and Health* 35, no. 1 (Spring 1996): 3-4.

"Staying Awake: Consciousness and Conscience." With Barry Ulanov. *Journal of Religion and Health* 35, no. 2 (Summer 1996): 91-92.

"Transference, the Transcendent Function, and Transcendence." *Journal of Analytical Psychology* 42, no. 1 (January 1997): 119-38.

"Teaching Jung in a Theological Seminary and a Graduate School of Religion: A Response to David Tacey." *Journal of Analytical Psychology* 42, no. 2 (April 1997): 303-11.

"Surviving in a Drifting Culture." *Journal of Religion and Health* 36, no. 1 (Spring 1997): 3-4.

"Two Requiems." With Barry Ulanov. *Journal of Religion and Health* 36, no. 3 (Fall 1997): 299-300.

"The Gift of Consciousness." *Princeton Seminary Bulletin* 19, no. 3 (1998): 242-58.

"Countertransference and the Self." Inaugural Issue, *Journal of Jungian Theory and Practice* 1, no. 1 (1999): 5-26.

"Afterword." *Gender and Psychoanalysis: An Interdisciplinary Journal* 4 (1999): 549-52.

"Chaos, Consciousness, and Plenum." *Journal of Religion and Health* 39, no. 3 (Fall 2000): 207-8.

"Hate in the Analyst." *Journal of Jungian Theory and Practice* 3 (Fall 2001): 25-40.

"Barry A. Ulanov: Eulogy." *Union Seminary Quarterly Review* 55, no. 1/2 (2001): 51-54.

"Ulanov, Barry, 1918-2000." *Journal of Religion and Health* 40, no. 1 (Spring 2001): 11-14.

"Terrorism." *Journal of Religion and Health* 41, no. 1 (Spring 2002): 41-44.

"Theology after Jung." *Journal of Jungian Theory and Practice* 8, no. 1 (2006): 61-68.

"Evil." *Quadrant* 36, no. 1 (Winter 2006): 71-89.

"The Space between Pastoral Care and Global Terrorism." *Scottish Journal of Healthcare Chaplaincy* 10, no. 2 (2007): 3-8.

Ann Belford Ulanov: Selected Bibliography

"Practicing Reconciliation: Love and Work." *Anglican Theological Review* 89, no. 2 (Spring 2007): 227-46.
"Losing, Finding, Being Found: At the Edge Between Despair and Hope." *Quadrant* 37, no. 2 (Summer 2007): 45-63.
"The Third in the Shadow of the Fourth." *The Journal of Analytical Psychology* 52, no. 5 (November 2007): 585-605.

Entries in Dictionaries and Encyclopedias

"Jung and Religion." In *The International Encyclopedia of Psychiatry, Psychology, Psychoanalysis and Neurology,* edited by B. Wolman. New York: Produced for Aesculapius Publishers by Van Nostrand Reinhold Co., 1977.
"Archetype." In *Routledge International Encyclopedia of Women: Global Women's Issues and Knowledge,* edited by C. Kramarae and D. Spender. New York: Routledge, 2000.
"Prayer, Psychology of." In *The New Westminster Dictionary of Christian Spirituality,* edited by Philip Sheldrake. Louisville: John Knox Press, 2005.
"Anima and Animus" and "The Transcendent Function." In *Edinburgh International Encyclopaedia of Psychoanalysis,* edited by R. M. Skelton. Edinburgh: Edinburgh University Press, 2006.